Praise for **WHO'S AFRAID OF THE BIG BAD JEW?**

Raphael Shore, a veteran fighter of antisemitism in all its ugly manifestations, has written a book which presents this ancient scourge through a modern lens. His insights, developed over many years of commitment to protecting the Jewish people, helps us understand the derivation of Jew-hatred, what can be done to stop it, and how it can be turned into a positive force. This is the right book at the right time and is a must-read for those seeking to master this complex subject.

Ambassador David Friedman

Former US Ambassador to Israel

Antisemitism—and its modern variant in the form of anti-Zionism—must be fought and defeated, first and foremost ideologically. With this book, Raphael Shore situates himself at the forefront of this war of ideas. At stake, is nothing less than the future of humanism and humanity. An extraordinary, eye-opening masterpiece.

Tal Ben Shahar

Author of Happier

This is a fascinating study on Jew-hatred, but most importantly this work is empowering. Something much needed in the Jewish world.

Ben M. Freeman

Author of Jewish Pride: Rebuilding a People

Here comes a book about the most depressing of topics - Jew-hatred throughout the ages - yet it's inspiring, uplifting. Without underestimating how evil it is, how twisted Jews' enemies are, Rabbi Raphael Shore pulls off the ultimate Jew-Jitsu: he explains that much of the hate comes because Jew-haters hate Judaism's empowering, soaring, disruptive message. Rather than succumbing to despair—like too many others—Rabbi Shore wisely, bravely, shows us that the best response to those who hate Jews is to embrace Judaism, appreciate its grandeur, and benefit from it. Bravo!!!

Professor Gil Troy

Author of Fearless Zionism and The Zionist Ideas

A must read for Jews who seek a deeper understanding of our plight which, as Shore explains in a brilliant twist, should be a source of strength and pride; and for non-Jews who know that antisemitism does not end with the Jews and who want to be on the right side of history.

Charles Jacobs

Author of Betrayal: The Failure of American Jewish Leadership

A genuinely erudite, deeply researched book, one filled both with information that is not widely known and with original insights.

Rabbi Joseph Telushkin
Author of Jewish Literacy

As a Muslim, I found this thought-provoking book invaluable in distinguishing facts from myths, which is crucial in today's world. This balanced and well-researched work, grounded in historical facts, dispels many stereotypes about the nature of antisemitism and the Jewish people.

Raheel Raza
Muslim Rights Activist and Director of the Council for Muslims Against Antisemitism

Who's Afraid of the Big Bad Jew explains antisemitism as a rejection of Jewish values of morality, justice and compassion and attempts to assimilate to avoid this hatred as fruitless. The more Jews assimilate the worse antisemitism becomes. It exposes antisemitism as not just a problem for Jews but a universal problem for anyone wanting to live in a just moral society. It is a wake up call for Jews to take on their mission of being a light unto the nations, teach universal values to the world and embrace their heritage. At a time when so many are struggling to understand the current surge of Jew hatred, this book provides a greater understanding of this cancer and how to respond to it.

Bob Diener
Author of *Biblical Secrets to Business Success* and Co-Founder of Hotels.com

Rabbi Raphael Shore's book 'Who's Afraid of the Big Bad Jew?' belongs in every Jewish home. It will remind us of the Almighty's teaching 'the heavens belong to G-d, but the earth was given to man'. It is in our hands to cure the sick, to educate the uninformed, to confront the haters. The holiness of Mt Sinai has been transferred to Jerusalem and to Klal Yisroel so that we, the ancestors of Abraham, Isaac, and Jacob, can make the world a better place worthy of the redemption of mankind.

Rabbi Marvin Hier
Founder of the Simon Wiesenthal Center and Co-Chairman of the Museum of Tolerance

Raphael poignantly shows that at the core of Jew hatred there is an element of envy that stems from the recognition of what Judaism has brought to the world. On a deeper level, it is a recognition of what the Jewish people have miraculously achieved, that so often the antisemites cannot achieve themselves. Any seeking to understand antisemitism and anti-Zionism today on a deeper level should absolutely read this book.

Emily Schrader
Journalist and Human Rights Activist

WHO'S AFRAID OF THE
BIG BAD JEW?

LEARNING TO LOVE THE LESSONS OF JEW-HATRED

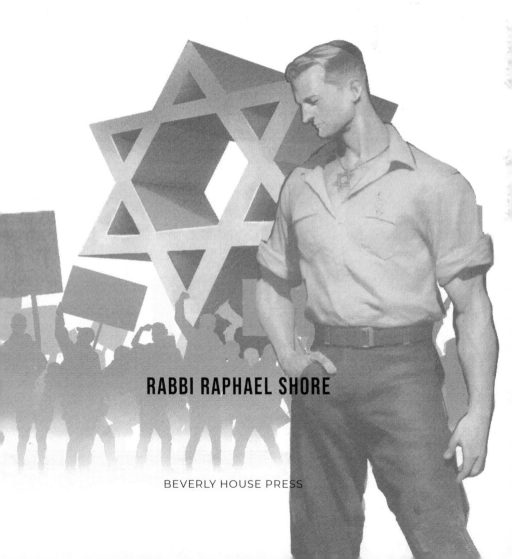

RABBI RAPHAEL SHORE

BEVERLY HOUSE PRESS

Published by

Beverly House Press

304 E. Pine St. #1058

Lakeland, FL 33801

www.BeverlyHousePress.com

ISBN 9781957466101

Printed in the United States of America

1st Printing, October 7, 2024

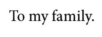

To my family.

Contents

Part Two
From Understanding to Action

WHO'S AFRAID OF THE
BIG BAD JEW?

LEARNING TO LOVE THE LESSONS OF JEW-HATRED

Introduction:

Who's Afraid?

No Jews Allowed. That was the sign my high school friends hung on the door of our usual weekend haunt... How blissfully ignorant had I been? As I was growing up, I never cared much, or thought about, my Jewishness.

I was not one to search for answers to life's mysteries (not even the obvious things)—I was more of the partying type. Perhaps I was even heading out the door of Judaism (or the Jewish People). Growing up happily in the small town of London, Ontario, Canada, among the northern snows, I gave little thought to things like that.

A lousy Hebrew school education at my family's conservative synagogue had convinced me that there was no compelling meaning to my Jewish identity, just some empty rituals and silly "Bible stories." But the wake-up call came on that fateful Friday night in 1978, when my long-standing "friends" locked the doors to the routine weekend party and told me, my brother, and our other Jewish friend, Stewart, that we were not welcome. I was shocked to the core (and it was then that I got into my first and only fistfight).

Stewart had regularly suggested to me that many of our "friends" harbored antisemitic feelings (maybe that is why the hockey jock guy laughed at me when he broke my finger playing soccer?), but I had always disagreed with him. Until then. Antisemitism was real. But what was there about us to hate? I was just like everyone else. Why would anyone hate me over a religion I did not practice or know anything about?

This startling reality that hit me at age 17 was experienced by Jews around the world recently when Hamas committed its cruel massacre of 1,200 Jews on October 7, 2023. The vicious attack, which included indiscriminate killing and raping, shocked people the world over. Equally horrifying was the post–October 7 explosion of hatred toward Jews and Israel. It was a wake-up call for Jews in Israel and around the world who thought that maybe antisemitism had died with the 6 million slaughtered in the Holocaust.

I began writing this book two years before the October 7 massacre. Truth be told, I had been sitting on it, unwritten, for more than 30 years, never feeling the time was right. After my personal Jewish wake-up in high school, I went on a journey of intellectual and spiritual exploration beginning with my university studies and continuing in yeshiva Torah study. I had hesitated to write because, although the conclusions are very meaningful, the ideas challenge conventional wisdom, sacred cows, and what I would call the 'orthodoxy' in much of academia and the Jewish world.

I am not afraid of speaking my mind, stirring controversy, or going against the mainstream, nor do I mind being disliked, but I didn't think the ideas would be heard, and I didn't want to waste my time and breath. With a generation more open to new ideas and enough distance from the Holocaust, I thought my somewhat radical approach could be considered objectively and not simply rejected due to cognitive dissonance.

That is my wish, at least—that with this book, I can help deepen our conversation around the meaning of both Jew-hatred and the Jewish People.

Jews are experiencing a new world—seeing a side of the world they either didn't know or thought no longer existed. As NYU student Bella Ingber testified to Congress, "Being a Jew at NYU is being surrounded by students and faculty who support the murder and kidnapping of Jews because, after all, as they say, resistance is justified. It is being surrounded by social justice warriors and self-proclaimed feminists, whose calls for justice end abruptly when the rape victims are Jews. Being a Jew at NYU is experiencing how diversity, equity, and inclusion is not a value that NYU extends to its Jewish students. Today, in 2023, at NYU, I hear calls to gas the Jews, and I am told that Hitler was right".[1]

Many Jews are now wondering what is happening. How do we make sense of this new reality? Is there something bigger behind the hate, or to being Jewish? These questions are on the minds of many, Jews and non-Jews, but cogent answers are hard to find.

Jewish identity, as it was presented to me and my generation, seemed to revolve around remembering the Holocaust and a few cultural tidbits like bagels and lox. For me, antisemitism was not a reason to be Jewish, and anyone can eat a bagel.

I wanted a positive reason to be Jewish, if there was one. And if there wasn't, well, then it was time to move on. I also wanted to be like everyone else. I thought I was—I played hockey, partied, and enjoyed everything my suburban Canadian life had to offer. But just when I thought I might leave Judaism behind, I began to discover reasons to stay.

At 20, my twin brother found God. I thought he was nuts... at first. We had always been competitive, and that didn't change with his newfound religiosity. We debated. I asked him a lot of questions and was surprised that he had intelligent responses. It got me thinking, for the first time, about deep life questions.

I reflected on being Jewish; although I did not believe in God, I had to admit there was an unarticulated sense in me that we, as Jews, were distinct in some way. Any time I met a fellow Jew, it felt a bit like we were family. To move forward, I needed answers to my basic Jewish questions:

1. Was there an explanation for my feelings of being part of a larger family?

2. Was there a reason for antisemitism, for the peculiar constancy of enmity against us?

3. How do we explain the outsized Jewish impact on the world?

4. How did we survive for so long?

I wanted to go beyond the conventional wisdom and insufficient narrative I had been given in Hebrew school, synagogue, and family holiday gatherings.

As I began my journey of exploration, one of my first stops for insight was reading about the Dalai Lama's investigation. I found he was asking some of the same questions, as described in the book *The Jew in the Lotus*.[2] Across two generations, from the 1950s to the 1980s, the Dalai Lama, the spiritual leader of Tibet, held a series of meetings with Jewish scholars and thinkers to learn the "secret" of Jewish survival.

The Tibetans, like the Jews, had been forced into a global diaspora by military invasion and religious persecution. Neither the Jews nor the Tibetans are unique in that regard. Human history is filled with the stories of ethnic and religious groups who were invaded, conquered, subjugated, and dispersed. In time, these groups usually faded away and were forgotten. But the Jews had survived for thousands of years as a people without a homeland. This mystery is what the exiled Tibetan religious leader hoped to learn so that he could help his people emulate the success and endure.[3]

He was not only impressed by Jewish survival—he was amazed that Jews had maintained a common culture, faith, identity, and brotherhood. And even more, they were successful; they not only survived, they thrived. The Dalai Lama wanted to know how the Jews did it. So did I.

What is it about the Jew that so much of humanity, for good or bad, remains mindful of them? And how do the Jews fit into the family of humanity?

I dove in to understand what being Jewish is about. I wanted to know how and why the Holocaust could have happened in the modern world—what were people thinking? I studied classical Jewish texts about the Jewish People and explored why antisemites say they hate Jews. I delved into texts some might avoid, including Hitler's *Mein Kampf* and everything he wrote or said that was available in English. Studying Hitler, I learned he had a clearly articulated ideology; this surprised me because I had always thought he was a raving lunatic. His own writings and speeches made it clear that the complete elimination of the Jews in Europe was, to him, the logical conclusion of his ideology.[4]

As I dug deeper, I made a second shocking discovery: the two worldviews—Hitler's ideology and Jewish philosophy—shared many common ideas. (I know that sounds crazy, but stay with me.)

What I observed was that they were almost like mirror images of each other, but one side had a positive view, while the other was negative. This strange insight will be unpacked in this book, but suffice it to say now that both sides touched on the most important questions about being human, and it is fascinating.

This book will explain the surprising root causes of antisemitism. But that is not why I wrote it. Sure, it's important to know why Jews are hated, because, as Harvard Professor Ruth Wisse said, "...as long as our actual awareness of the roots and character of anti-Semitism ... remains shallow and poorly informed, it will not lessen the clear and present danger".[5] Understanding Jew-hatred is not this book's purpose. My interest lies in the meaning of it all; this book answers why the Jews have been hated (in a very unconventional way) to reveal the more important, and positive, why—the why of the Jewish People[6]. And what it means for Jews, and all of humanity.

• • •

Thousands of years ago, the Jewish story began when a wanderer, our forefather Abraham, traveled more 2,000 miles to what is today the land of Israel. Like Abraham, I began a journey from even farther away—both geographically and spiritually—that eventually brought me to Israel to question who I was, what my purpose was, and what the content of my life should be.

Abraham left behind a booming civilization with its magnificent towers, great temples, and vast markets because he understood there was more. I, too, had a deep feeling that there was more. My journey led me to discover the profound meaning of my Jewish identity. I ended up becoming a rabbi[7], getting married, and raising a family with my wife in Israel. Because of all I've experienced and the people I've met along the way, I believe that sharing what I've learned can help all Jews understand more about both who they are and why much of the world is reacting the way they are (with hatred and double-speak), once again, today. My main reason for writing Who's Afraid of the Big Bad Jew? is to lay out clearly what has been quite concealed in this generation: the mission and purpose of the Jewish People (and humanity, actually), and how these lessons and ideas can enhance our lives today.

In the process, we will explore the deeper reason for antisemitism, including why the Holocaust happened. When the Torah describes an earlier attempt to destroy the Jews, and how God transformed the sorcerer Balaam's curses into blessings, the Talmud adds that, "From the blessing of that wicked person (Balaam) you can ascertain what was in his heart."[8] This book reveals the inverse: that from the curses of Hitler and other Jew-haters we can learn about our blessings.

After 3,500 years of existence and 2,000 years of exile and oppression, the Jewish People have remarkably survived, returned home, and, as the Dalai Lama recognized, continued to thrive. But with the passage of time, the stresses of persecution, perhaps some negative Jewish social or educational experiences, and today's social pressure towards universalism, many Jews have (understandably) become indifferent and fairly uninformed about what we stand for. After October 7, with so many questions raised and so few answered, can we Jews provide the Dalai Lama—and ourselves—a coherent answer on what our secret is? And do these answers have relevance and meaning for you and me today?

These are not uniquely Jewish questions. They are fundamentally human ones.

Who's Afraid of the Big Bad Jew? is a helpful read for all concerned people who care for their society's health, because Jew-hatred is not just a Jewish problem; its very existence is, in essence, a barometric reading of the moral health of a society. In other words, the rise of antisemitism is a harbinger of moral decline. As Rabbi Lord Sacks often said, "The hate that begins with Jews never ends with Jews."[9] The Jewish People are the proverbial canary in the coal mine, the bird that is destined to be the first victim and alerts others to the impending lethal danger of gas leaks—but they are never the last victim when a society has lost moral clarity and conviction.

This book shares my personal journey of discovery and flips antisemitism on its head, shedding light on its profound insights for Jewish identity and its broader implications for civilization. In doing so, I hope that it serves as a beneficial guide toward personal and collective empowerment.

Part One

Unmasking the Enemy:
The Roots of Jew-Hatred

1

The October 7 Reveal

As I see them from the mountain tops,
gaze on them from the heights;
there is a people that dwells apart,
not reckoned among the nations.
– Numbers 23: 9

WHO'S AFRAID OF the big, bad Jew? Apparently, more than a few people.

No people have been as hated—and for as many reasons—as the Jews. It has been said that if you want to understand someone, look at their enemies. If you ranked the most evil people throughout world history, you'd see that the Jews have been hated by the majority of them. So, we must be doing something important.

One thing we can learn from antisemites is that the Jewish People matter. After all, insignificant peoples and states are not despised, they are ignored. The Jewish People are never ignored, because, clearly, we matter. Ironically, it is the dogged persistence and vehement intensity of their hatred and slander which proves it.

Rather than let that tear us down, we are going to use it to make ourselves stronger. In this book, we will explore together why the Jewish People matter, not just to validate our own existence, but to learn why the Jewish People matter to all of humanity.

While this book will answer why Jews are hated, it is about more than antisemitism. We will explore antisemitism as a means of understanding the mystery of the Jews. You see, Jew-haters may be evil, but they aren't always stupid, and we will carefully study some of them to see if we can gain insight from their thoughts.

In explaining the root cause of antisemitism, this book will illuminate for you the essence of the Jewish People.

Patterns of Hate

What if I told you that what happened on October 7, 2023, was not an aberration in Jewish history—it was part of a pattern? I saw it coming, and you could have too.

On that holy day of Simchat Torah, the radical Islamist Hamas terror organization carried out the largest and most violent pogrom since the Holocaust and reminded the world, once again, that Jew-hatred is still alive. It was the third-deadliest terror attack in modern history.[10]

Hamas and some other Palestinians, with the help and support of Iran, brutally murdered more than 1,200 Jews. Almost all of them were civilians—including babies. They went about systematically raping, torturing and dismembering many. They took more than 250 people including women, elderly, and children, as hostages back to Gaza where they paraded and cheered (and the majority of which, at the time of this writing more than 10 months later, have yet to be returned). In American terms, if we proportionate the population, it would be the equivalent of more than 30,000

Americans murdered. For comparison, the terror attack of 9/11 took a tenth of that—only 3,000 victims.

The revelation that Jew-hatred was still a powerful force in the human heart came as a shock to many. But some people were less surprised by the latest explosion of antisemitism. I take no particular pride in saying that I was one of those who, although saddened and horrified by the brutality, was not bewildered. I knew the signs of what was happening from watching history play out over the last two decades.

I have produced six feature-length documentary films on the threat of radical Islam that have been seen by more than 100 million people over the past 15 years. And, I've produced another three films about the new antisemitism on campuses under the title *Crossing the Line: The Intifada Comes to Campus.* These films revealed that the double standards, demonization, and delegitimization[11] strategies used against Israel on campuses are clear indicators, identified by human rights activist Natan Sharansky, that many anti-Israel advocates have "crossed the line" to antisemitism. That may sound obvious today, after all we have seen since October 7, but at the time, this idea was a novel insight, and many mainstream Jews and organizations challenged me for 'overreacting' and 'scaremongering'.

It was through these films that I tried (in retrospect, quite unsuccessfully) to alert the Jewish People not only that anti-Israel sentiment was widespread and growing, but that it had become the new form of Jew-hatred. I also tried to warn about the corresponding intense pressure on young Jews, leading to a dramatic deterioration in Jewish identity. Unfortunately, my impact was limited.

Recently, a friend asked me how I had been so prescient in my career. After recovering from my surprise at the question, I responded that I am a very regular person; all I did was listen and take seriously what the Islamists who hated us had been saying. I respected them enough to believe them at face value, to believe they meant what they said, and I did not choose to ignore them or project my Western attitudes onto them.[12]

I did not say, "that's not what they mean; they just need to say that because…" or "they just want a better economic situation for their family" or "they just want a little land of their own and then they will welcome peace" because that is not what they were saying—neither their leaders, their teachers, nor their imams (Muslim religious leaders). When the Palestinian Authority, considered by many to be moderate because they are less extreme than Hamas, legislates a "pay to slay" program and spent $300 million in 2023—10% of their annual budget—to reward their people who kill Jews, I am honest enough to say that these folks are not moderate.

Sadly, I was in the minority and part of only a small club of activists who took what those Jew-haters were saying at face value. Major organizations that were supposed to be the Jewish world's bellwether chose for decades to minimize Islamic antisemitism and focus almost exclusively on hate from the far right, skinheads, and the like.

Despite serious distribution efforts, my films about the the growing problems on campus were not shown much at the main Jewish student organizations, which preferred to minimize matters and promote the idea that the Oslo peace process was a success.[13] Meanwhile, Israeli leaders fawned over Arafat and worked hard to sell us that those 1,000 murdered in the second intifada's terror attacks were "sacrifices for peace". They tried to convince us that we had true peace partners, despite Arafat's consistent statements in Arabic—and the bus bombs—that forcefully belied this.[14]

By doing so, our leaders helped lull the Jewish People—and the rest of the world—to sleep. After all, if our political, organizational, and thought leaders were telling us not to worry about Islamic

Jew-hate, then I guess we were safe. Then came October 7, and out of the carnage, everyone could see that their "concept" had been terribly mistaken.

This is not the first time Jews have chosen denial in the face of an unpleasant reality. A friend recently shared with me how his grandparents had prepared for his father's bar mitzvah in Budapest in January 1944, as if life was normal—two months later, they were shocked as they, along with 400,000 Hungarian Jews, were shipped off to Auschwitz.

In 1939, 1944, and 2023, there were some who were not surprised by the horrors that followed, but they were the minority; we consistently want to be convinced, understandably, that we live in a new, tolerant world, or perhaps that we have succeeded in becoming invincible, but these false hopes indicate that we Jews have a propensity for denial.

Jews have many virtues, and that is what this book is about, but we are human, as well, and like most people, our strengths are also our weaknesses; we are kind-hearted and compassionate, we love life, and we want to believe all people are like us—merciful and peaceful. But sometimes others have radically different values, and listening to them is not easy. Believing them is even harder. It's as though people tell themselves: "They couldn't *really* mean that they want us dead, or our country wiped out. Clearly we are misunderstanding—let's give them the benefit of the doubt."

It is certainly hard to face hatred head on—not just because it reveals that dark side of humanity, but because it means that Jews still cannot rest; we must live with the reality that we will continue to be chased and persecuted.

It is hard to accept that, despite our desire and efforts for peace, yet another generation of young Jews will need to fight for the defense of their country—or else be annihilated—and that peace will remain elusive because the other side's Jew-hatred is so strong that it has not yet come to terms with living side by side with Jews.

We had hoped and prayed that with our return home to our historical homeland, our 2,000 years of pain and persecution would end together with our exile, but October 7 revealed to our generation that antisemitism is still here, and still intense, both in Israel and around the world.

Why the Jews?

Let's try to understand why Jewish hatred exists. It is very perplexing and enigmatic because so many different reasons have been given to explain and justify it.

So Many Reasons for Antisemitism

American Jews have had other recent wake-up calls—not just the 2018 Pittsburgh Tree of Life synagogue attack where 11 were killed, but in 2019, a white supremacist opened fire in a synagogue in the small city of Poway, California. Months later and thousands of miles away, a black supremacist attacked a congregation with a machete in Monsey, a New York town with a large Jewish population.

The two bigots of different races on opposite sides of the United States disagreed on which of them belonged to the master race, but both hated Jews enought to attack and kill.

The Poway shooter credited Hitler and accused the Jews of a "meticulously planned genocide of the European race." The Monsey slasher claimed that Jews had usurped the true "Ebinoid Israelites" and searched for "German Jewish Temples" to attack. One killer saw Jews as the enemies of white Europeans, while the other saw Jews as white Europeans. But both were convinced that the Jews posed a threat to their identities—and to the world.

These two attacks were part of a 14% surge in antisemitic hate crimes in 2019 resulting in more than 1,000 victims. Even though Jews are less than 2% of the American population, 60% of all religious-based hate crimes targeted Jews.[15] In all, 88% of American Jews say that antisemitism is a problem, 82% believe that it's rising, and 25% say they have personally experienced an antisemitic incident.[16]

All of that was before October 7, when anti-Jewish religious hate crimes were already six times more common in the US than the next-largest category.[17] Since then, the numbers have exploded.

On college and university campuses, the number of antisemitic incidents rose by more than 700% since the the previous year.[18] The ADL recorded a total of 2,031 antisemitic incidents in the US in the two months following the attack of October 7. The numbers were up from 465 incidents during the same period in 2022, representing a 337% increase year-over-year.[19]

Britain has recorded thousands of antisemitic incidents after the outbreak of the war in Israel, making 2023 the worst year for UK antisemitism since they began recording such data.[20] And a 2024 survey found that 96% of European Jews experience antisemitism in their daily lives.[21] One poll shows that a billion people around the world harbor antisemitic attitudes (see figure on next page).[22]

From Eastern Europe to Sub-Saharan Africa[23], and from Asia to South America, a few million Jews somehow generate the resentment and hatred of 100 times that number of people.

The enigmatic nature of antisemitism makes it so that people, like the two synagogue attackers, who agree on nothing else—who would even be willing to kill each other—are even more willing to kill Jews. Nations, creeds, and ideologies who can agree on nothing else will agree to hate the Jews.

Sunni Muslim and Shia Muslims hate each other intensely, but that has not prevented the Sunni Hamas from cozying with their patrons, the Islamic Shia Republic of Iran. Much like arch enemies Hitler and Stalin, who both plotted to massacre Jews, or the biblical Midianites and Moabites, historical rivals who united to oppose the Jewish return to Israel from Egypt, this has always been the case. Today, in the US and Europe, the progressive leftist campus activists join hands with radical Islamist supporters in an odd couple red-green alliance, and despite being diametrically opposed on most core values, they come together to fight against the Jewish State.

Figure 1. Global Distribution of Antisemitic Attitudes: *The map shows the percentage of adults harboring antisemitic attitudes across various regions. The highest prevalence is in the Middle East & North Africa (74%), followed by Eastern Europe (34%) and Western Europe (24%). The global index score indicates that 26% of the world's adult population, equating to 1.09 billion of the 4.1 billion adults surveyed, hold antisemitic views.*

In 1843, Karl Marx[24], author of *The Communist Manifesto*, ranted, "What is the worldly religion of the Jew? Huckstering. What is his worldly God? Money... Money is the jealous god of Israel, in the face of which no other god may exist."[25] Almost a century later, in 1935, Joseph Goebbels, the propaganda boss of Nazi Germany, denounced, "It was the Jew who discovered Marxism. It is the Jew who for decades past has endeavored to stir up world revolutions through the medium of Marxism[26] To the Nazis, the Jews embodied Judeo-Bolshevism and, to their arch-enemy Communists, Judeo-Fascism.

The inherent contradictions of the two synagogue killers have always been with us. In the decades leading up to the Holocaust, the greatest mass slaughter of Jews in history, Jews were accused of having invented both religion and atheism, of being nationalists and internationalists, radicals and bourgeois, for inflicting on mankind morality and immorality, capitalism and socialism.

Antisemitism is filled with paradoxical contradictions. The Jews are seen as both powerful and weak. The Jews are accused of being utterly worthless *untermenschen*, or subhuman as the Nazis called them, and yet are deemed to be exerting "too much influence," engineering human history and current events in a world where they constitute only 0.2% of the population.

When the financial crisis hit Asia in 1997, Prime Minister Mahathir of Malaysia blamed an international Jewish conspiracy. "The Jews rule this world by proxy,"[27] he insisted. The coronavirus pandemic led to a record number of antisemitic incidents in the UK, Alt-Righters in America took to calling it the "Jew Flu," and Palestinian Prime Minister Shtayyeh claimed that Israeli soldiers were "trying to spread the virus through the door handles of cars."[28]

There is no accusation too implausible for antisemitism to take root.

Antisemitism is reinvented in every generation—Jews are called god-killers, they are condemned as an impure race, and in modern times they are labeled as colonialist oppressors. As the economist George Gilder explains, "Today this choice (of being antisemitic or not), with all its relentless implications, is focused not on the Jews in the neighborhood but on the Jews as a nation (Israel)."[29] In other words, antisemitism has morphed again, and now is often cloaked in the "legitimate" dislike of Israeli policies[30] the complexities of which we will explore further as we go through our texts.

The Jews were taunted as cowards in Europe, even when they had fought bravely in every European army, from that of the Czar in the farthest east to the United Kingdom in the west. And yet, when they fought for themselves in their regained ancient homeland, they were dubbed as *warmongers* and *savages*. The Jews are accused of terrorism when they fight for their freedom. And then accused of oppression once they had won it.

When Israel fights, it's condemned. When it withdraws, as it did from Lebanon and Gaza, it is ignored and denounced. Philosopher Eric Hoffer said it wryly in a memorable 1968 *Los Angeles Times* article: "Other nations, when victorious on the battlefield, dictate peace terms. But when Israel is victorious it must sue for peace. Everyone expects the Jews to be the only real Christians in this world."[31]

The sheer scope of global opposition to Israel, a tiny democratic nation the size of New Jersey that is nevertheless the nearly exclusive focus of UN Security Council condemnations[32], appears entirely irrational except from the perspective of anti-Jewish bias.

The eternal hatred of Jews, often leading to genocide, has flowed through the bloodied rivers of civilization for thousands of years. It began in Egypt, where Jewish children were drowned, continued to ancient Persia with a decree for physical annihilation, and persisted through the Greek campaign of cultural genocide. The

Roman Empire's destruction of Jerusalem and the subsequent cruel exile, the persecution in Europe under Christianity, and the horrors of the Holocaust are all part of this dark history. Today, this hatred fragments into numerous streams, flowing globally through the multigenerational wars and radical Islamic terror of the Arab-Muslim world.

Jews remember some of these episodes in Passover, Purim, Chanukah, and many other feasts and fasts. These traditions serve as poignant reminders that Jew-hatred has endured as long as there have been Jews. As we celebrate our improbable victories over more powerful oppressors, we often summarize our survival with the catchphrase, "They tried to kill us. We won. Let's eat." We belittle our own battles and victories because they have become predictable. We know that the bigotry is nothing new. As Tom Lehrer sang in National Brotherhood Week, "Oh, the Protestants hate the Catholics/And the Catholics hate the Protestants/ And the Hindus hate the Muslims/ And everybody hates the Jews."

Science fiction writer Dan Simmons mused, "What common element will bind 2001 and 3001? The answer, when it arrived, hit me with the full nausea of certainty. *The one constant thread between today and a thousand years from now will be that someone, somewhere, will be planning to kill the Jews.*"[33] (his emphasis)

Simmons's answer appears absurd in the fantastic milieu of flying cars and spaceships, and yet it is historically inescapable as the one constant that endures across different eras and cultures.

"No Jews Allowed" Redux

Antisemitism is embraced by madmen, but it also seems to make great men mad.

After urging that synagogues be burned and rabbis be banned

from teaching, the 16th-century theologian and founder of the Christian Reformation, Martin Luther, agonized, "What will happen even if we do burn down the Jews' synagogues and forbid them publicly to praise God, to pray, to teach, to utter God's name? They will still keep doing it in secret."[34]

Luther, whose antisemitism would later inspire the Nazis, was obsessed with the idea that even if the synagogues were destroyed, the Jews would go on praying. This same obsession drove the Spanish Inquisition to cruelly target Conversos, the Jews who had converted to Christianity by force rather than be killed at the stake. For 700 years they went after Conversos, convinced they were worshiping their God in secret.

Hitler mirrored this fear a few hundred years later, when he demanded that Germany and Europe must become *judenrein*— free of Jews.

Today, the populations under both Hamas and the Palestinian Authority were rated in the 2023 annual ADL survey as the most Jew-hating on the planet with an astonishing antisemitic rate of 93%[35]. It's no surprise that they continue to insist that their territories be 100% Jew-less, just as the Nazis demanded last century.

Even in the supposedly progressive world of 2024, the Palestinians uphold two horrifying laws: one that rewards Palestinians with escalating financial rewards and a life pension for killing Jews, and another that mandates the death penalty for anyone selling land to a Jew.[36]

Almost every European country has at one point in history kicked their Jews out[37] including England, Spain, Portugal, France, Hungary and Lithuania. But even after Jews are expelled or killed, the obsession remains. The Jews never seem to be far enough away for those that hate us.[38]

Today, even in nations where there are almost no Jews, antisemitism thrives. Despite most Jews being dead or gone after 90% of Poland's 3.3 million[39] Jewish population were murdered, hatred remains. Today, a country doesn't need a Jewish population for antisemitism to thrive.

We see this holds true especially in the Arab Muslim world. Despite the fact that most of the region's Jewish population of a million souls fled from fear or were driven out of nations like Egypt, Morocco, Yemen, and Iraq almost 100 years ago, antisemitism is rampant throughout the region.[40]

Not So Surprising for Judaism

For many well-informed Jews, this remarkable persistence of Jew-hate is hardly surprising. Jewish tradition is intimately familiar with the double standard and the catch-22 game of antisemitism. A story in the *Midrash*, a compendium of Jewish thought encapsulated in stories or parables, tells of the second-century Roman Emperor Hadrian encountering two Jews:[41]

> The first Jew greeted Hadrian.
>
> "Who are you?" demanded the emperor who had brutally destroyed Israel and replaced its name with that of 'Palestine'.
>
> "I am a Jew," came the reply.
>
> "How dare a Jew pass before Hadrian and greet him. Cut off his head," the emperor ordered.
>
> The second Jew did not greet Hadrian.
>
> "How dare a Jew pass before Hadrian and not greet him. Cut off his head," he commanded.

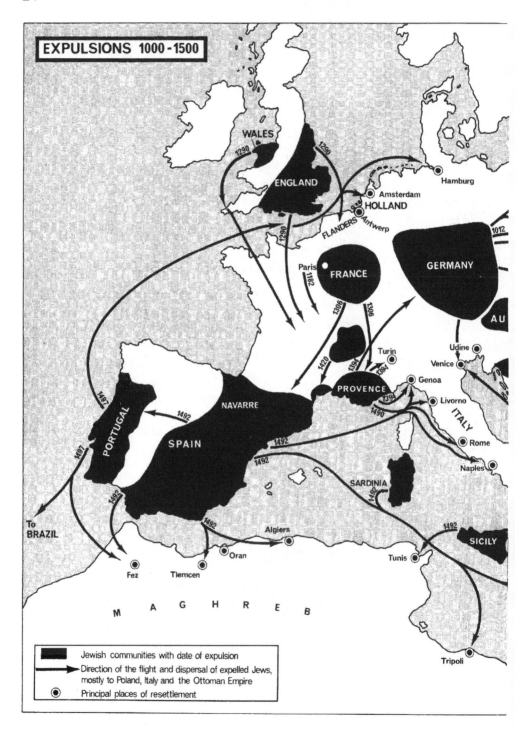

EXPULSIONS 1000-1500

WALES
1290
1290
ENGLAND
Hamburg
1290
Amsterdam
HOLLAND
FLANDERS
Antwerp
1290
Paris
1182
FRANCE
GERMANY
1012
AU
1306
1306
Turin
Udine
Venice
1420
1394
1394
Genoa
PROVENCE
1394
Livorno
1497
NAVARRE
ITALY
1492
Rome
PORTUGAL
SPAIN
1492
1490
1497
Naples
1492
1492
SARDINIA
To
BRAZIL
1492
1492
1492
Algiers
1492
Oran
SICILY
Fez
Tlemcen
Tunis
Tripoli
M   A   G   H   R   E   B   B

■ Jewish communities with date of expulsion
➤ Direction of the flight and dispersal of expelled Jews,
mostly to Poland, Italy and the Ottoman Empire
◉ Principal places of resettlement

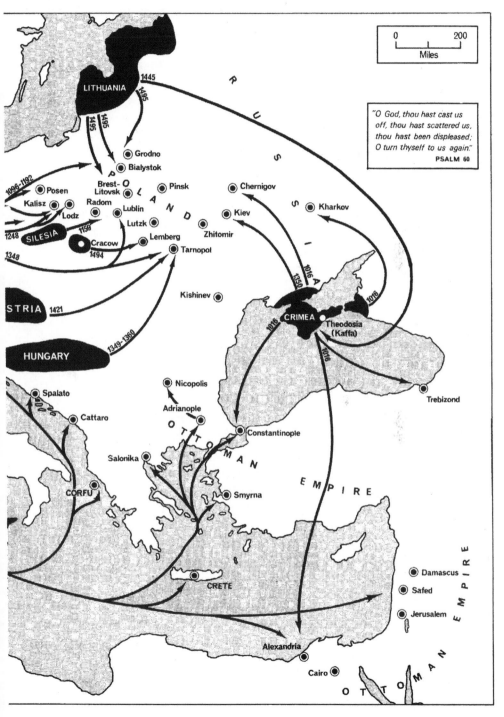

Figure 2. Map of Jewish Expulsions from 1000-1500 CE.[52]

When asked why he had killed both the Jew who had greeted him and the Jew who had not, the emperor retorted, "I do not need your advice about killing the people I hate."

The Common Denominator: Jews Are What You Despise

From the Hellenist Greeks to the Crusaders and the Nazis, and from the Communists to Iran and the Muslim Brotherhood, authoritarian ideologies often seem to have two things in common:

1.   An obsession with conquering the world

2.   Hatred of the Jews

Despite these groups having diametrically opposed worldviews, their primary common enemy remains the Jew. Historian Robert Wistrich articulates this bizarre phenomenon in his epic work, *Antisemitism: The Longest Hatred*:

> …whether it be fear of pollution by alien 'inferior' races; the angst provoked by class struggle, ethnic and religious conflict, the leveling tendencies of mass societies; the hatred of capitalism or Communism (etc.)…(they all conclude that the)… principle evil is not in ourselves. It comes from the outside…the mythical Jew.[42]

It is astonishing that the target is always the Jews. Antisemitism is unique in its universality, intensity, and longevity. Yet, it consistently presents with a similar theme: Jews are seen as more than just a disliked group—they are perceived as a mortal threat to civilization. It is this exaggerated belief that so often drives Jew-hatred beyond mere racism to genocide.

Author Dara Horn summarizes the elasticity and the 'how' of Jew-hatred as traced in historian David Nirenberg's book *Anti-Judaism*:[43]

> ...this deep neural groove in Western thought becomes difficult to dismiss, its patterns unmistakable. If piety was a given society's ideal, Jews were impious blasphemers; if secularism was the ideal, Jews were backward pietists. If capitalism was evil, Jews were capitalists; if communism was evil, Jews were communists. If nationalism was glorified, Jews were rootless cosmopolitans; if nationalism was vilified, Jews were chauvinistic nationalists. "Anti-Judaism" thus becomes a righteous fight to promote justice.[44]

Antisemitism's persistence and intensity throughout history reveals a deeply rooted hatred that transcends time and ideology. This is the 'how' of antisemitism. But the unyielding animosity demands a closer examination to understand why Jews have been uniquely targeted across centuries and cultures.

Reasons or Excuses?

Knowing the perplexing *how* of Jew-hate only begs the question further: why is it the Jews who perform this bizarre role in history? We need to go deeper and understand why the Jews are consistently "chosen".

It is not enough to say that Jews become the opposite of a society's values; even if true, it doesn't fully explain the issue. We see that there seems to be an infinite number of possible 'reasons' to hate the Jewish People. But, what is so strangely compelling about them that brings together so many diverse peoples, cultures, and religions around a murderous obsession? The ultimate goal of antisemitism is eliminating Jews; the "reasons" seem to be secondary.

Many contradictory and imaginative excuses have been made to explain the hate, but the big question persists: *Why do so many people and nations want to see the Jewish People wiped out*?

Why, even today, just 80 years after the Holocaust, are not only millions of Islamists, but also many college professors, calling for the elimination[45] of the only Jewish state?[46]

Why, when we envision life in the year 3001, must we also envision antisemitism? What is behind the incredible exceptionalism of antisemitism and, by extension, of the Jews?

The Three Possible Explanations

There are three possible answers to the above questions:

1. It's not about the Jews.

2. The Jews are really bad.

3. It's about the Jews.

Let's think about each of these possibilities:

It's not about the Jews at all. It has become the accepted 'explanation' of antisemitism and is the actually the reason most commonly given. The claim is that we are being used as scapegoats, which means it's just a bad coincidence that when a society needed to blame some group, we were there for them to use. It means that despite what antisemites may say are their reasons for hating Jews, those reasons are not really what bothers them. Conventional wisdom would have us believe that it's simply xenophobia, a garden variety of bigotry and "dislike of the unlike";[47] the Jews were at the wrong place at the wrong time. Sometimes this idea is expressed as "antisemitism is a virus," a disease that is seemingly unknowable.

The Jews are really bad. This answer assumes that everything that antisemites say we are—a bothersome force, an evil influence, deserving of persecution in every generation—is true.

It's about the Jews. The Jews are not so bad, and Jew-hatred is not an unfathomable disease, but there is something deeper, beyond the contradictory smears, the double standards and the obsessions, that has fueled antisemitism for thousands of years.

Which one is the answer?

The conventionally accepted explanations of antisemitism are inadequate: Either they only identify the external excuses, or they give up on explaining it by saying Jews are convenient scapegoats, but these explanations don't reach the heart of the matter. As Douglas Murray said, "this can't be a coincidence."[48] These attempts to explain Jew-hatred as being unrelated to the Jews is what Dennis Prager and Joseph Telushkin have called the 'dejudaization of Jew-hatred."[49]

If antisemitism is a "mutating virus," as it is popularly called today, then let's behave as doctors do. Let's stop being distracted by the myriad and contradictory symptoms, and instead search for the root cause of the virus.

To get to the answer, I have done what it seems I do well and, sadly,[50] somewhat uniquely:[51] I listen to the Jew-haters and take seriously what they say, rather than interpreting and having them mean what I *want* to hear.

I will share with you what I have learned from a most surprising source. You see, it turns out that history's worst and most-famous Jew-hater provides an unexpected explanation of who the Jews are.

And through exploring the dark corridors of Adolf Hitler's mind, we will unearth a paradoxical affirmation of the Jewish People's significance.

2

Hitler's Chosen People—The Irony of Antisemitic Insight

Then Balak said to Balaam, "What have you done to me? Here I brought you to damn my enemies (the Jews), and instead you have blessed them!" Balaam replied, "I can only repeat faithfully what God puts in my mouth."
–Numbers, 23:11–12

"Rational" Antisemitism

ADOLF HITLER CONSIDERED himself a "rational antisemite."[53] He considered most Jew-haters in history to be "emotional antisemites" who would not come to the necessary, logical conclusion to deal with the "Jewish problem."

Hitler had a plan to solve the problem. He was a very evil person—he hated and killed many people and groups—but it was the Jews he was most obsessed with, and only for them did he mobilize the German nation to commit genocide. What was he so concerned about, and why were the Jews Hitler's chosen people?

As we analyze this together, you'll learn that Adolf Hitler was afraid of the Jews. Hitler's Holocaust was driven not just by hate, but by fear of a Jewish victory over Germany in an unseen war. In short, Hitler believed that "Jewish ideas" and values were harmful to human progress. He saw that these values had been adopted by European civilization and incorporated in society. For the sake of Europe—indeed, all human progress—Hitler took on the task of uprooting these foreign, destructive ideas at their source.

As early as 1919, Hitler's first written political document distinguished between "emotional" antisemitism and "rational" antisemitism, where the "ultimate goal" would "unalterably be the elimination of the Jews altogether."[54] A year later, he called for eradicating the Jews' "root and branch."[55] He claimed to have studied the Jewish "problem" for years to understand its nature.[56]

In the spring of 1933, in response to a protest against new Nazi laws by Italy's Ambassador in Berlin, Hitler declared:

> No one understands this problem better than I do, because I have made a thorough study of it and I know how dangerous the Jews in Germany are…I refuse to alter a single point in my programme…to rid the world of the Jewish pest.[57]

Five years after calling for a "rational antisemitism," Hitler contended, "I have been much too soft" and was now convinced that only "the most severe methods of fighting" would do. The fight against the Jews, he argued, was a "vital question not just for our people but for all peoples. For Juda is the plague of the world."[58]

Based on his assessment of the problem, he ultimately proposed and executed a ruthless "final solution." Sure, Hitler opined, many Jew-haters throughout the ages persecuted the Jews, keeping them as second-class citizens and/or killing them in pogroms and acts of terror; some, like the Romans, the Inquisitors, and Chmielnicki even led murderous campaigns that killed hundreds of thousands and perhaps millions. But in the past couple of millennia, only he conceived and implemented a final solution, determined to accomplish the total destruction of the Jewish People. In his view every single Jew had to die: genocide.[59]

Why? In what way was this solution "rational"? What "problem" was he trying to solve?

On the surface, Hitler seemed incredibly irrational, and his antisemitism seemed compulsive and emotional.

Wasn't He Crazy?
The Insanity Distraction

Before we dive into what Hitler defined as the "problem," let's first note something very important that creates a lot of cognitive dissonance against hearing what might be rational about Hitler's worldview.

We have been taught—even conditioned, I would say—to believe that the Holocaust was unknowable and that Hitler was a lunatic, and therefore his thinking could not be at all coherent. After all, he was a racist, was very mercurial, and made some questionable military decisions. Most historians agree that Hitler mismanaged the war with a series of overreaches: a pre-emptive assault on the Soviet Union,[60] which had been his ally at the time and was supplying his war machine with crucial aid; his unwillingness to give up Stalingrad at any cost; and a miscalculated pre-emptive declaration of war on the US.

And even as the German military was in retreat in 1944, thousands of trains that might have saved his soldiers' lives and prolonged Germany's ability to continue fighting were instead diverted to kill the Jews. Even beyond the perplexing choice of using scarce resources to kill Jews instead of fighting the war, it is beyond puzzling that a military superpower would embark on such a grandiose program of persecution, to deploy so much energy and resources hunting down a tiny minority group scattered around Europe that posed no military threat to him.

In 1945, while his armies were being crushed by the American and Russian forces he had unnecessarily begun wars with, he put a gun to his head and pulled the trigger.

Hitler's racism and antisemitism seemed irrational in other ways, as well.

The world war that he provoked in 1939 required building bonds with other murderous antisemites, no matter how different they might outwardly seem. That included a man Hitler hosted as an honored guest of the Nazi state from 1941 until 1945—Haj Amin al-Husseini, the Grand Mufti of Jerusalem. He is considered by many to be the father of Palestinian terror and the grandfather of Hamas, an offshoot of the Muslim Brotherhood that he helped build in the 1920s and '30s.

In 1941, the Mufti had a private meeting with Hitler, to convince the Führer of the need to wage war on the Jews, only to be informed bluntly that antisemitism was as fundamental to the Nazi worldview as it was to the Islamist who would later be dubbed "Hitler's Mufti."

Hitler told al Husseini to take his assurance and "to lock it in the uttermost depths of his heart," promising him that when the extermination of the Jews of Europe was complete, Germany would reach the Middle East and its objective would "be solely the destruction of the Jewish element."[61] Nazi Germany would not undertake this invasion to conquer the land only, but to kill the Jews.

There was room in Hitler's outlook for a diversity of races and religions, albeit some to be subjugated by his Aryan master race,

Figure 3. Hitler and the Mufti of Jerusalem.
Bundesarchiv, Bild 469-1987-004-09A | Heinrich Hoffmann | CC-BY-SA 3.0

but there was no place for tolerance with the Jews, who had to be eradicated.

With all of this disjointed decision-making, can there be any sense to Hitler's obsession with the Jews?

Most people think not. Scholars have overwhelmingly dismissed Hitler's fixation with the Jews as either irrational or tactics for propaganda, manipulations for political purposes. For example, in the classic *Hitler: A Study in Tyranny*, historian Alan Bullock concludes that Hitler's "...dictatorship was barren of all ideas save one - the further extension of his own power and that of the nation with which he had identified himself." According to Bullock, "...the sole theme of the Nazi revolution was domination...dressed up in the doctrine of race...It is this emptiness, this lack of anything to justify the suffering he caused...which makes Hitler...so barren a figure."[62]

The conventional wisdom has become that the Holocaust was an unknowable aberration, as historian Isaac Deutscher describes, "... it is the absolutely unique character of this catastrophe. It is not only a matter of time and of historical perspective. I doubt that in a thousand years people will better understand Hitler…".[63] The meaning is clear: Hitler's antisemitism made no sense, Jews were the unlucky scapegoat in a mad megalomaniac's irrational war for power.

It is easy to dismiss Hitler as a madman.[64] He was incredibly evil, and so it goes against our sensibilities of decency to judge him as sensible in some way.[65] But this accepted approach has distracted people from searching for the essence of what drove the Holocaust. Hitler claimed to have a coherent and consistent worldview that informed his decisions, and so, before dismissing him, it behooves us to listen. And when we listen, we will see from his own spoken and written words that there was a method to his madness.[66]

Hitler's Worldview: A Method to His Madness

Hitler's *weltanschaulich*, which is best translated as "ideology" or "worldview," was an encompassing philosophy—he expressed it clearly and openly. It provided the German people with a purpose and a cause. He explained why it was necessary to exterminate the Jewish People.

Let's unpack his worldview, one step at a time, in his own words.

The starting point for understanding lies in what Hitler told the Mufti that day in 1941, that his primary fight was not against armies, but ideas:

> Germany was at the present time engaged in a life
> and death struggle with two citadels of Jewish power:
> Great Britain and Soviet Russia…theoretically there
> was a difference between England's capitalism and
> Soviet Russia's communism; but in practice the

> Jews in both countries were pursuing a common
> goal. This was the decisive struggle...ideologically
> it was a battle between National Socialism and the
> Jews.[67]

The worldview of Nazi Germany was a struggle against Jewish ideas and philosophy, which were embodied in the physical existence of the Jews. We will soon see why England and Russia were considered to be reflecting Jewish power, but the main takeaway here is that to Hitler, the movements of armies, the thunder of artillery, and the roar of warplanes, were an expression of a deeper ideological struggle between the Third Reich and a tiny, fragmented people.

The Jews were seemingly too small—less than 1% of the population[68]—and weak—they had no military—to pose any threat to a Nazi war machine that plundered westward across Europe and then eastward to the USSR. And yet, the Jews were seen as the prime enemy that threatened Germany's future and Europe's entire civilization.

In his 1925 autobiographical manifesto, *Mein Kampf*, Hitler had already defined Germany as the vanguard of a revolutionary global mission in fighting the Jews: "If Germany frees itself from this embrace (of Jewry), this greatest of all dangers to the peoples can be regarded as crushed for the entire world."[69]

Only the Jewish People needed a "final solution" because they were the biggest threat.

How could this small and despised group of people be victorious over the might of Germany?

Hitler's answer was that the Jews could win the war of ideologies.

The Nazi Idea:
Survival of the Fittest—for Nations

Hitler's grand plan was to build a rejuvenated human order built on "natural" European values that had been lost, forgotten, or, more to the point, replaced by Jewish ones. He borrowed from an intellectual movement popular in his days: Social Darwinism. While Darwin in the 1850s had identified "survival of the fittest" as the governing principle that drives evolution—i.e., progress of the animal kingdom—Social Darwinism, which arrived soon after and became popular in late-19th-century Europe, asserted that the same rules apply to humans.

Just as in the jungle, where struggle and combat are the filtering tools for survival, allowing the fittest to endure while the weak are eliminated (thus guaranteeing progress), so it was with humans. Social Darwinism asserted that these laws of nature also govern human development; instead of animal species, it is nations, people, or races that evolve and develop through the struggle for survival and domination.[70]

In *Mein Kampf,* Hitler often returned to this theme:

> The ultimate wisdom is...a man must never fall into the lunacy of believing that he has really risen to be lord and master of Nature...he must...realize how much his existence is subjected to these laws of eternal fight and upward struggle. Then he will realize that in a universe where planets revolve around suns, and moons turn about planets, where force alone forever masters weakness, compelling it to be an obedient slave or else crushing it, there can be no special laws for man.[71]

If conflict, power and force are nature's best drivers to evolve and develop mankind's strength and vitality, then Hitler understood that mankind was in deep trouble if they did not observe these Natural Laws:

> The earth continues to go round, whether it's the man who kills the tiger or the tiger who eats the man...Men dispose of one another, and one perceives that, at the end of it all, it is always the stronger who triumphs. Is that not the most reasonable order of things? If it were otherwise, nothing good would ever have existed. If we did not respect the laws of nature, imposing our will by the right of the stronger, a day would come when the wild animals would once again devour us... and finally nothing would exist on earth but the microbes.[72]

As he surveyed Europe in the early 20th century, Hitler concluded that mankind was now in peril. Over the preceding millennia, humanity had been diverted from a *natural* process in which the strongest triumphed, and instead had bought into a diametrically opposite value system of soft "ethical ideas" that protected the weak and sick, had compassion for the underdog, and placed morality above strength as the highest virtue. The results of this experiment gone wrong were, much like wild animals caged in a zoo that become depleted of their vitality, a diminished, worn-out, domesticated Europe.

For Hitler, his ethics and morality were sourced in struggle, survival, and victory, as he wrote in *Mein Kampf*: "Mankind has grown great in struggle, and only in eternal peace does it perish."[73] In August 1941, he declared a logical conclusion of this worldview: "For the good of the German people, we must wish for a war every fifteen or twenty years."[74]

A logical corollary of this worldview was the necessity for

inequality. Addressing a meeting of the German diaspora abroad, Hitler was paraphrased saying, "Forget all you have learned hitherto. We do not seek equality, but mastery. We shall not waste time over minority rights and other such ideological abortions of sterile democracy."[75]

If nations or people are like species, then another inescapable inference is that the individual does not have intrinsic value. Hitler sought to usher in a moral system that mirrors nature, where, just as the "fly is snapped up by a dragonfly, which itself is swallowed by a bird,"[76] individual people would be disposable and only the survival of the nation mattered. Hitler said, "The life of the individual must not be set at too high a price."[77]

Consistent with this philosophy were various German laws enacted to evolve the ideal German *volk* (regular Germans). For example, the July 14, 1933 Law for the Prevention of Progeny of Sufferers from Hereditary Diseases, empowered the National Socialists to sterilize the sick. In January 1940, a full-scale euthanasia campaign was launched, and by August 1941, the Nazis had disposed of 70,273 of their own Aryans.[78]

Hitler said, "If I can accept a divine Commandment, it's this one: 'Thou shalt preserve the species.'"[79] Social Darwinism became the scientific justification for the Nazi belief in the inequality between peoples and nations.[80]

Enter the Jews—and the Opposite Ideology

In the natural world, the stronger overcomes the weaker, and so it would be among human beings if not for the Jews. According to Hitler, "It is Jewry that always destroys this order."[81]

What was the Jewish "insolent objection" to nature's laws, in Hitler's worldview?

The ideas that intellectually oppose Hitler's *weltanschauung* are those that assert that humanity stands outside the social Darwinian construct—that man is not a mere animal, an expendable fly to be disposed of. Against this Nazi worldview stood the Jewish idea that man is also a spiritual being with infinite value and that there exist moral imperatives and humanitarian values—e.g., to help the poor, weak, and oppressed (rather than to eliminate them) and to strive for human rights and peace (not war).

The Jewish worldview emphasizes that humanity transcends the social Darwinian construct, asserting that humans are spiritual beings with infinite value and moral imperatives.

Hitler argued that Nature knows nothing of the notion of humanitarianism which signifies that the weak must be protected, especially at the expense of the strong. Unless humankind abandoned these humanistic ideals and reverted to the rule of natural law, it would surely be destroyed.[82] Hitler's *weltanschauung* understood the world to be fighting over values, between the "effeminate pity-ethics" of humanitarianism that believes in the equality of mankind against the "aristocratic principle of Nature" where might makes right.[83]

Hitler and the Nazis sought to resurrect a "hierarchy among nations"[84] based on struggle (*kampf*), dominated by the powerful, to renew humanity. However, historical progress had been interrupted because "It is Jewry that ...constantly provokes the revolt of the weak against the strong."[85]

Hitler believed that everything except nature's law of raw force was a human delusion, specifically a Jewish delusion:

> It is always primarily the Jew who tries and succeeds

> in planting such mortally dangerous modes of
> thought in our people…who can make them think
> he has found a way to play a little trick on Nature....[86]

Hitler saw himself as restoring a pagan civilizational imperative that the Jews had sabotaged.[87] To be clear, like so many evil people before and after him, Hitler honestly thought he was doing good; he believed he was acting for the benefit of his nation and all humanity. "I would prefer not to see anyone suffer, not to do harm to anyone. But when I realize that the species [Aryans] are in danger, then in my case sentiment gives way to the coldest reason."[88]

In sharp contradiction to the social Darwinian Nazi worldview, the Judaic outlook placed humanitarianism at the forefront, emphasizing compassion and human rights, rather than brute force. "Eternal Nature inexorably avenges the infringement of her commands,"[89] Hitler argued in *Mein Kampf*, and that was what he was doing "by defending myself against the Jew" who had undermined the "privilege of power and strength."[90]

The Vision:
A New Nazi Man and World Order

The new, ideal Germany Hitler envisioned would live by the laws of Nature. Hitler was paraphrased by Hermann Rauschning, a ranking member of the Nazi party who abandoned the movement in 1935 after becoming privy to the underlying logic and consequences of Adolph Hitler's worldview:

> In my great educative work (the Nazi movement),
> I am beginning with the young. Look at these
> young men and boys! What material! With them
> I can make a new world. I want to see once more
> in its eyes the gleam of pride and independence of

the beast of prey...In this way I shall eradicate the thousands of years of human domestication.[91]

The Führer considered that Weimar Germany was corrupted and needed to die, and the main culprit for destroying Germany was Judaism, which had spread a set of ideas based on love and tolerance, not violence and fear.[92] The defeat of Jewish ideas would usher in a new world order through "...this historic struggle which, for the next 500 or 1,000 years will be described as decisive, not only for the history of Germany but for the whole of Europe and indeed the whole world."[93]

Not Just Hitler

While Hitler was the deadliest practitioner, Hitler's *weltanschauung* was not original; rather, much of his antisemitic worldview was already well-known and popular in Germany.

In *The Myth of the 20th Century*, considered after *Mein Kampf* to be the most important Nazi manifesto, the chief ideologue of the Nazi Party, Alfred Rosenberg, laid out the desperate need to reset European civilization by destroying what he characterized negatively as "the human concept":

> The dogmas of an all-embracing love and of the equality of all human beings before God on the one hand and the doctrine on the other of democratic 'human rights' founded neither on race nor on national honor...These (humanitarian) dogmas thus became the protector of all things and being inferior, ill, crippled, criminal and rotten...A nation whose central idea was (instead) honor and duty, would not preserve decadents and criminals, but would eliminate them.[94]

Judaism and the Jews had altered the world's core values. As a result, it had become impossible for man to revert to a world based on Nature's laws of honor, power and even savagery without having to grapple with an inner conscience and a God that demanded that he overcome his base nature. In other words, the Jews had imposed *humanity* on mankind.

This was the mighty clash of opposite ideological titans on which the Nazi *weltanschaulich* was founded. Out of the confrontation between the *human concept* and the *honor concept*, a new age of mankind could arise. Only the destruction of these Jewish ideas would allow the evolution of mankind through *kampf*, or conflict.

Exterminating the Jews would wipe out the debilitating ideas and values of ethical monotheism. "A people of culture permits no one the right to assess its creations as good and bad, true and false," Rosenberg argued.

This "honor" ideology was not a secret. Young Germans were indoctrinated in anthems like this:

> We are the joyous Hitler Youth.
> We need no stinkin' Christian virtue.
> Our Führer is our savior and future.
> The Pope and Rabbi shall be gone.
> We wish to be pagans once again.[95]

Genocide was meant to recalibrate mankind by reverting its worldview. The Nazis did not fight simply to conquer lands (*lebensraum*), but also to defeat morality. They committed atrocities to conquer the human feelings within themselves. They directed the worst of these atrocities at the people they blamed for having invented the idea. The overwhelming success of Jewish values and its worldview in influencing Western civilization over the past two millennia demanded that Hitler make a historical reckoning.

Another Enemy: Christianity

Hitler understood that the Jews invented the "human concept," but their success in impacting the world was not single-handed. It was entirely consistent that Hitler considered Christianity an enemy ideology as well. It was a Jewish ideology—not just because its founder, Jesus, was a Jew, but because its core values of God, love, equality, brotherhood, compassion, and so on, were Jewish.

Hitler dismissed the Bible as "Jewish mumbo jumbo."[96] In this ideological war, Hitler saw Christianity as the prime conveyor of Jewish ideas and values to the world, and so it had to be challenged and defeated.[97] Although Christian antisemitism had thrived in Germany for more than 1,000 years, the Nazi form of Jew-hatred was also vehemently opposed to Christianity.

"The heaviest blow that ever struck humanity was the coming of Christianity,"[98] Hitler privately observed. "The man of the isles pays homage to the forces of nature. But Christianity is an invention of sick brains,"[99] he commented on one occasion, and on another called the religion a "disease."[100]

Hitler observed that, 1,900 years earlier, Jews had brought Christianity into being and thereby collapsed the Roman Empire and halted human progress. Without Christianity, the "Roman Empire, under Germanic influence, would have developed in the direction of world domination."[101] Christianity was built on a foundation of humanitarian Jewish ethics, but, "The law of selection justifies this incessant struggle by allowing the survival of the fittest. Christianity is a rebellion against natural law, a protest against nature. Taken to its logical extreme, Christianity would mean the systematic cultivation of human failure."[102]

Hitler's personal secretary, Martin Bormann, described the opposition between Nazism and Christianity when he said:

"National Socialist and Christian concepts are incompatible...Our National Socialist worldview stands on a much higher level than the concepts of Christianity, which in their essentials were taken over from Judaism..."[103]

Hitler had a "solution" in mind for Christianity, too. In a private discussion in July, 1941, he declared that, "In the long run, National Socialism and religion will no longer be able to exist together."[104] In November, he said, "The Church must be made to understand that her kingdom is not of this world."[105] Even more ominously, Hitler predicted that "The precept that it's man's duty to love another is theory, and the Christians are the last to practice it."[106]

But in a Christian country, Hitler and the Nazi elite had to be careful about sharing publicly their true views. In contrast to his "solution" to the Jewish problem, which was genocide, Christianity, he believed, would rot and die on its own, without substantial Nazi coercion:

> When I was younger, I thought it was necessary to set about matters with dynamite. I've since realized that there's room for a little subtlety. The rotten branch falls off itself. The final state must be: in St. Peter's Chair, a senile officiate; facing him, a few sinister old women...[107]

Hitler was prepared to be patient, as he said:

> ...the main thing is to be clever in this matter and not to look for a struggle where it can be avoided. So it's not opportune to hurl ourselves now into a struggle with the Churches. The best thing is to let Christianity die a natural death.[108]

In the short term, Christianity would be allowed to exist in Nazi Germany, but in the long run, this situation could not be tolerated:

"One is either a German or a Christian. You cannot be both."[109] Therefore, the endgame was clear, as Hitler wrote: "The war will be over one day. I shall then consider that my life's final task will be to solve the religious problem. Only then will the life of the German nation be guaranteed once and for all."[110]

Another Mortal Threat: Bolshevism/Marxism/Communism

Hitler had another archenemy, in addition to Judaism and Christianity: Bolshevism (Marxism/Communism). This relatively new ideology, which strived (at least in theory) for the brotherhood of all mankind, had taken over Russia and was spreading quickly and aggressively all over Europe.

Hitler considered Bolshevism/Communism another Jewish ideology, not just because its founder, Karl Marx, was a Jew, or because so much of its leadership, like Leon Trotsky, were Jews, but because it was another successful deployment of the "human concept." The notion of universal brotherhood was, to Hitler, simply Judeo-Christian humanitarian values minus God:

> Of old, it was in the name of Christianity. Today, it's in the name of Bolshevism. Yesterday, the instigator was Saul; the instigator today, Mordechai. Saul was changed into St. Paul and Mordechai into Karl Marx. By exterminating this pest, we shall do humanity a service of which our soldiers can have no idea.[111]

Just as Hitler saw Judaism and Christianity as revolts against the laws of nature, so was Marxism:

> "The Jewish doctrine of Marxism rejects the aristocratic principle of Nature and replaces the

eternal privilege of power and strength by the mass
of numbers and their dead weight...If, with the
help of the Marxist creed, the Jew is victorious over
the other peoples of the world, his crown will be the
funeral wreath of humanity..."[112]

Addressing an audience in Munich, Hitler stated:

"Economically he [the Jew] dominates the peoples;
politically and morally he subjugates them.
Politically he accomplishes his aims through the
propagation of the principles of democracy and
the doctrine of Marxism... From the ethical point
of view the Jew destroys the peoples in respect to
religious and moral considerations. Anyone who is
willing to see that, can see it; and no one can help
the person who refuses to see it."[113]

Just as Judaism and Christianity could not exist simultaneously
with National Socialism, so did he believe that Bolshevism was an
ideology that must be completely destroyed. In 1926, Hitler said:

"We are convinced that a final showdown will
come in this fight against Marxism... for two
Weltanschauungen (worldviews) are fighting each
other and there can be only one outcome! One will
be destroyed and the other will win..."[114]

In March 1941, a military directive went out instructing the
German Army to kill all Russian education officers, rather than
consider them legally protected POWs, because:

"This struggle is one of ideologies and racial
differences and will have to be conducted with
unprecedented, merciless and unrelenting
harshness...The (Russian) commissars are the

bearers of an ideology directly opposed to National Socialism. Therefore the commissars will be liquidated.[115]

Faced with criticism for this brutal behavior, Field Marshal Keitel clarified:

> These scruples (the ethical desire to protect Russian POWs) accord with the soldierly concepts of a chivalrous war. Here [in this war, on the other hand] we are concerned with the extermination of an ideology. That is why I approve of and defend this measure (to kill the officer POWs).[116]

In July 1941, Hitler stated unequivocally that, "What matters is that Bolshevism must be exterminated...Moscow, as the center of the doctrine, must disappear from the earth's surface."[117]

Hitler's three mortal enemies were connected ideologically, and he was consistent in his thinking on them from the start of his career until the end. Because the Russian battle was against an ideological enemy, Hitler emphatically had stated already, in June 1931, that, "Only an anti-Semite is a true anti-Communist."[118]

The Consistent Either-Or Worldview Pieced Together

Hitler had a very clear and consistent *Weltanschauung*. Now we are in a position to understand what he was saying to the Islamic Mufti in 1941, which at first blush seemed so irrational, as he wrote in *Mein Kampf*: "This was the decisive struggle...ideologically it was a battle between National Socialism and the Jews." The primal struggle of the world war was more about ideology than power and territory, and the only two heavyweight contenders were the Aryan Germans and the Jews.

In a 1922 NSDAP (Nazi party) meeting, Hitler had declared, "Here too, there can be no compromise—there are only two possibilities: either victory of the Aryan or annihilation of the Aryan and the victory of the Jew."[119] Twenty years later, his outlook remained unswerving. In a Berlin speech on January 30, 1942, Hitler warned, "We realize that this war can only end either in the wiping out of the Germanic nations, or by the disappearance of Jewry from Europe."[120]

This worldview informed Hitler from his first political writing in September 1919[121] to his final written testament to the German people before killing himself in April 1945, in which he pledged the nation to continue fighting the Jews as their first priority. He asserted, in a vain attempt to keep his philosophical dream alive, "In a ghastly conflict like this, in a war in which two so completely irreconcilable ideologies confront one another, the issue can inevitably only be settled by the total destruction of one side or the other."[122]

Hitler died as he had lived, relentlessly obsessed with the Jews.

As we've seen, there was method to the evil Nazi madness: Nature dictated that the strong conquer the weak, but the Jews disrupted that paganistic world order through the conviction that there was something more powerful and important than physical force— the idea that man is not an animal but a spiritual being, and that therefore the law of the jungle—conquest, war, and oppression—is morally wrong.

The Jewish idea was winning. Therefore, the Jews had to be eliminated. As the SS Chief, Heinrich Himmler, stated in 1943, "We had the moral right, and the duty, toward our nation to kill this people which wished to kill us."[123]

Explaining the "Strange" Decisions

For Hitler, genocide of the Jews was not a peripheral undertaking of WWII; it was a core mission. As historian Lucy Dawidowicz says in *The War Against the Jews*, "The final solution transcended the bounds of modern historical experience. Never before in modern history had one people made the killing of another the fulfillment of an ideology... (and not to achieve some kind of instrumental ends)."[124]

And so there was a logic in keeping the trains rolling to Auschwitz, even as the Soviet forces advanced. Within the context of the Nazi worldview, these decisions were completely consistent. As French philosopher and political scientist Raymond Aron pointed out:

> As for genocide...I would say that its apparent irrationality results from a false perspective... If one is prepared to admit that the liquidation of the Jews...was Hitler's primary aim, the industrial organization of death becomes rational as a means toward this end, genocide. Once the genocide had been established as the aim, the materials, the men, and mostly the means of transportation needed for this enterprise had to be diverted from the logistics of the armed forces.[125]

Similarly, the war's economic considerations were not a factor in the face of the priority of genocide, even though the war effort was being harmed by the Holocaust's machinery. As historian Saul Friedlander observed, "The 'Final Solution' meant a loss for the German war economy, which was compensated only to a very small degree by the partial exploitation of Jewish slave labor and the property seized from the victims."[126]

In 1941, Alfred Rosenberg's Ministry of Occupied Eastern

Territories (Ostland/Poland) removed all doubt and ambiguity on this matter. In response to a mass-murder directive, a subordinate asked for clarification: "Please advise me as to whether your request of October 31 is to be interpreted as an order to liquidate all Jews in Ostland. Is that to be done regardless of age and sex and economic interests (such as the need of the Wehrmacht for skilled labor in munitions factories)?" Rosenberg answered flatly: "In reply to your letter of Nov. 15, 1941. Economic interests are to be on the whole disregarded in the solution of the (Jewish) problem."[127]

For Hitler, the genocide of the Jews was a central mission of WWII, not a side issue. This explains why the Nazis continued transporting Jews to Auschwitz even as Soviet forces advanced, prioritizing the extermination of Jews over the war effort's logistic and economic needs.

Next, we will explore Hitler's idea of Jewish DNA, delving into how he believed Jewish ideology to be rooted in their beings, further fueling his genocidal determination.

Hitler's Idea of Jewish DNA

Hitler's understanding of the Jew went another important step further. He believed that Jewish ideas were an essential and inescapable characteristic of their race.

This is why Hitler considered the "Jewish problem" more serious than the Christian and Marxism "problems." This led him to conclude that the "solution" for the Jews was much more challenging and radical—only the "Jewish problem" required genocide.

On July 21, 1941, Hitler told Croatian Foreign Minister Kvaternik, one of the founders of the brutal Ustasha Movement responsible for some of the worst atrocities of the Holocaust, "If only one country for whatever reasons tolerates a Jewish family in it, that family will become the germ center for fresh sedition. If there were no longer any Jews in Europe, the unity of the countries of Europe would no longer be disturbed."[128]

Hitler believed that every Jew was intrinsically connected with Judaism and Jewish ethics, irrespective of their beliefs and education. Therefore each one represented a serious threat. In order for the German nation to defeat the human concept and establish the new world order, every Jewish man, woman, and child—regardless of nationality, profession, influence, or religious beliefs—had to be eliminated.

Hitler explained on several occasions that the various *human* ideologies were alien to the German/European character, but:

> ...for the last three centuries the country [Germany] has been...subjected to the influence... of Christianity—(but) Christianity is not a natural religion for the Germans, but a religion that has been imported and which strikes no responsive cord in their hearts and is foreign to the inherent genius of the race.[129]

On the other hand, according to Hitler, "The Jew...has always been a people with definite racial characteristics and never (just) a religion."[130] Therefore:

> ...the Jew can never become a German. If he wanted to become a German he would have to give up becoming a Jew. That he can not do. The Jew can not become a German at heart for a number of reasons: First, because of his blood; second, because of his character; third because of this will, fourth because of his actions. His actions remain Jewish and he works for the greater 'idea' of the Jewish people.[131]

Hitler argued that the Jewish characteristics were embedded in the Jew as part of their nature. "The internal expurgation of the Jewish spirit is not possible in any platonic way, for the Jewish spirit is a product of the Jewish person. Unless we expel the Jewish people soon, they will have Judaised our people within a very short time."[132]

As with his overall *weltanschauung*, these notions were not Hitler originals. Dietrich Eckart, one of the founding members of the German Workers' Party which later became the Nazi Party, was one of Hitler's mentors. In one of their conversations, Hitler explained why Martin Luther's proposal of some 200 years earlier to burn synagogues and Jewish houses was an insufficient solution:

> Even if there had never been a synagogue or a Jewish school or the Old Testament, the Jewish spirit would still exist and exert its influence. It has been there from the beginning, and there is no Jew, not a single one, who does not personify it.[133]

To the Nazis, a Jewish atheist or convert to Christianity was as bad as any other kind of Jew. The Jewish idea could not be separated from the body or soul of the Jew: "Even when recreant Jews abjured God…," Rosenberg argued, "…they only put in His place what was essentially the same concept under other names. This they called humanism, liberty, liberalism."[134]

The Nazis saw the religious outlook, with its moral demands for restraint and compassion, as a necessary product of the Jewish person; it was in their blood. There was no way to uproot this misguided value system from European civilization without destroying the Jews who not only created it, but embodied it.

Nazi ideologists thus regarded the notion of secular Jewry as oxymoronic. As Alfred Rosenberg wrote:

> …we find this method of the Talmud exactly

reflected again in the spiritual frame of mind of our Jewish journalists and lawyers. They act in accordance with the Talmud even when they know nothing of it, for it was not the Talmud which made the Jews, but the Jews that made the Talmud.[135]

To Hitler and the Nazi ideologists, this intrinsic Jewish character also explained the Jewish development of socialist ideals for a utopian brotherhood of man. Rosenberg put in bluntly in his 1920 *Race and Race History*:

> Communistic thinking had been formed long before Marx. However, the clever Jew welded it together and molded it into a rigid form. Later, we will speak about the Jewish spirit and about that determination which represents the center of the Jewish character.[136]

Since every Jew was a "super-spreader" of the humanism of Judaism,[137] the Nazis deduced that genocide was the only real solution, because even when Jews abandon religion, they continue to propound its moral and ethical teachings in manifold secular and intellectual ways. Judaism, Christianity, and Bolshevism were variations on the same theme—some more, some less religious—of creating a humane world. And put together, the "Jewish ideas" had successfully transformed Europe.

The accusations leveled by Nazi propagandists against the Jews were often contradictory, blaming them simultaneously for capitalism and Marxism, for religion and atheism, for morality and immorality. Despite these contradictions, the Nazi leadership maintained a consistent understanding of the deeper ideological war that motivated them. They believed with absolute clarity of conviction that their revolution was the world's final chance, the last battle against the Jewish idea.

Furthermore, Hitler was confident that eliminating the Jews would prevent any other group, religion, or power from reviving those ideas. He believed that if he could destroy the root—the Jewish People—he would eradicate everything that stemmed from them, "The Jew plays in nature the role of a catalyzing element. A people that is rid of its Jews returns spontaneously to the natural order."[138]

To summarize Hitler's worldview,

1. World War II was about ideology.

2. European man was meant to develop by adhering to 'natural laws' of survival of the fittest, which, as social Darwinism maintained, propels the 'evolution' of man.

3. An opposing ideology of 'humanitarianism' had challenged this ideology and achieved near victory.

4. This victorious ideology was created by the Jewish people.

5. Christianity and Communism/Bolshevism were also enemy and 'Jewish' ideologies because they were fundamentally humanistic.

6. Jews were different because the ideology was inside their spiritual makeup.

7. The hour was late since he was losing, but Hitler took upon himself the mammoth task of saving Germany and Europe by starting a war to eliminate the enemy ideologies and recalibrate Europe. To do this, the elimination of every Jew was necessary.

Fear of Jewish power lay at the heart of the Holocaust. Hitler's war was driven by fear of a Jewish ideological victory: "The mightiest counterpart to the Aryan is represented by the Jew."[139] He was not just afraid, he was terrified. This is why he always spoke of his fight with the Jews as a war of self-defense, one in which he was not confident of victory:

> When over long periods of human history I scrutinized the activity of the Jewish people, suddenly there arose up in me the fearful question whether inscrutable Destiny, perhaps for reasons unknown to us poor mortals, did not, with eternal and immutable resolve, desire the final victory of this little nation.[140]

Was Hitler correct to fear the Jews?

3

The Disrupters—The Dual Recognition of Jewish Impact

God said to Abram, "Go forth from your native land
and from your father's house to the land
that I will show you. I will make of you a great nation,
and I will bless you; I will make your name great,
and shall be a blessing. I will bless those who bless you,
and curse the one who curses you; And all the families
of the earth shall be blessed through you."
–Genesis, 12:1–3

HITLER'S MAIN CHARGE against the Jews was that they were disrupting the world on a massive scale. On reflection, this was not a delusional perception. My research led me to an unsettling conclusion: Hitler was right.[141]

I recognize that this statement is disturbing, and I have no doubt we all have a strong impulse to recoil at the idea that someone so evil was right.

In this chapter, we will review the incredible impact that the Jewish People have had on civilization. This influence has not gone unnoticed by our detractors, as the fear of Jewish influence stretches far back in history. We will also examine a strange and astonishing phenomenon: both antisemites and those who appreciate Jews agree on the significant impact of the Jewish People. When I say that the Jews are "disrupting," I don't mean it negatively; I mean that they have changed the status quo.

This analysis is not meant to validate the antisemitic viewpoint but to highlight a critical intersection where Jewish philosophy and its fiercest antagonism meet. It reveals an ongoing ideological war over the essence of being human and the different ways of responding to Jewish impact.

What Did Nietzsche See?

In his 1888 autobiography *Ecce Homo*, Friedrich Nietzsche, one of the great German philosophers of the 19th century, wrote of his understanding that Judeo-Christian morality was 'weak'. He argued that its values like compassion, kindness and equality, were a great harm to humanity. He considered this insight one of his greatest contributions, "Have you understood me?...[it is] that which defines me, that which makes me stand apart from the whole rest of humanity . . . the unmasking of Christian morality is an event which is unequalled in history."[142]

Nietzsche's vocabulary of "superiority and degeneracy" was adopted as a central part of the Nazi political lexicon. He formulated the notion that the Jews had inflicted "slave morality" on the world, primarily through Christianity, which had overthrown the morality of mastery, of might, and of natural superiority: "It was, in fact, with the Jews that the revolt of the slaves begins in the sphere of morals; that revolt which has behind it a history of two millennia, and which at the present day has only moved out of our sight, because it has achieved victory."[143]

By successfully "subverting the natural order," he concluded that "Everything is obviously becoming Judaized, or Christianized, or vulgarized".[144] To Nietzsche, the French Revolution, the American Revolution, and even the idea of democracy, with its obsession for freedom and equality, were direct results of the moral revolution that the Jews started and Christianity spread: "The democratic movement is the heir to Christianity."[145]

While it is a matter of scholarly debate whether Nietzsche hated Jews, what is indisputable is that he identified the power of Jewish ideas, loathed Jewish values, and abhorred the fact that they had upended European civilization.

Similarly, Wilhelm Marr, whose bestselling book in 1873 coined the term "Antisemitism" (*Antisemitismus* - until then it was called, more accurately, hatred of Jews[146]) and led to the birth of the influential League of Anti-Semites, concluded that the Jews had "taken over the world," rising to positions of leadership in every sphere of German life. "We harbor a resilient, tough, intelligent, foreign tribe among us, who knows how to take advantage of every form of abstract reality." He bemoaned, "...the Judaization of the Germanic world..."[147]

Writing in *The Victory of Judaism over Germandom* over a decade before Hitler was even born, Marr said that, "Not individual Jews, but the Jewish spirit and Jewish consciousness have overpowered the world."[148]

German anti-Judaism, from Nietzsche to Marr and Hitler, was founded on the idea that the Jewish worldview had transformed everything. The fundamental crime of the Jews was not so much the smear that they wanted to control the world, but that their values, success, and way of thinking were influencing and even dominating Europe.[149] The fear of a Jewish victory seemed, at first blush, paranoid and irrational. But what they were all seeing was Jewish influence.[150]

What Did Regular Germans See?

Regular Germans, the *volk*, were also seeing Jewish influence in a myriad of other ways.

For example, more than half of German doctors joined the Nazi Party early.[151] For them, what the Nazi movement offered was quite clear: There would be no more Jewish doctors for them to compete with.

The fear of Jewish doctors had a long history. During medieval times, Church decrees had banned Jewish doctors from treating non-Jewish patients. The University of Vienna in 1610 claimed that Jewish physicians killed every 10th Christian patient. And Martin Luther, the German father of Protestantism, warned, "If they (the Jews) could kill us, they would gladly do so, aye, and often do it, especially those who profess to be physicians,"[152]

In pre–World War II Weimar Germany, every effort to keep Jews out of medicine ultimately failed. In 1907, 6% of German doctors were Jewish, but by the time the Nazis took power in 1933, almost half of Berlin's doctors were Jewish despite the Jewish commuinty comprising only 2.5% of the capital's population. Jews excelled across German sciences so that by 1938, a quarter of the German Nobel Prizes were won by Jews.

In 1933, likely partially swayed by Jewish impact, 44% of Germans democratically voted for Hitler's anti-Jewish Nazi Party and brought him to power.[153]

Jewish Influence Goes Way Back

Fear of Jewish impact is not a modern invention, as we see in ancient Egypt over 3,000 years ago. Despite Jews being a small minority, the biblical pharaoh tells the Egyptians, "Behold, the people of the children of Israel are too many and too mighty for us," leading to Jewish enslavement and eventual murder of all male Jewish babies.

"If the Egyptians went to the theater, it was full of Jews; if they went to the circus, again, the place was full of Jews," notes the Yalkut Shimoni, a 13th-century compilation of biblical commentaries. The Jews had become successful and joined the Egyptian elites, transforming Egypt in the process.

Joseph had risen to power as the second-in-command in Egypt, and his reforms helped make Egypt a superpower. However, his skills and talents, and those of his descendants, led to resentment and conspiracy theories. As a result, the Egyptians turned the successful Jews, who had originally arrived in the form of Joseph as a slave, back into slaves.

The story of Egyptian antisemitism mirrors that of European antisemitism and the various iterations in between. The ancient Egyptians, like the League of Anti-Semites of 19th century France and Germany, recognized and resented Jewish success. The Nazis also resorted to slave labor and mass murder.

Antisemitism attempts to control or eliminate Jewish success, but on a deeper level, the 'problem' of the Jews was not just their success, but their transformative impact on society.

Not Just Germans: What Did Others See?

The American author and economist George Gilder observed that no explanation of anti-Jewish feelings can ignore "...the obvious and massively disproportionate representation of Jews in almost every index of human achievement."[154]

After WWII, Jews made up 15% of the USSR's scientists and engineers despite representing only around 1% of the population.

After the death of Stalin in 1953 and the end of his murderous persecution of Jewish scientists, their numbers increased to 25%.[155]

Outsized Jewish achievement in the US was also met with restrictions and barriers. In 1919, Jews made up 20% of the student body of Harvard, 13% of Yale, and 40% of Columbia. Between 1921 and 1925, 45% of the students admitted to New York City medical schools were Jewish. The response was a quota system that dropped the number of Jewish medical students in New York City to 25%.[156] Today, as well, American colleges have conspired to reduce the numbers, and their efforts have been successful, reducing the percentage of Jews in elite schools from around 25–35% to closer to 10%.[157] Nevertheless, Jews represent 37% of the American Nobel Prize winners.

In fact, Jews have won 40% of all the Nobel Prizes in Economic Sciences, including 37 awards in the 54 years since it was established. Israelis are the fifth-largest recipients of Nobel Prize awards despite being only the 100th-largest country in population. Globally, 29% of all Nobel prize winners have been Jewish since the awards began in 1901. That is 11,500% more than would be expected based on Jews being one-fifth of one percent of the world's population.[158]

The remarkable achievements and influence of Jews in various fields have been both celebrated and resented throughout history. This outsized success often fuels antisemitic sentiments, demonstrating a long-standing tension that persists to this day.

It's Not Just About Success; It's About Influence

Jewish doctors, writers, and politicians shook the class system. Their appearance reminded French Catholic traditionalists and

German nationalists that the old order had fallen away. And these new Jewish thinkers took down more than just the class system.

A Jewish doctor in Vienna named Freud founded a new way of viewing and treating mental disorders. A Jewish patent clerk in Switzerland named Einstein reimagined the nature of the universe. And more prosaically, Jewish businessmen were reinventing finance and retail.

Karl Marx, the grandson of a rabbi, but loathing all things Jewish, would help birth the ultimate anti-capitalist movement. Ironically, within a generation, Jew-haters would indict Jews for both capitalism and socialism.

Jews were neither intrinsically capitalists nor socialists; they were at their core innovative disruptors, dissatisfied with what they saw around them, and pursuing a better world, be it through free markets or by supporting the rights of the weak and poor. And this drive was felt for millennia.

When Emperor Marcus Aurelius of Rome visited Israel 2,000 years ago, he remarked, "O Marcomanni, Quadi, and Sarmatae (German tribes that Aurelias warred with), at last I have found people more restless than you." The Roman philosopher Seneca would complain that so many had adopted the Sabbath that, "The customs of this most base people have so prevailed that they are adopted in all the world, and the conquered have given their laws to the conquerors."[159]

Like Hitler and Marr, Seneca was complaining that Jewish ideas had proved too compelling. The Romans gave the world methodologies, but as we shall see, Jewish restlessness changed how we think.

Next, we will delve into how Jewish influence has shaped civilization over centuries.

A Broad Look at Jewish Disruption

For thousands of years, Jews were powerless militarily. Their power was that of ideas.

The Jew in exile oftentimes gained wealth and power, if only temporarily, by finding new commercial techniques. They would turn the legal restrictions that prevented them from many trades and professions to their advantage, by using creativity and resilience to invent new ones.

Excluded from local trades, Jews built mercantile networks spanning vast portions of the world at a time when mapmaking was in its infancy. And, slowly, they positively influenced the world.

Behind the discovery of America lay the talents of Jewish mapmakers like Rabbi Abraham Zacuto, the inventor of the brass astrolabe, and financiers like Luis de Santangel, the *converso* (forcibly converted) finance minister of the Spanish Crown.

Economist Thorstein Veblen explained the Jewish role in science by stating that the Jews achieved brilliance because they stood outside mainstream society: "He becomes a disturber of the intellectual peace, but only at the cost of becoming an intellectual wayfaring man, a wanderer in the intellectual no-man's-land, seeking another place to rest, farther along the road, somewhere over the horizon."[160]

As outsiders in every society, Jews had a different perspective, free from the status quo and its cultural norms, which enabled them to adapt and add value with their unique vision.

The Jews were not limited by the narrow cultural horizons of any specific place because they had been forced to wander the world. As we will see, their minds and souls often lived in another world entirely. This willingness—and necessity—to find their own way fostered a rugged individualism that is an essential part of Jewish disruptiveness. This unique perspective has transformed societies in many ways, including the modern technological revolutions.

Behind much of the computer renaissance lay John von Neumann's mathematical genius, Hedy Lamarr's wireless communications, Russell Kirsch's pixel, and the development of packet switching by Leonard Kleinrock and Paul ("Pesach") Baran. Companies like Google, Oracle, and Facebook, with Jewish founders, and the larger infrastructure behind the computer revolution and the internet, draw from the pioneering research of many Jewish scientists.

Jewish refugees fleeing persecution in Czarist Russia, the Soviet Union, and Nazi Germany became the scientists who kickstarted everything from the atomic bomb to the space program and the digital revolution. Within a decade, Albert Einstein could be found laboring on his theories of the universe, Niels Bohr was putting into place some of the building blocks of quantum mechanics, while fellow Nobel prize winner Eugene Wigner was leading a team working on the Manhattan Project's effort to build a nuclear bomb. Led by J. Robert Oppenheimer, 6 of the 8 project's scientists were Jewish.[161]

While Biblical Joseph may have been the first famous Jew to interpret dreams, Freud and most of the fathers of psychoanalysis were also Jews (except for Carl Jung). Later contributors included a disproportionately large number from the Jewish community: Alfred Adler, Erik Erikson, Bruno Bettelheim, and Erich Fromm, among others.

Jewish psychologists were instrumental in founding many branches of modern psychology. Nearly all of the major theorists of the Gestalt school were Jews. Maslow developed his famous hierarchy of needs and was one of two cofounders of humanistic psychology; Holocaust survivor Viktor Frankl developed logotherapy, based on the idea that finding meaning in life is the primary human motivational force; Martin Seligman founded positive psychology, the science of happiness; and Daniel Kahneman won a 2002 Nobel prize for his work on the psychology of decision-making. A 2002 study published in the *Review of General Psychology* found that 40% of the 99 most influential psychologists of the 20th century were Jewish.[162]

Can we picture the world without Einstein's Theory of Relativity and Freud's Psychoanalysis, without cruise ships (invented by Albert Ballin), lasers (Theodore Maiman), jeans (Jacob Davis— not to mention Levi's), stainless steel (Hans Goldschmidt), the microprocessor (Stanley Mazor), or, on a lighter note, without Hollywood (Goldwyn, Warner, Fox, Mayer), comic books (*Superman, Batman, The Incredible Hulk, Captain America,* and so on[163]), or Las Vegas (Bugsy Siegel)?

From Wall Street to Silicon Valley, from Hollywood to the Space Age, from the women's rights movement (Betty Friedan, Gloria Steinem) to civil rights, there is no major modern revolution in technology, sociology, and business that doesn't have plenty of Jews on board.[164]

The '60s in America might have looked different without the vision of the "Frankfurt School" of intellectuals, Adorno, Marcuse, and Fromm; the inspiration of counterculture leaders Lenny Bruce and Alan Ginsburg; and poet laureate of the generation, Bob Dylan (Robert Zimmerman). Approximately 30-50% of the members of the SDS (Students for a Democratic Society)—the major student civil rights organization of the '60s, were Jews;[165] the two most well-known student activists were Abbie Hoffman and Jerry Rubin.[166]

Mark Twain said it well:

> If the statistics are right, the Jews constitute but one
> percent of the human race.[167] It suggests a nebulous
> dim puff of stardust lost in the blaze of the Milky

> Way. Properly, the Jew ought hardly to be heard of,
> but he is heard of, has always been heard of...His
> contributions to the world's list of great names in
> literature, science, art, music, finance, medicine,
> and abstruse learning are also way out of proportion
> to the weakness of his numbers.[168]

Jewish influence has significantly shaped various aspects of civilization, from scientific advancements to cultural revolutions. Their creative approaches, born partially from being outsiders, have driven innovations and transformed societies throughout history. As we continue learning, we'll discover that Jewish philosophy has played an even greater role as it shaped ideas of morality and the best ways for humanity to live.

The Biggest Influence: Mindset

Beyond social justice movements, science, economics, psychology, or the ubiquitous brands of our consumer society, this story goes much deeper: Can we imagine human civilization as we know it without the Jews?

Thousands of years ago, Jewish philosophy began to change history, transform convictions, and shape what the world thinks and believes. The impact of the Bible on Western democracy,[169] art, literature, Christianity, Islam, and the moral heritage of mankind has been enormous.

Starting with Abraham, the Jewish patriarch, a wave of fundamental rethinking has swept around the globe, washing across continents, transcending oceans, and eventually reaching every part of the world. The contemporary historian Paul Johnson pondered the condition of the human race had the Jewish People never existed:

> Certainly the world without the Jews would have

been a radically different place. Humanity might eventually have stumbled upon all the Jewish insights. But we can not be sure... To them we owe the idea of equality before the law, both divine and human; of the sanctity of life and the dignity of the human person; of the individual conscience and so of personal redemption; of the collective conscience and so of social responsibility; of peace as an abstract ideal and love as the foundation of justice and many other items which constitute the basic moral furniture of the human mind. Without the Jews it might have been a much emptier place.[170]

Born and raised in a world transformed by this Jewish intellectual legacy, we never think to question the implausibility that a seed planted by Abraham has so upended the world. Thomas Cahill wrote in *The Gifts of the Jews: How a Tribe of Desert Nomads Changed the Way Everyone Thinks and Feels* that "Their worldview has become so much a part of us that at this point it might as well have been written into our cells as genetic code".[171]

The ideas of the Jews, beginning with Abraham and then the Torah, were, as Twain said, puffs of stardust that changed the world.[172] The secret of the Jewish disproportionate impact is in the world of ideas, often intangible ideas, from the discovery of God[173] to charting the outer realms of physics and psychology that revolutionize the world.

Over the millennia, the Jews were often guided by their Torah, but they were not always motivated by any consciously religious impulses. They often invented, built, bought and sold, envisioned, and explored without giving any thought to God or even the basic morality of the Ten Commandments. But what so often characterizes Jews (and I am not saying Jews have a monopoly on this attribute, just that it seems Jews have a predilection for it) was a drive for more, or for a better or different way to do things, from the secrets of the universe to better economic and political systems for mankind.

From the patriarchs to the prophets, from Abraham to King David, from lesser-known scientists like Norman Abramson, the father of modern wireless networks, to Abraham Silverstein, NASA's space flight chief who set up the manned space program that took mankind to the moon, Jews have sought a better way.

As former UK Chief Rabbi Lord Jonathon Sacks said in *Radical Then, Radical Now*, "For Judaism, faith is cognitive dissonance, the discord between the world that is and the world as it ought to be".[174] The Jewish men and women transforming the history of mankind, usually for good but sometimes for bad, were not primarily grappling with power. At the heart of their struggles, their rise and fall, lay their attempts to come to grips with what the world should be.

What Abraham sought from the very beginning was the best way for people to live. Thousands of years later, his descendants are still searching for the same thing that their patriarchal forefather undertook a long journey to find.

Explaining Jewish Impact

Jewish influence has been so strong historically that it is not surprising that it has led to numerous conspiracy theories. Observers are often astonished by the prominence of so many Jews throughout history, and conspiracy theories provide a convenient way to explain the outsized disruptive Jewish influence. Kanye West is a prime example of this type of antisemite who marvels at Jewish influence and concludes nefarious motivations.[175] Instead of recognizing the hard work behind Jewish success, he attributes it to a conspiracy:

Jewish people have owned the Black voice. Whether
it's through us wearing the Ralph Lauren shirt, or
it's all of us being signed to a record label, or having
a Jewish manager, or being signed to a Jewish
basketball team, or doing a movie on a Jewish
platform like Disney.[176]

In the minds of this type of Jew-hater, the massive influence
wrought by Jews can only be explained as part of a master plan.
They imagine a secret club meeting daily over bagels and lox to
determine the fate of the world. This is not a new idea; *The Protocols
of the Elders of Zion* forgery became one of the world's bestselling
books in the 1920s.[177] An epilogue to the *Protocols* fantastically
reads, "According to the records of secret Jewish Zionism, (King)
Solomon and other Jewish learned men already, in 929 B.C.,
thought out a scheme for a peaceful conquest of the whole universe
by Zion."[178]

Henry Ford, the Jew-hating automotive pioneer,[179] embraced
the *Protocols*, translating and distributing them to millions of
Americans. "German Jews, French Jews, English Jews, American
Jews. I believe that in all those countries except our own the Jewish
financier is supreme,"[180] he declared.

How can millions believe something as absurd as conspiracies
like the *Protocols*? The answer lies in the remarkable prominence
and influence of Jews throughout history. People felt the impact of
Jewish influence and latched onto these convenient yet ridiculous
explanations.

This influence also explains why many people dramatically
overestimate the actual number of Jews. Compared to the 2.3
billion Christians, 1.8 billion Muslims, 1.1 billion Hindus, and half-
billion Buddhists, there are only about 15 million Jews, making
up roughly 0.2% of the global population. Yet, in one survey,
one-third of respondents believed that Jews made up as much as

10% of the world population, equating to about 800 million Jews. Additionally, 18% thought Jews represented more than 10% of the world population,[181] overestimating by 5,000%.

In the United States, one in five Americans thinks that 20% of the population is Jewish[182], translating to 60 million Jews, whereas the actual number is around 5 million. Similarly, one in five Japanese and Kenyans believe Jews make up about 10–20% of the global population.[183]

How can so many be so wrong about Jewish population numbers? These exaggerated estimates are because people see and *feel* their impact and influence, rather than the actual numbers. What these estimates do accurately reflect is just how often people all over the world hear about the Jews. As one pithy slogan says, "Jews are news."[184]

Mark Twain cleverly noted this phenomenon over a century ago, "When I read in the C. B. (*Encyclopedia Britannica*) that the Jewish population of the United States was (only) 250,000, I wrote the editor, and explained to him that I was personally acquainted with more Jews than that."[185] If there seems to be more Jews than there really are, it's because ideas are the ultimate force multiplier of human civilization. Jewish ideas and contributions amplify their presence far beyond their actual numbers.

At the start of this chapter, we asked whether Hitler's perception of Jewish influence was founded or irrational. We have now seen that Hitler was observing something very real. There was and is little doubt in the minds of many even casual observers that the Jews have dramatically impacted civilization and continue to do so. It is not Hitler's or anyone else's delusion to be awe-struck at Jewish influence.

But let's take a step further and ask: Does Jewish disruption cause Jew-hatred? Is antisemitism the only possible reaction?

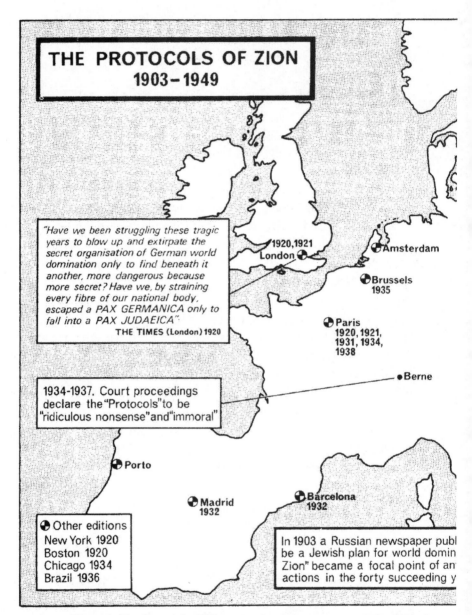

THE PROTOCOLS OF ZION
1903–1949

"Have we been struggling these tragic years to blow up and extirpate the secret organisation of German world domination only to find beneath it another, more dangerous because more secret? Have we, by straining every fibre of our national body, escaped a *PAX GERMANICA* only to fall into a *PAX JUDAEICA*".
THE TIMES (London) 1920

1920, 1921
London

Amsterdam

Brussels
1935

Paris
1920, 1921,
1931, 1934,
1938

• Berne

1934–1937. Court proceedings declare the "Protocols" to be "ridiculous nonsense" and "immoral"

Porto

Madrid
1932

Barcelona
1932

Other editions
New York 1920
Boston 1920
Chicago 1934
Brazil 1936

In 1903 a Russian newspaper publ
be a Jewish plan for world domin
Zion" became a focal point of an
actions in the forty succeeding y

Figure 4. The Protocols of Zion. *In 1903 a Russian newspaper published what claimed to be a Jewish plan for world dominion.

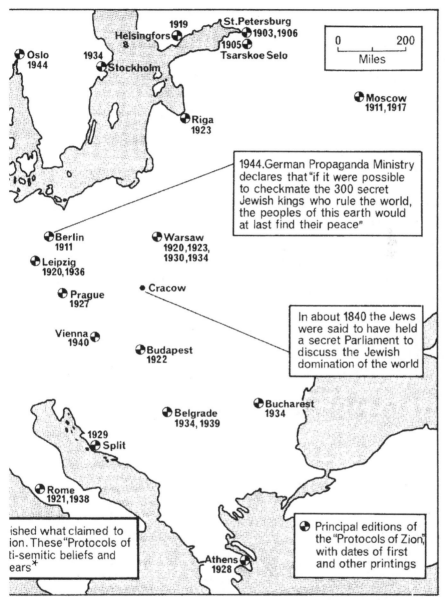

1919
St.Petersburg
Helsingfors
1903,1906
1905
Tsarskoe Selo

Oslo
1944

1934
Stockholm

Moscow
1911,1917

Riga
1923

1944.German Propaganda Ministry declares that "if it were possible to checkmate the 300 secret Jewish kings who rule the world, the peoples of this earth would at last find their peace"

Berlin
1911

Warsaw
1920,1923,
1930,1934

Leipzig
1920,1936

Prague
1927

Cracow

In about 1840 the Jews were said to have held a secret Parliament to discuss the Jewish domination of the world

Vienna
1940

Budapest
1922

Belgrade
1934, 1939

Bucharest
1934

1929
Split

Rome
1921,1938

...ished what claimed to ...ion. These "Protocols of ...ti-semitic beliefs and ...ears*

Athens
1928

Principal editions of the "Protocols of Zion," with dates of first and other printings

0   200
Miles

These "Protocols of Zion" became a focal point of anti-semitic beliefs and actions in the forty succeeding years.[195]

The Israel Test

Economist George Gilder explains that when people subconsciously feel or consciously realize Jewish disruptiveness, success, and influence, they face what he calls the "Israel Test"[186]: in an open environment where success is based on merit, and in the face of competition from Jews, do people respond to Jewish achievement with admiration and appreciation, or do they resent it and become antisemitic?

This is no small challenge. Gilder relates that he personally faced his "own Israel Test" growing up: "As a youth I learned first-hand the temptations of antisemitism,"[187] when he lost his school's editor-in-chief position to a Jew, and again when his family business, Tiffany and Company, was "...surrendered to Jewish entrepreneurs."[188] As a self-identified elite WASP, he reluctantly admitted, "I suppose we knew also that Jewish intellectuals and entrepreneurs were challenging the preeminence of WASPs in American cultural and commercial life."[189] The Israel Test, Gilder formulated, "...revolves around a fact that is recognized by most people in some form…but is rarely acknowledged openly or explored for its consequences; in any rivalry with intellectual dimensions, disproportionate numbers of the challengers and of the winners will be Jewish."[190]

In observing that "Virtually none of the significant scientific and technological achievements of the 20th century would have been possible without critical contributions by Jews," Gilder concludes that "The envy of excellence leads to perdition, the love of it leads to the light."[191] And therein lies the Israel Test: "As with all nations and cultures faced throughout history by the plain facts of Jewish excellence and success, we have a choice. We can resent it, or embrace it as a divine gift to the world."[192]

Jew-haters from Haman to Hitler, and from Arafat and Khamanei to Kanye fail the Israel Test. However, this jealous response to

Jewish success is not *the* sole reason for Jew-hatred. Being poor, ghettoized, legally relegated to second-class status, and even enslaved—experiences endured by Jews for more than 2,000 years—never brought relief from antisemitism.

Jewish success does not have to provoke hatred. Many good people, like Gilder, observe the same reality and respond with admiration. John Adams, the second president of the United States, wrote glowingly of the Jewish People, "They are the most glorious nation that ever inhabited this Earth. The Romans and their Empire were but a Bauble in comparison of the Jews. They have...influenced the affairs of Mankind more, and more happily, than any other Nation ancient or modern."[193]

Thomas Cahill wrote:

> The Jews started it all—and by "it" I mean so many of the things we care about, the underlying values that make all of us, Jew and gentile, believer and atheist, tick. Without the Jews, we would see the world through different eyes, hear with different ears, even feel with different feelings...we would think with a different mind, interpret all our experiences differently, draw different conclusions from the things that befall us. And we would set a different course for our lives.[194]

Cahill, Adams, Johnson, Twain, and Gilder are philosemites— they admired the Jewish People and their impact. However, others, whom we call antisemites, react negatively to this influence.

The Bizarre Point of Agreement

Amazingly, we arrive at a bizarre and astonishing phenomenon: both antisemites and philosemites agree on the power of Jewish disruption. They disagree on their response to it.

Jewish impact cannot be explained as a coincidence, nor can antisemitism. The uniqueness of the Jewish People is the best explanation for their success and influence. It was also Hitler's reason to murder them.

4

Hitler Was Right to Be Afraid of the Big, Bad Jew

The peoples hear, they tremble;
Agony grips the dwellers in Philistia.
Then the clans of Edom were dismayed;
The tribes of Moab—trembling grips them;
All the dwellers in Canaan are aghast.
Terror and dread descend upon them;
Through the might of Your arm they are still as stone—
'Till Your people cross over, God...
–Exodus 15:14–16

As WE DELVE deeper, an even more remarkable and mind-bending revelation emerges. Not only do both Jew-haters and Jew-lovers acknowledge the power and influence of the Jews, but Nazism and Judaism share many basic foundational ideas. Astonishingly, these two worldviews—Jewish philosophy (*hashkafa*) on the one side, and Hitler's *weltanschauung* on the other—are mirror images of each other, with the two standing on opposite moral corners. As we explore further, we'll uncover striking parallels—and profound differences—that define these opposing perspectives that have shaped history in unimaginable ways. Jewish philosophy and tradition would say that Adolf

Hitler was right about the nature of man's struggle and the Jewish People's disruptive impact, but he was dead wrong morally.

Nietzsche, Hitler, and many others believed that a Jewish worldview had transformed Western civilization. The Nazis believed that the Jews invented world-changing ideas for devious purposes, to weaken and devastate humanity. Jews, on the other hand, believed that they were given a set of powerful ideas as part of a divine mission.

Before we unpack what Jews have traditionally said about who they are, their philosophy, and their mission (Chapter 6), let's take a cursory look at how the two worldviews compare.

Comparing the Two Worldviews

To Hitler, man was just another animal in an uncaring, random social Darwinian universe.[196]

To the Jews, man (all human beings) is a being created just short of the angels, in the image of God, souls of infinite value.

According to Nazi ideology, one great conflict drove all of human history: the battle over humanity's self-definition—the "honor" concept of nature which Hitler sought to revive versus the Jewish "human" concept. The future of humankind depended on adherence to nature's laws of might and survival, and so necessitated the defeat of the humanitarian values of love, brotherhood, and tolerance that Jews had taught and that had become pervasive in Western civilization.

Judaism agrees with Hitler (and Nietzsche) that humanity is engaged in a battle that strikes at the core of the human condition. It is the battle of soul versus body, good versus evil, holy versus profane. In Nazi words, this was the conflict between the "human concept" and the "honor concept."

Jewish tradition agrees with Nietzche that it was they who disrupted and transformed a world comfortable in "the master morality." In fact, 3,800 years ago, a deep-thinking genius named Abraham searched philosophically, and what he found changed the world. This is where the Jewish story begins, with the first Jew.

Abraham's discovery of God[197]—infinite yet personal—was humanity's greatest discovery. And Abraham went further. He questioned, formulated, and articulated a complete system of philosophy and ethics that was world-shattering. These principles became the foundations of Judaism; Abraham had accessed the Divine life principles that seven generations later were concretized at the great revelation of the Torah at Mount Sinai.[198]

Judaism believes that all human history—and, thus, every individual human life—is the story of this battle with the human condition. And that salvation, both personal and global, is dependent upon the victory of the human concept. Best-selling author Rabbi Jacobson says it well:

> The struggles to integrate the Divine and the
> human, matter and spirit, body and soul, the inner
> and the outer, are as old as history itself. The tension
> between these opposing but complementary forces
> lie at the root of all conflict: inner (personal) and
> outer (social and political).[199]

Hitler said, "No nation will be able to withdraw or even remain at a distance from this historical conflict."[200]

The Nazis believed that spirituality dehumanizes man, while Judaism holds that man humanizes the universe. The Torah illustrates this worldview eloquently through the story of Rebecca.

While still in her womb, Rebecca's twins fought desperately, causing her such anguish and pain that she sought out a prophet to explain the unusual nature of her pregnancy. The prophet revealed that she was carrying two diametrically opposed leaders. The 19th-century Jewish philosopher Rabbi Shimshon Raphael Hirsch explained the prophetic response:

> Rebecca was informed that she carried two nations in her womb who would represent two different forms of social government. The one state would build up its greatness on spirit and morals, on the humane in humans, the other would seek its greatness in cunning and strength. Spirit versus strength, morality versus violence oppose each other, and indeed, from birth onwards will they be in opposition to each other...The whole of history is nothing else than a struggle as to whether spirit or sword, or, as our sages put it, whether Caesarea or Jerusalem is to have the upper hand.[201]

Judaism and Nazism share a common worldview: there is another world war, one more significant than the battles fought with guns and tanks—an epic ideological struggle. The Nazis fought on the side of brute force and the Jews on the side of love. One side wielded the might of a vast army and empire; the other commanded an empire of the spirit. The Nazis sought to destroy the moral power of the Jews with raw force, through degradation and deprivation, killing millions, and yet they could not achieve their goal.

The cults of personality of totalitarian regimes, with their claims of master races and utopian visions, are futile attemps to manufacture the illusion that their power can overcome human failings. Their followers are taught that they do not need to engage in a personal reckoning if they believe in the power of the Führer or the Beloved Leader and devote all their energies to fighting for him.

Judaism offers no such escape from personal responsibility. Instead, it demands, as the essence of faith, a morality that comes from a constant dialogue with a personal God.

Hermann Rauschning, a former Nazi, tried to alert the world to these ideas. As the President of the Senate of the Free City of Danzig[202] from 1932-4, he had several conversations with Hitler, which led him to subsequently reject the Nazi movement and make his way to the US. He wrote several books before and during the war in a desperate attempt to show the free world that Nazism was a serious threat, warning:

> The new element (Nazism) is, at the same time, of immemorial age. It is the demon of destruction, which had been banned from our normal life by civilization. It is the craving, suddenly grown to immense urgency, to throw off domestication and all civilized restrictions...Be not deceived: this urge to return to the primitive is felt not only by the Germans. Among the masses everywhere there is the same strong desire to throw off the burdens and obligations of a higher humanity.[203]

Throwing off the Yoke

This is the same human struggle that author Fyodor Dostoevsky so powerfully described through the character of Ivan Karamazov in his novel *The Brothers Karamazov*. Set in Spain during the bloody days of the Christian Inquisition, Jesus appears and is arrested by the Grand Inquisitor, who proceeds to lecture him. The Inquisitor argues that Jesus' mistake and sin was expecting too much of humanity; by placing on people the moral burden of freedom and a moral code, he demanded too much. For this sin, the Inquisitor plans to burn Jesus at the stake for imposing the Judeo-Christian worldview:

> You want to go into the world...with some promise of freedom which they (humanity) in their simplicity and innate lawlessness cannot even comprehend, which they dread and fear—for nothing has ever been more insufferable for man and for human society than freedom![204]

Ivan had identified man's discomfort with the burden of personal responsibility:

> Instead of taking over men's freedom, you increased it still more for them! Did you forget that peace (of mind) and even death are dearer to man than free choice and the knowledge of good and evil? There is nothing more seductive for man than the freedom of his conscience, but there is nothing more tormenting either[205]

Jesus' mistake was that he had, "...overestimated mankind...I swear, man is created weaker and baser than you thought him!... Respecting him so much, you behaved as if you had ceased to be compassionate, because you demanded too much of him... Respecting him less, you would have demanded less of him, and that would be closer to love, for his burden would be lighter. He is weak..."[206]

That struggle continues today, on the global scale of world power and within each of us.[207] Modern German historian Robert Pois describes the human temptation to abandon this ethical call in favor of a less burdensome "call to Nature":

> ...the notion that humans, having certain powers over nature, are themselves responsible for it in some way (rather than simply adjusting to certain 'natural laws' beyond their control), places a great burden upon them. It has been, and is, a far easier choice to see man as not being apart from nature, much less above it, but of nature.[208]

This conflict is the fault line of the human condition: on this point, the Torah, Hitler, Dostoevsky, and Nietzsche agree. Hatred takes root precisely against the "terrible burden" of "freedom of choice."[209] The existentialist philosopher Jean-Paul Sartre also recognized that it is on this fault line where the heart of Jew-hatred lies.

Throwing off the Jewish Yoke

Having lived in Paris through the Nazi occupation during World War II, Sartre wrote *Anti-Semite and Jew* in 1944, charging that antisemitism stems from something fundamental in human nature--the fear of the responsibility of being human:

> We are now in a position to understand the anti-Semite. He is a man who is afraid...of himself, of his own consciousness, of his liberty, of his instincts, of his responsibilities, of solitariness, of change, of society, and of the world...In espousing antisemitism, he does not simply adopt an opinion, he chooses himself as a person. He chooses the permanence and impenetrability of stone, the total irresponsibility of the warrior who obeys his leaders...antisemitism, in short, is fear of the human condition."[210]

Rauschning also saw firsthand that this inner struggle explains why the Nazis targeted the Jews:

> In the hatred of the Jews there is an instinctive element that points to a reaction against the author of those tablets of commandments in which the evil was separated from the good and the separation attributed to a divine will...Consequently, antisemitism is always most clearly manifested at times of spiritual crisis, of human insecurity, not

only because at such times men need diversions, but because men are tiring of the burden of a higher life.[211]

When Christians hate Jews—as the Church did quite extensively in the Middle Ages—it can be seen as the base side of man revolting against the imposition of a system of moral responsibility by Jesus, which was based on Jewish ideas. The 19th-century Jewish philosopher Franz Rosenzweig explained this, "Whenever the pagan rises in revolt against the yoke of the cross, he vents his fury on the Jew."[212]

Similarly, on the eve of World War II, Sigmund Freud suggested in *Moses and Monotheism* that, "The hatred for Judaism is at bottom hatred of Christianity."[213]

The Nazi Revolution was a modern rebellion against the call to civilization—the call to Sinai. During and after World War II, the Arab and radical Islamic worlds, including Hamas and Iran today, picked up the baton *(See Figure 5 on page 88-89).*[214]

The Call of Mount Sinai

Three thousand years ago, the Psalmist King David prophesied about how the world would chafe at the ethical responsibilities of Jewish values:

> Why do the people gather, and the nations talk in vain? The kings of the earth take their stand and the lords conspire secretly, against G-d and his anointed (the Jews), saying: 'Let us cut their cords [of the moral burden] and cast off their ropes.[215]

This is why the Talmud states, in a play on words, that at Mount Sinai, "Sinah," the Hebrew word for hatred, came into the world.[216]

While Jew-hate certainly predated Sinai, it now had a powerful new motivator aimed at the Jews. It was there, at the dawn of a new era in human history, when the Ten Commandments and the Torah were given, that antisemitism took on its profound significance.

Hitler said it directly, as quoted by Rauschning, "The Ten Commandments have lost their validity."[217]

Perhaps not all Germans were aware of the depth of Nazi ideology,[218] even if they supported Hitler and disliked Jews. However, the German nation was educated in these lessons, as illustrated in the Nazi Youth song "Jews Out, Away With the Pope":

> No, we have not bled
> anonymous and without fame,
> So that the German race will be Judaised
> through Christendom again.
> We are free from the mountain of Sinai,
> The sun circulates, you leave us alone.[219]

Dostoevsky's Inquisitor's harsh message to Jesus is the same one that antisemites have been asking the Jews over the centuries: "Why have you come to get in our way?"[220] Jew-hatred is the instinct to get Jews and everything they represent out of the way.[221]

This stark similarities and contrasts between Nazi ideology and Jewish values highlights the enduring struggle between brute force and moral responsibility. Both philosophies agree that this is the human story.

Summing up Human History based on the Nazi and Jewish Worldviews

Beginning with Abraham, a spiritual revolution emerged that introduced a new outlook into the world. This revolution was so

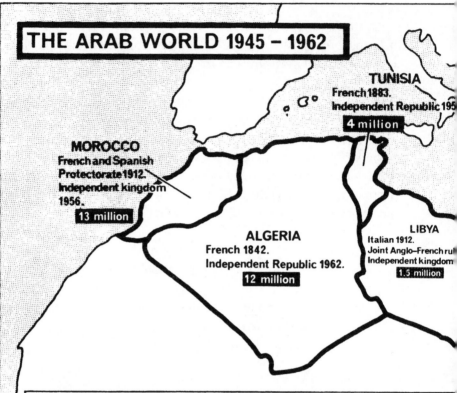

THE ARAB WORLD 1945 – 1962

TUNISIA
French 1883.
Independent Republic 195

4 million

MOROCCO
French and Spanish
Protectorate 1912.
Independent kingdom
1956.

13 million

ALGERIA
French 1842.
Independent Republic 1962.

12 million

LIBYA
Italian 1912.
Joint Anglo–French rul
Independent kingdom
1.5 million

In February 1945 an Arab League was established, with British encouragen
to promote Arab unity.   It rapidly became a platform for united Arab acti
against the Jewish community in Palestine.   After 1945 it also tried to prev
Germany paying Reparations to Jewish victims of Nazi persecution. It sub
quently became the chief opponent of the State of Israel (established in 19

*"Never has the Arab nation commanded such elements of freedom,
strength and opportunity as those which now lie in its hand. With
its twelve Sovereign States, its vast territory, its great resources of
manpower and wealth, it has realized ambitions beyond the wildest
expectations of recent years. Is the world really asking too much if it
demands of this vast empire that it live in peace and harmony with a
little State, established in the cradle of its birth, sustaining its life within
the narrowest territory in which its national purposes can ever be
fulfilled?"*

ABBA EBAN, FOREIGN MINISTER OF ISRAEL, 1958

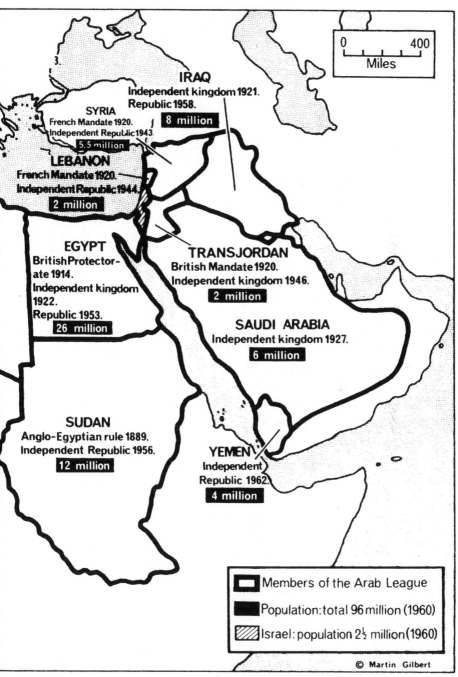

Figure 5. Formation of the Arab League.[249]

successful that 3,700 years later, one of the most powerful nations in the world, Germany, launched a campaign of genocide to eradicate it.

Hitler observed, with fear and disgust, that most of the modern world had embraced the ideas brought to the world by Abraham and the revelation at Sinai. These Jewish teachings promote values that are now widely accepted: classic Western liberalism, rejecting the primitive ideals of "might makes right," and instead striving for equal and human rights and the dignity and sanctity of life. They advocate for caring for the oppressed and downtrodden, promoting universal education, creating social welfare programs to help the sick and needy, encouraging tolerance, working to end racism, and fostering peace and the end to violence and war. These ideals, which are fundamental to Judaism, were not widely accepted when they were first introduced.

It is no coincidence that one of the freest countries in human history has a verse from the Hebrew Bible inscribed on its Liberty Bell, "Proclaim liberty throughout all the land unto all the inhabitants thereof."[222] It is also no coincidence that the global institution tasked with working for world peace, the United Nations, takes its vision from the Jewish prophet Isaiah: "They shall beat their swords into plowshares, and their spears into pruning hooks; nation shall not lift up sword against nation, neither shall they learn war any more."[223]

But over the thousands of years that it took humanity to get to where it became self-evident that "all men are created equal,"[224] there has been resistance every step of the way. There is a body-soul push and pull through history; as the lofty and holy ideas are slowly and painfully integrated into civilization, they are simultaneously resisted. The pushback is called *antisemitism*.

In his novel *The Portage to San Cristobal of A.H.*, the literary critic and philosopher George Steiner imagines a scenario where Adolf

Hitler survived World War II and hides in Argentina. Jewish Nazi hunters eventually capture him. Unable to extradite Hitler to Israel, they organize an improvised trial on the spot, and give the evil one a chance to justify his actions and explain why he committed genocide. Hitler offers a fascinating defense:

> You call me a tyrant, an enslaver. What tyranny, what enslavement has been more oppressive, has branded the skin and soul of man more deeply than the sick fantasies of the Jew? You are not God-killers, but God-makers. And that is infinitely worse. The Jew invented conscience and left man a guilty serf.[225]

The medieval scholar Rashi, reflecting on the Torah's careful choice of words in the war of the Jews against the people of Midian, explains that those who fight the Jewish People are simultaneously fighting God.[226]

This helps us understand the Torah's prediction given to Abraham: "those who bless you will be blessed, and he who curses you will be cursed; all the nations will be blessed through you"[227] It is much more than a metaphysical promise; it is a description of the natural consequences of a societies' values. Those societies open to and appreciative of Jewish values will be blessed by modeling these values, thereby becoming free, open, and tolerant societies; those closed to these ideas are usually repressive and undemocratic societies.

And to the extent they are repressive regimes, they will not like Jews and Israel. As mentioned before, this conflict can be seen today in the Middle East, as Gilder explains:

> The central issue in international politics, dividing the world into two fractious armies, is the tiny state of Israel. The prime issue is not a global war of

civilizations between the West and Islam or a split between Arabs and Jews. These conflicts are real and salient, but they obscure the deeper moral and ideological war. The real issue is between the rule of law and the rule of leveler egalitarianism, between creative excellence and covetous "fairness," between admiration of achievement versus envy and resentment of it.[228]

From medieval Christendom to Nazi Germany, from Soviet Russia until the modern Islamic Republic of Iran and much of Palestinian society today—they all fail the Israel Test and share the same traits: brutal authoritarianism and obsessive antisemitism.

This message of freedom, equality, and love threatens every totalitarian leader and ideology. It is why the bad guys always fight the Jews. Abraham's discovery of morality, social responsibility, and the universe threatened the greatest empire of his time. In reaction to his success in spreading his wisdom, the Midrash records that the world's most powerful tyrant, Nimrod, tried to kill Abraham by having him thrown into a fiery furnace.[229] It is why Hamas cannot accept a Jewish State beside them, and why the Palestinian Authority, like Hitler, cannot allow for Jews to live in their prospective future state.[230]

Throughout human history, Cain kills Abel, man kills man, Esau hunts Jacob, Pharaoh plots the destruction of the Jews, and countless tyrants mimic this pattern across thousands of years. The Ten Commandments, the Torah, and the Jewish mission were meant to break this cycle of blood and hate for all of humanity. Antisemites wage war on the Jews to protect the primitive values that the Jews disrupted.

Hitler and the Nazis sought to cast off conscience and the divine truths of morality by committing horrifying crimes against the Jews, only for Germany to be haunted by those crimes for generations. Rauschning quotes Hitler declaring, "Yes, we are barbarians! We want to be barbarians! It is an honorable title. We shall rejuvenate the world!"[231] Renowned psychologist Erik Erikson, in his famous book *Childhood and Society*, quoted Hitler as saying, "...conscience is a blemish like circumcision—and that both are Jewish blemishes."[232] The primordial message of God to Cain was that there is no escape from morality.

The Man on the Other Side

Abraham's discovery set him apart, philosophically, from all of humanity. As the Midrash says, "The whole world was on one side (*ever*), and Avram was on the other side."[233] And so, he became known as *HaIvri*—the Hebrew—which means "the man on the other side." This has been the essence of being Jewish ever since. His descendants have made a habit of challenging the status quo and have so often been seen as different, despised, ridiculed, and persecuted.[234] As Rabbi Sacks says, "Judaism is a living protest against the herd instinct. Ours is the dissenting voice in the conversation of humankind."[235]

The great poet Leonard Cohen, famous for baring his soul through song, spoke about facing antisemitism and the human reaction to being challenged:

> The world is hostile not only to the Jewish writer... the world is hostile to the writer, the world is hostile to the poet, the world is hostile to any man who will hold up a mirror to the particular kind of mindless chaos in which we endure. That is the glory of the poet, that is the glory of the writer, that is the glory of the Jew: that he is despised, that he moves in this mirrored exile, covered in mirrors, and as he passes through the communities that he sojourns, he reflects their condition, his condition.

To me, his destiny is exile and his vocation is to be
despised.[236]

The Jews may have been physically weak at times in their history,
but their ability to disrupt and spread a vision of the world as it
could be makes them perhaps the single most influential people in
the human story. Jewish philosophy and history clearly implicate
themselves as the perpetrators of the crime that Hitler and others
blame them for—the crime of gifting and transforming the world
with humanitarianism and ethical monotheism.[237] As Rosenzweig
said pithily, "The Jew must pay for his blessing."[238]

There is a Midrash that teaches a parable that at Sinai, God offered
the Torah to all the peoples of the world.[239] Every nation responded
by asking what the moral demands were, and, upon hearing the
unwanted restrictions, they politely declined.[240] Only the Jews,
usually famous for asking questions, unhesitatingly accepted to do
what God asked of them when they declared, "we accept to do,
and we will strive to understand..." regardless of the unknown
lifestyle demands being made of them, and in full knowledge that
accepting these divine gifts came with a high price of responsibility
and suffering.

Ivan Karamazov said it clearly: "Is it the fault of the rest of feeble
mankind that they could not endure what the mighty endured? Is
it the fault of the weak soul that it is unable to contain such terrible
gifts?"[241]

The *Why* of Jew-Hatred

And so we return to our opening question: Why, in every generation,
are so many people trying to wipe out the Jewish People? Here is
what I think Jew-hatred is, and what it is not.

At times, Jew-hatred can certainly be your run-of-the-mill

ignorant racism. It can be a legitimate gripe against Jews who deserve to be disliked—for example, when they act immorally, as the Jewish People have had their fair share of scoundrels. But taken in totality over Jewish history, in its genocidal passion in every generation, including today's anti-Israel frenzy, Jew-hatred is *not* like other forms of xenophobia. Jew-hatred is not because we are easy scapegoats;[242] it is not because of the "dislike of the unlike"[243] or because our blood is impure; it is not because we killed Jesus or drink Christian blood; it is not a mysterious virus; and it is not because we are white colonialists who stole Palestinian land.[244]

Jews are hated for every possible—and often opposite—external reason, which tells us that these are not the real reasons.[245] Most Jew-haters do not have Hitler's clarity on what the real "Jewish Problem" is, and perhaps because so few lack a deep understanding of what is bothering them, they reach for the day's values to justify and moralize why they hate Jews.[246] But make no mistake: next year, they will hate us again, and this time for a different reason, because the stated reasons are just excuses, and they do not get to the root of what they hate about Jews.

That is what Jew-hatred is not. If you only learn what antisemitism is not from this book, I believe it would be a solid contribution because there is so much confusion on the matter. These misunderstandings do a disservice—not just to dealing with the hate, but also to Jewish identity.

What is the reason that evil always seems to find and target the Jews?

There are certainly levels. It is a reaction against Jewish strength, as manifested in Jewish success and influence. It is a reaction against the Jewish predilection to push for change and improvement, the drive for more. It is created by the hostility of people and belief systems—religious, racial, or ideological—that fear Jewish success, Jewish disruption, and competition. It is the rebellion against

Jewish ideas and ideology, especially the unwelcome imposition of monotheism and its moral demands. At its deepest level, Jew-hatred is the revolt against God and the people who represent Him, against those who were commissioned to bear the ancient moral truths.[247] It often comes from a deep feeling many have that Jews are somehow very different.[248] As we will see in Chapter 6, Jew-hatred is the struggle to destroy the awesome spiritual potential of humanity by wiping out the Jews.

I think that Hitler articulated the uncomfortable disruptive power of the Jewish People. It is a phenomenon that many people feel but cannot articulate. Hitler understood the Jews with icy clarity. But there was one thing he could not fathom.

5

Purim and the Lesson That Hitler Did Not Understand

God promised (Jewish survival) in the Torah: "I will not reject them"; this was in the days of the Chaldeans. "Nor will I abhor them"; this was in the days of the Greeks. "To destroy them utterly"; this was in the days of Haman. "To break My covenant with them"; this was in the days of the Romans. "For I am the Lord their God"; this will be in the future, when no nation or people of a foreign tongue will be able to subjugate them further.
–Talmud, Megilla 11A

THERE WAS ONE thing that Hitler struggled with: the indestructibility of the Jews.

The Eternal Jew

As the preparations for the Holocaust were underway, the Nazis unveiled a new film, a propaganda masterpiece, *Der Ewige Jude*, (German for 'The Eternal Jew'). Although the Nazis intended the title as a slur, it was the very eternity of the Jews that challenged Hitler's ideas about the nature of reality.

Figure 6. Eternal Jew poster on wall.
Courtesy of The U.S. Holocaust Memorial
Museum. Provenance: Samuel Schryver.

Both the Jews and the Nazis clung to powerful ideas of eternity: heaven, on the one hand, and the 1,000-Year Reich on the other. The Holocaust was a clash between these two opposing concepts of eternity. Despite the overwhelming might of the Nazis and the physical helplessness of the Jews, Hitler feared the victory of the "eternal Jew."

The Jews had compounded their "crime" of spreading their ideas into the world by refusing to vanish like other peoples. Somehow, the eternal Jew had survived and thrived for more than 3,000 years. Hitler and the Nazis could only attribute the Jews' unnatural existence and impact to a vast conspiracy extending across thousands of years.

When Julius Streicher, the Nazi leader whom the Nuremberg prosecution said had "educated the whole of the German people in hatred," fell into American hands when the war ended, he explained to his interrogator that:

> The German people will not be free of the danger of the Jewish plague until the Jewish question is liquidated in its entirety...The danger of the plague infecting the German people will continue to exist as long as there is a seed of this pestilence anywhere in the world.[250]

Asked for clarification from the perplexed interrogator, Streicher answered that the Jewish question would not be solved as long as any Jew lives because of the "Biblical covenant between the Lord and Abraham and to the circumcision of the Jews as a sign of it."[251]

Purim Fest

In December 1941, when Hitler made the catastrophic decision to declare war on the United States, he accused "President Roosevelt and the Jews" of "preparing a second Purim."[252] He was referring to the Jewish holiday that commemorates the improbable victory of the Jews throughout the Persian Empire 2,500 years ago against Haman and his genocidal designs.

In January 1944, as Berlin was being bombed, Hitler delivered a radio address warning that if the Nazis lost, there would be "a second triumphant Purim festival."

In 1946, when Julius Streicher was led out to the gallows with nine other Nazis sentenced to death at the Nuremberg Trials and came face-to-face with the rope that would end his life, he screamed, "Purim Fest 1946."[253]

The Nazis had a special obsession with the Jewish holiday of Purim.

In 1941, in the Polish town of Zduńska Wola, the Nazis had decided to create their own twisted version of Purim. They demanded that the Jews choose 10 of their own by lot to be hanged to avenge the death of Haman's 10 sons (who were hanged in the wake of his failed attempt to exterminate the Jews).[254]

At their hanging on Purim morning, the assembled Jews were told that these 10 were being executed in revenge for Haman. But "when the 10 condemned men learned that their deaths would save the Jewish community, they were filled with a strange joy and sang as they stepped up to the gallows."[255]

The Jews who died knew their deaths were *al kiddush Hashem*, sanctifying the name of God. They found meaning in their deaths because they knew they were part of a great ongoing story—of their own lives and their people—of Jewish strength of the spirit, and that victory would come in due time.

There was no singing when 10 Nazis, including Streicher, were hanged for their crimes on October 16, 1946. Streicher and his fellow Nazis found no such comfort or meaning in their deaths. They knew they had lost the world war over humanity's core values. In the battle for the soul of humanity, the law of dominance and power that Hitler sought to restore was defeated by the Jewish ethos of human dignity that has shaped civilizations.

The frenzied cry of "Purim Fest" suggests that Streicher saw the modern re-creation of the Purim story, that again, in the latest attempt at genocide, the Nazi Hamans end on the gallows. The Nazis had worked to disprove Purim and Jewish destiny, only for Streicher to realize in the closing moments of his life that he was the latest actor in the ongoing Purim story.[256]

Why were Hitler and the Nazis so obsessed with this particular Jewish holiday?

Streicher testified at Nuremberg that he had studied the Torah and read the work of Jewish scholars. He was intimately familiar with the Purim story. It seems that when people like Streicher studied the Torah, they naturally gravitated toward the figure most like themselves.

Haman seeks to exterminate the Jews. He advises the king that they are unlike any other people; they are a disruptive element, being scattered throughout the kingdom, and following their own laws.[257] "All this (power and wealth) is worth nothing to me as long as I see Mordechai the Jew sitting at the King's gate,"[258] Haman wails at a crucial moment in the Book of Esther. Despite being the second-most-powerful man in the world's mightiest empire, he could not tolerate one Jew refusing to acknowledge that power, his power, was everything.

Similarly for Hitler, the military conquest of all Europe was meaningless to him if one Jew remained alive. In his declaration of war against America, Hitler was deploying Hamanesque rhetoric about the danger that the Jews posed to the world.

Just as Haman gave up his wealth and power in a bid to exterminate the Jews, Hitler sacrificed Germany, its soldiers, and the war he had begun to his obsession with destroying the Jews. Hamas and the radical Islamists prefer killing Jews and destroying Israel over the value of protecting their own people and building a prosperous society for them.

Jewish History Disrupts Natural Law

The essence of Purim is the story of reversal. It's a holiday celebrated with costumed masquerades and with the tradition of drinking *"Ad d'Lo Yada,"* until the drinker cannot distinguish between Haman and Mordechai. This commemorates the genocidal plot that was turned upside down, transforming Purim from a day of "sorrow to rejoicing, and from mourning into a holiday."

Reversal—strength becoming weakness, and weakness turning into strength, the victim emerging triumphant and his killer falling victim to his own plot—is a fundamental Jewish idea. It pervades not only Purim, but the entire Jewish story.

The implausible survival and civilizational influence of the Jews through thousands of years of persecution, despite an enduring hatred with no parallel, reverses the natural course of events. The Nazis believed that nothing is mightier than nature, while the Jews insisted that God is above nature, and that He created us to rise above our physical nature and the natural course of events. Hitler believed that the insolent Jewish insistence that "man conquers nature" was a trick, but the trick proved to be another reversal of the natural order.

When God lifted Abraham above the stars in an early prophetic vision, He was showing him that his people will not be subject to the normal, "natural" rules and patterns of history. As the 19th-century philosopher known as the Malbim explains, "Abraham's descendants will shine light to the world, as the stars do; they will be eternal, as the stars are; and yet they will be 'above the stars'— i.e. not subjected to the normal earthly laws of cause and effect." [259]

American founding father Alexander Hamilton observed the same phenomenon 3,800 years later:

> Progress of the Jews, from their earliest history to the present time, has been and is entirely out of the ordinary course of human affairs. Is it not then a fair conclusion that the cause also is an extraordinary one—in other words, that it is the effect of some great providential plan?[260]

Jewish history is a series of unexpected reversals in which the revolutionary messages and beliefs of a tiny, despised people somehow become adopted by most of the world. The Nazis began the 1940s on top of the world, but half a decade later, they had fallen as thoroughly as Haman.

To his credit, Hitler did suspect that there were mysterious forces working in the Jews' favor when he declared that "Destiny, perhaps for reasons unknown to us poor mortals...desire(d) the final victory of this little nation."[261] How else to explain their outsized influence on all sectors of modern Germany, their dramatic impact on world history—indeed, their very survival?[262]

Adolph Hitler was right to fear the Jews. The Jewish People are the Burning Bush that will not be consumed:

3,300 years ago: The superpower of the day, Egypt, brutally enslaved the Jewish People for over 200 years. The Jewish People emerged with the Torah to share with the world its lessons of love, freedom, and justice.

2,500 years ago: The superpower of the day, Persia, declared genocide. The Jewish People survived and rebuilt the Second Temple in Israel.

2,200 years ago: The superpower of the day, Greece, declared war on Torah and the Jewish religion. The ragtag Jewish militias defeated them and gained newfound independence.

2,000 years ago: The superpower of the day, the Roman Empire, crushed Jerusalem, destroyed the Second Temple, slaughtered over a million people, and exiled the survivors. They expected that to be the end of the Jewish story. It wasn't.

For 1,300 years: The European Christian empire relentlessly persecuted the Jews through pogroms, forced conversions, inquisitions, ghettos, and economic exclusions to prove that the Jews were now despised by God. Instead, Jews adapted, survived, and built study halls and spiritual kingdoms in the ghettos and wastelands they were afforded.

For 1,400 years: Jews under Islam were—together with Christians—given the status of *dhimmi*, legally second-class citizens. While they fared better in Islamic lands than under the Christians, their inferior status often led to persecution.

100 years ago: The Russian Communists declared

Judaism obsolete and Zionism illegal. About 80 years later, one million Soviet Jews emerged and "made *aliyah*" to Israel, helping it become the Start-Up Nation.

About 90 years ago: Hitler decided humanity needed a "final solution to the Jewish problem." He built the superpower of the day and executed mankind's most ruthless and systematic genocide. The 1,000-Year Reich crumbled, and the Jews emerged and re-established the State of Israel.

After World War II: The Arab and Islamic world, the one Nazi ally that escaped undefeated and unrepentant, carried on the battle in Hitler's shadow. After failing to "throw the Jews in the sea" in the Independence War of 1948, the Arabs, Islamists from Saudi Arabia to Iran, and Palestinians, with some European help, have continued with 75 years of constant terror, wars, boycotts, and diplomatic delegitimization. The Jews prevailed and built the only democracy in the Middle East.

Mark Twain said in 1899 that "All things are mortal but the Jew; all other forces pass, but he remains. What is the secret of his immortality?"[263]

The Secret

We began this book with the Dalai Lama's search for the Jewish secret to survival and success, exploring how the Jews remained a cohesive people with a common identity, values, and culture.

Now, we know the secret.

Hitler understood the secret too. In 1941, after sharing it with the Mufti, he asked him to "lock it in the uttermost depths of his heart." Hitler told the Mufti, "This was the decisive struggle... ideologically it was a battle between National Socialism and the Jews."

World War II was the last-gasp historical grab for power by an almost defeated foe—it was now or never, and Hitler knew it. In an NSDAP speech in 1922, he already articulated that, "Here too, there can be no compromise—there are only two possibilities: either victory of the Aryan or annihilation of the Aryan and the victory of the Jew."[264] The Nazis knew it was an either-or war and the Germans were humanity's last chance to defeat the Jewish worldview.

It cost 60 million lives fighting—although many were not conscious of it—over which ideology would rule, but Hitler's was rejected.[265] The Holocaust and 100 years of Arab Islamic Jew-hatred are the world's most recent negative reactions to the Jewish story. Millions of Jews have been killed for it, and millions of individual Jews opted out or were forced out along the long journey, but overall, the Jewish People have bravely held on.

This is the mystery that the Dalai Lama and Mark Twain wondered about: The Jewish People are a superpower in humanity's primal, spiritual world war.

The great Russian writer Leo Tolstoy wondered:

> "The Jew is the emblem of eternity. He whom neither slaughter nor torture of thousands of years could destroy, he whom neither fire nor sword nor inquisition was able to wipe off the face of the earth, he who was the first to produce the oracles of G-d, he who has been for so long the guardian of prophecy, and who transmitted it to the rest of the world—such a nation cannot be destroyed. The Jew is as everlasting as is eternity itself.[266]

The Jews have endured the most severe persecutions while wielding improbable influence over the course of human events because they are the carriers of information so potent that it has drawn both vehement opposition and begrudging respect from nations, even as the clarity of its contents has dimmed in collective memory.[267]

For most of the past 2,000 years, the Jews have fought with the only weapons available to them—what the Torah calls "Jewish weapons" of the spirit: prayer, Torah study, ethical observance, and belief in God and His Plan. King David summarized it: "They call on chariots, they call on horses, but we call on the name of the LORD our God."[268] The prophet Zecharia declared: "This is the word of God to Zerubbabel: 'Not by might, nor by power, but by My spirit, said the Lord.'"[269]

Recently, the Jewish People, much to the chagrin of much of the world who seem to love dead Jews more than live ones,[270] have added a physical army to their spiritual arsenal, as they had for centuries during the First and Second Jewish Commonwealths. But Hitler also understood that Jewish power was not primarily physical: "The Jewish State has never been spatially limited in itself; it was universally unlimited in respect to space, but was restricted to the collectivity of the race."

The question remains: Why are the Jews indestructible?

The answer, in short, is that the Jewish People are essential to fulfilling the world's purpose—God's plan requires an indestructible people. In the following chapters, we will explore the deeper aspects of Jewish identity and philosophy, uncovering the profound reasons behind the Jewish People's survival and the world's reaction to them.

6

The Why and How of the Jewish People

I call heaven and earth to witness for you this day:
I have put before you life and death, blessing
and curse. Choose life, so that you and
your offspring will live (to full self-actualization).
–Deuteronomy, 30:19

THE STORY OF Jewish survival, unique and amazing as it is in human history, is not our essential story. Our essential story is based on the worldview that began with Abraham, which we have only briefly touched upon. As we will now see, the Jewish worldview explains—and predicts—both the mystery of the Jews and the reaction against them.

Let's explore what Jews have traditionally said about their identity, philosophy, and mission. Jewish thought is rich and deep, so bear with me, as this exercise will take a few pages to unravel. We will see that the Jewish People are indestructible because they are essential in helping the world fulfill its purpose, and so God's plan requires an indestructible people.

But first, a caveat. In these few pages, for several reasons, we cannot do justice to the scope and depth of ideas that have occupied the Jewish People for thousands of years:

1. The ideas are so vast that they have engaged the cleverest Talmudic minds of each generation in lifetime learning efforts, yet these scholars feel they have barely scratched the surface. Simplifying these complex concepts might even be a disservice.

2. Any translation of Hebrew into English loses the nuance of meaning.

3. Misconceptions abound before we even begin, due to our cultural associations of Judaism with religion and Jewish thought with theology, when the Torah is neither. Judaism is not a religion as commonly understood, nor is Jewish philosophy merely theology.[271]

I present these ideas with no politically correct varnish, knowing that some people do not agree or believe in these principles, and that they may be uncomfortable and possibly even offensive to some. I lay down the classical Jewish outlook so that we can compare it to what we have learned about Jewish impact and antisemitism; the relationship is astonishing.[272]

The Jewish Worldview:
The Hidden World and the First Jew

In Hebrew, the world is called *Olam*, which comes from the same root word as *elem*, meaning "hidden." This tells us that in creating a material world, God hid Himself, a phenomenon known in the mystical Kabbalistic tradition as *tzimtzum*. The void created by hiding the spiritual world enables man's search and his opportunity for growth. Amid the philosophical chaos and seeming anarchy of everyday existence, human beings must seek answers to life's most important mysteries.

Around 3,800 years ago, a man named Abraham searched, and the God he found was not just the God of the rain or of the harvest, though He controlled the natural order. It was a power that existed outside the universe, outside of time and space. One might think that God was therefore unknowable with no natural way to relate to Him, and some might have been daunted by that realization—but not Abraham.

The First Jewish Disrupter

Abraham became the first Jew, and he was the paradigmatic Jewish disrupter. Maimonides describes the early years of Abraham's life:[273]

> After this mighty man was weaned, he began to explore and think. Though he was a child, he began to think [incessantly] throughout the day and night.
>
> He had no teacher, nor was there anyone to inform him. Rather, he was mired in Ur Kasdim[274] among the foolish idolaters. His father, mother, and all the people [around him] were idol worshipers, and he would worship with them. [However,] his heart was exploring and [gaining] understanding.
>
> Ultimately, he appreciated the way of truth and understood the path of righteousness through his accurate comprehension. He realized that there was One God who controlled the sphere (heavens), that He created everything, and that there is no other god (power) in existence apart from Him. He knew that the entire world was making a mistake.
>
> Abraham was 40 years old when he became

(deeply) aware of his Creator. When he recognized and knew Him, he began to formulate replies to the inhabitants of Ur Kasdim and debate with them, telling them that they were not following a proper path. He broke their idols[275] and began to teach the people that it is fitting to serve only the Eternal God of the world.

At the age of 75, Abraham had risen to such a spiritual height—in character development and intellectual understanding (the Talmud records that "Abraham fulfilled the entire Torah" even before it was given[276])—that he experienced his first prophetic revelation.[277] God's first command to the man who reintroduced the world to Him was to become a wanderer: "And God said to Abram, 'Go, leave your native land, your birthplace, and your father's home, to a Land that I will show you.'"[278]

"*Lech lecha*," God said, which means "go forth" and implies that "going will be for your own good."[279] What seemed at first like a punishment of exile from the life and world he knew was actually a carefully designed personal-growth program for Abraham: The challenges and tests ahead of him, including this one, were designed to help him achieve personal greatness and self-actualization.

Abraham probably needed God's reassurance to leave everything behind, and God promised that his family would continue his work and be a blessing to all humanity:

> I will make of you a great nation,
> and I will bless you;
> I will make your name great,
> and you shall be a blessing.
> I will bless those who bless you
> and curse the one who curses you;
> And all the families of the earth
> shall be blessed through you.[280]

To accomplish the mission he was being assigned, Abraham would have to trust God and go on a difficult spiritual journey without a clear destination. This was to become the archetypal Jewish—and human—journey.

Abraham accepted God's command and took his family to Canaan (Israel). It was a faith that would carry him from a wandering exile to becoming the father of all monotheistic religions. He set out to live in a relationship with the loving God who created him, to follow the ethical principles that derived from this worldview, and to teach his discoveries to everyone.

By asking the ultimate existential questions and making a total commitment to live with the answers no matter their consequence, Abraham chose his destiny. He chose to be 100% accountable to God, and that decision enabled him to become the father of a people who would be expected—and challenged—to continue the important and perilous journey. The mission undertaken by Abraham was not just to reduce the number of gods to one, but to spread the knowledge that God transcended the universe that He had created, and that despite the vast differential between man and God, human beings could reach Him.[281]

Abraham's Philosophy 101:
The Jewish *Why*

What specific ideas did Abraham discover? He learned, with incredible depth, who is God and what is Man. Abraham reasoned that a loving Creator brought into existence the universe and all life, including humans—conscious beings who could aspire to receive not just the enjoyment of the things we ask for in our daily lives, but also the pleasure of spiritual life and godliness. He understood that there is nothing we can offer God. Everything in the universe already belongs to Him. God did not create mankind so that we would give Him "things" like sacrifices, praises, or prayers; nor did He need us to build things or send him checks.[282] Abraham grasped that Man does not supply God with His needs. What we give God is someone He can give to.

King David sang of how God created a world with many types of creatures, beings of pure spirit, known as angels, and creatures of flesh, or animals.[283] But the goal, the purpose, was man, a hybrid being of spirit and flesh, whose resultant free will could bridge the worlds of the physical and the spiritual and create something new and awesome.

A divine soul was breathed into a material body. Man is made in the *Tzelem Elokim*, the image of God, but physically, he is a biological creature with the same impulses and drives as any animal. Man is therefore pulled, internally, in two opposing directions and can become either one. This unique spirit-animal that God made can enjoy all the sensory pleasures of life while also contemplating the nature of existence. He is free to choose his life's path and make the moral and philosophical decisions that will define him[284] and the world.

The spiritual soul that God miraculously grafted onto a physical body reaches instinctively for a hidden world and a spiritual connection beyond the earth and sky, while the body is driven by the animalistic desires that pull a human being into the depths of the material world.[285] Rabbi Simon Jacobson gives an analogy:

> Look closely at the flame of a candle, and you will see an approximation of your soul—the flame licking the air, reaching upward, as if toward God. And yet the wick pulls it back to earth. Similarly, your soul is constantly reaching upward, while your body holds you back with its insistent demands for physical sustenance or gratification. The question for each of us is, Do we choose to be the flame that rises upward or the wick that holds us down?[286]

Abraham understood that life is God's gift to man. And that man's purpose and deepest happiness comes not only from enjoying the world, but from finding the purpose of our lives and building ourselves into giving, loving people connected with our souls and God. God created man to enjoy the ultimate pleasure of becoming a spiritual being, as articulated in the Jewish philosophy classic *The Path of the Just* by the Italian Rabbi and mystic Moshe Chaim Luzzatto:

> Our sages have taught us that man was created to delight in God and to derive pleasure in the radiance of the *Shechina* (The Divine Presence). For this is the true delight and the greatest pleasure that can possibly exist.[287]

Man's job is to live a life of the spirit while in our bodies and to avoid becoming purely physical beings, like an animal.

The Why of Free Will: Choosing Is Not Easy

Rabbi Luzatto explains more about the body-soul dynamic in the classic philosophy primer *The Way of God*:

> And since each one of them naturally inclines to its side—meaning to say, the body towards physicality and the soul towards spirituality—it comes out that there is a war between them in such a way that if the soul wins, it will raise the body with it; but if man allows the physical to win in him, the body will surely be lowered and the soul will be lowered with it. Man has the ability to humble his physical [side] before his spiritual [side] and acquire his perfection.[288]

Rabbi Jacobson clarifies the deep purpose of man's unique design:

The true goal of life is to challenge ourselves in order to refine this material world. Life is synonymous with challenge, and challenge is synonymous with the potential for good and evil, and our ability to choose between the two. Without the possibility that we may fall temporarily, there would be no independence to life, and therefore no meaning.[289]

Climbing the Ladder

The challenges people overcome and the choices they make are more than just inner struggles; they allow them to move up to higher levels until they become more than just souls trapped in a physical reality. Along this spiritual journey called life, one can experience the pleasure that comes when our physical and spiritual worlds unite, elevating spiritually while bringing the body along to enjoy the sublime spiritual pleasures. This is what Judaism calls a life of *dveikut*, or "cleaving to God."

Rabbi Jacobson puts it succinctly: "This means uniting the body and soul to fulfill the mission for which we were all put on earth: to lead a meaningful, productive and virtuous life by making the physical world a comfortable home for spirituality and Godliness."[290]

This Abrahamic notion—where our body is our partner, not our enemy—was and remains a very unique idea compared to many other religions:

> We were created to transform this material world into a more refined place and to introduce a higher dimension: Godliness. So while the ultimate goal of our work may be spiritual growth, the fact that God placed us in a material world means that we reach that spiritual plane through physical labor.[291]

The *Why* of Being Jewish

Abraham chose a life of the spirit that has infinite potential but that also includes a rigorous demand to refine a person's ethical and moral character. He was asked to become holy, to bring God's light into the world, and to establish a family that would become a people whose conduct and teachings would sanctify God's name in the world.

The great 18th century Talmudist Rabbi Chaim of Volozhin explains in his seminal work of Jewish philosophy and mysticism, *Nefesh HaChaim*, that sanctification—transforming of the self and the world to holiness—is the highest opportunity of life:

> This is the meaning of "God created man in His Image"[292]: that just as God is the One who empowers All existence in all of the worlds (physical and spiritual), arranging and controlling them all each moment per his Will, similarly God willed it that man is enabled to exert control such that he is the one who opens and closes a myriad of powers and worlds according to the detail of his behavior in all that he does each moment…(through) his actions, speech, and thoughts.[293]

Abraham chose this life because he understood that the actualization of human potential to this high level was our purpose; it was the reason that God created man with an eternal soul. Thus, his children, the Jewish People, were tasked as messengers to help humanity in their journey of self-actualization and self-transformation[294], to make their lives and the world a spiritual abode. This is the *why* of being Jewish.

Dealing With High Expectations

What God is asking of the Jews—indeed, of all people[295]—is to become "superhuman." This does not mean flying through the air with a cape or toppling buildings with their hands, but rather transcending human limitations to do the impossible. The real impossibilities holding people back aren't outside; they're inside.

Faced with high expectations, it's natural for people to protest that too much is being asked of them. "We're only human," they sometimes protest when asked to do difficult tasks, especially things that seem impossible. Those "impossibilities" aren't rooted in the laws of physics but in people's self-definition and in their belief in their own limitations. Transcending these limitations is what makes them superhuman.

Leaping into the air and flying would be much easier than complete self-transcendence and living in an alternate and invisible spiritual world while walking through this material world. But we know it can be done because Abraham did it. And God says in the Torah:

> For this commandment which I command you this day, is not hidden from you, nor is it far away. It is not in heaven, that you should say, "Who will go up to heaven for us and fetch it for us, to tell us, so that we can do it?" Nor is it beyond the sea, that you should say, "Who will cross to the other side of the sea for us and fetch it for us, to tell us, so that we can do it?" Rather, this matter is very close to you; it is in your mouth and in your heart, so that you can do it.[296]

The *Why* of Human Life

The Abrahamic ideal for humanity, the *why* of human existence, is to perform the superhuman feat of spiritual self-transformation by harmoniously balancing a connection to God while inhabiting a physical body and world.

The *How* of Being Jewish

Likely, only a few individuals in human history have achieved this at the highest level. Jewish philosophy maintains that for an entire people to approach such a lofty level requires spiritual refinement unattainable by man's choices alone.[297] The Jewish People would need certain experiences and tools to have a chance at fulfilling their mission.

To make the impossible possible, God provided the Jewish People with several divine tools: the Torah, *mitzvot* (commandments),[298] the land of Israel,[299] and suffering/antisemitism.[300] Each one of these is a deep concept deserving of full explanation, but for our purposes, given the need for brevity, we will explain two of these divine tools.

The First Divine Tool: The Torah

Why were the Jews given these Five Books, and how does the Torah help accomplish the mission?

The traditional Jewish understanding—in fact, the most important article of Jewish belief[301]—is that 3,300 years ago, 50 days after a slave nation was liberated and left a mighty civilization in shambles, Moses led the Jewish People to the Mountain to hear God speak to them.

The *Book of Exodus* describes the almost 200 years[302] of Egyptian slavery and oppression that preceded the moment at Sinai when they heard God proclaim the first two of the Ten Commandments and establish Moses as their prophet who would bring the rest of God's instructions to them. In one powerful moment, 600,000 adult men, plus women and children, became prophets. It was the most unique event in human history.

The Jewish People stepped outside time and space, the world stopped in its tracks, and the boundaries between heaven and earth evaporated. God delivered a message that transcended the boundaries of the senses and spoke directly to the souls of the waiting Jews.

Mount Sinai introduced a new worldview for humanity. The Ten Commandments[303] and the whole Torah were more than a set of laws: the written Five Books of Moses and the detailed Oral Law (the explanation of every word, letter, and law, which was subsequently partially written down in works such as the *Mishnah* and *Talmud*), were received by Moses over 40 days. To the millions standing at the foot of the mountain, to their descendants over time, and through them to the billions of humanity, God revealed His purpose, His ethical code, and the science of the spiritual world. [304]

The Torah was a revolution in human affairs. Its moral and philosophical principles changed how people lived. But even as it gave much, it also demanded much. Judaism tells us what kind of people God wants us to be: "Judaism is a religion given by God to define man, while the other faiths were created by man to define God," wrote Rabbi Samson Raphael Hirsch, the 19th-century scholar and leader.[305]

The earth-shattering events of Sinai created two enduring impacts that help the Jewish People in their mission:

1. Jews began a love affair with learning Torah.

2. The transformative experience of Revelation altered Jewish souls.

Effect #1: A Love Affair With a Book

The Jewish People have had a 120-generations-long love affair with learning. They became the people of the Book by treasuring it, studying it constantly, memorizing it, and passing it carefully from generation to generation.

Rabbi Joseph Soloveitchik, one of the foremost Jewish scholars of the 20th century, described Torah study as a "symposium of generations" where young boys argue and revive the debates between religious scholars who lived and died long before the discovery of America. "We belong to the same 'Mesorah' community, where generations meet," he said, using the Hebrew word for the transmission of heritage. "Where hands, no matter how wrinkled and parched dry (old) one hand is, and how soft (young) the other hand is, shake, and unite—and The Great Dialogue continues."[306]

Even today, tens of thousands study a page of *Talmud* every day in the *Page of Talmud a Day* program. It takes 7.5 years to learn through the entire 2,711 dense pages of the Talmud. And when they finish, they celebrate with a *Siyum*—which means completion and begin again— but now with deeper insights, and thousands more joining.

Figure 7. Siyum HaShas 2019. Celebrating the completion of reading the Talmud.
13th Siyum HaShas In MetLife Stadium by Shemtov613.[334]

There are many levels and aspects of Torah learning.

Torat Chaim: The Torah's full name means "an instruction manual for living" to the fullest, offering wisdom for happiness and a guidebook that shows us the mindset that will help us navigate life's challenges.

Moral Code: The Torah defines ethical behavior down to the minutest detail, expressing and defining our *core values*. It contains an entire *justice system* and legal code covering all aspects of life.

Intellectual Development: The Torah *develops us intellectually through its rigorous and relentless "question and answer"* learning method, helping us to pursue truth. It *transforms us spiritually* by providing wisdom and power tools like prayer, meditation, and the *mitzvot* (commandments) to transcend our physical limitations.

The Torah revolution began by changing the Jews themselves. The Torah did not aim at a political revolution; it ushered in a revolution in moral consciousness. This primal book is not a passive experience; it is meant to change who we are. The Torah would not have changed the world otherwise.

The Torah informs us not only how to make the most of our lives, but also *why we live*.

The Torah tells us *who and what we are*. It reaches our minds and our souls, speaking to us both on a conscious and unconscious level that touches the deepest part of who we truly are.

Rabbi Luzzatto says:

> Torah study is a necessary matter. Without it, it is impossible to arrive at (proper) action (defining

how to be good)...However besides all this, there is a great function in study towards the perfection of man...Among the (spiritual) influences that are brought from God for the needs of His creatures, [Torah study] is the most precious and sublime of all that can be found in existence...and the greater the understanding, the greater the level of influence that will be brought down through it.[307]

To learn Torah is to study God's world. It is the science of the spiritual world.[308]

In the command (mitzvah) for Jews to learn the entire Torah[309], we are called on to become philosophers, PhDs of God and life. Every Jew is challenged not only to become a scholar, but to internalize its ethical and spiritual truths. The Torah is the teacher, the interface with the Divine.

Effect #2: A Soul-Bending Experience

When God spoke directly to the Jewish People, the revelation was a wave of raw, spiritual power that no human being could fully endure[310], and this created the second permanent impact of Sinai: The soul of every Jew was transformed.

The mind- and soul-blowing experience of the Revelation is described in the Torah as synesthesia—they "saw the sounds and heard the sights,"[311] and this altered spiritual state changed Jewish souls forever. They experienced a level of holiness so high and powerful that they would never be the same again. The Talmud says that at Sinai, the souls of all Jews were, in a spiritual manner, genetically changed.[312]

Scientists have recently discovered that experiencing high levels of stress can change our DNA, and that these effects are passed on from parents to their children. This is called *epigenetics*. Judaism says that in a similar way, there is spiritual epigenetics—when a powerful spiritual experience is imprinted on and passed on in the DNA of our souls. The great 19th-century kabbalist Rabbi Yosef Chaim of Baghdad explained that

> The awesome holy fire that shone down from Above at the Sinai Revelation caused a spiritual cleansing of all the souls standing there; the burning power of it spontaneously repulsed and cast away contaminations.[313]

Sinai was burned into our souls. Even 3,300 years later, even when some Jews have lost conscious clarity of the mission, their spiritual DNA still pushes them to accomplish, disrupt, and transform.

The gift of Torah, then, is the first tool that God gave the Jews to help them accomplish their difficult national mission. The second divine tool we will explain is more difficult to understand.

The Second Divine Tool: Suffering

God promised Abraham that his descendants would be given the Torah and the land of Israel but that the necessary preparation involved an unpleasant and lengthy descent in a foreign land. He also promised that the Jewish People would experience much more persecution in the centuries to come.

The third prophecy Abraham received from God is called the "Covenant Between the Parts," and in it, God revealed the special covenantal relationship He would have with Abraham's children, and the special role they would play in history. The prophecy also informed Abraham of the very painful future his descendants will endure before they receive the Torah:

"And [God] said to Abram[314], 'Know well that your
offspring shall be strangers in a land not theirs,
and they shall be enslaved and oppressed for four
hundred years.'"[315]

Why was suffering part of the package? It is certainly counter-
intuitive that the people earmarked by God for a unique role
should also be earmarked for persecution. And to be fair, Judaism
says that negative prophecies, those dealing with suffering, did not
necessarily have to come to fruition. While there was a chance to
accomplish the mission without this, it seemed unlikely from the
outset, which raises the following question: Why did God decree
this, and how does it help?

This requires some serious unpacking (and I can acknowledge up
front that even the unpacking, the answers remain emotionally
difficult to appreciate).

The Spiritual Crucible

Abraham's descendants would have to be refined not only in
spiritual aspiration, but in the fires of persecution. The sublime
and admittedly difficult-to-grasp idea is that the Jews needed to
become spiritually refined by breaking down and extracting some
of their physicality, as metal is refined in a smelting furnace. Just as
the smelter uses heat to drive off impure elements and leave the pure
metal behind, God refines the Jewish People through a historical
process that removes physicality and allows the attainment of
holiness[316]: "But you God took and brought out of Egypt, that iron
blast smelting furnace, to be God's very own people, as is now the
case."[317]

Interestingly, I was once told this lesson by an older friend of mine
who survived the Holocaust, in an intimate conversation we had a
few years before he passed on in 2010. He explained to me the core

lesson he learned from his four years of suffering in Auschwitz: The Nazis not only enslaved and killed the Jews, they degraded them in every possible manner—to the point that he knew in his dry bones that he was not a body, that his soul was above—and so he could never be truly enslaved. That knowledge, he revealed to me, gave him the power to survive.

The Rebbe of Slonim clarifies this deep idea:

> This is the explanation of all of the Exiles that the Jewish People pass through, that their purpose was to refine and purify the Jews. This was so they will be prepared to fulfill their exalted role in history to create a spiritual abode for God's presence in our material world…And this was the primary goal of the Egyptian Exile, to purify them, not from sin, but to purify their souls so they will be capable of receiving the Torah.[318]

In addition to the purifying power of suffering, hatred of Jews has a second function.

Another Way Suffering Is a Tool for the Jewish Mission

As we have seen, antisemitism is often a reaction to the Jewish mission, to Jewish success, and to the ways that we change the world. When the Jews fulfill their role, they help spread awareness of God throughout the world. That awareness includes the understanding that life is a gift from God that has purpose and meaning, which is lovely but also carries serious duties and obligations due to a higher moral code. When Jews spread God's message of ethical monotheism, moral responsibility, and human dignity, they are often resented.

But what happens when they don't? When the Jews fail to live up to the national challenge that our forefathers accepted at Sinai, Jew-hatred emerges to ensure that the Jewish People cannot disappear or fade away.[319]

With the fate of humanity hanging on the Jewish mission, failure is not an option. God created the world for a purpose, and He will see it through, allowing humanity to exercise its free will. When antisemites choose to hate and persecute Jews, they are using their free will; simultaneously, antisemitism acts as a divine tool, strengthening the Jewish People and keeping them focused on their mission.[320]

God has made antisemitism the final defense of Jewish exceptionalism and uniqueness. When Jews try to abandon that exceptionalism, antisemitism forces them back. Throughout history, surges of Jewish assimilation were met with swells of antisemitism. We have seen that play out in the last two centuries, and we can see it all around us today.

Most German Jews in the late 1800 and early 1900s believed that assimilation would end the dislike of the "other." Some, like Moses Hess, writing in *Rome and Jerusalem* 17 years before the term *antisemitism* was invented, knew that it would not work: "Even baptism itself does not save from the nightmare of Jew-hatred."[321]

The knowledge of how antisemitism is a divine tool explains how a Rabbi in 1920 could predict the coming of a German antisemitic eruption more than a decade before it arrived. Rabbi Meir Simcha HaKohen of Dvinsk, writing in his famous book, the *Meshech Chochmah*, well before the Nazis had any influence, warned that the German Jews who had tried so hard to emulate (and assimilate into) their host culture would instead be reminded painfully by the Germans that they are Jews:

The Jew forgets his roots and sees himself as a

> natural citizen [of Germany]. He forsakes the study of his own religion… he thinks that Berlin is Jerusalem, learning from the corrupt among his neighbors, not even from the upright among them…

> (And so, I predict that)… a tempestuous wind and storm will blow (from Berlin), uprooting him from those people…there, he will know that he is a stranger…He will know that his roots are those of the People of Israel.

> Through this (Divine historical process) the Jewish People will (always) remain and grow stronger. This is the way of the Jewish people, from the day they began their wanderings.[322]

Rav Simcha was not a prophet. But he knew Torah[323] and so he knew the script; he knew God's tools, and he had read the prophet Yechezkel:

> And what you have in mind shall never come to pass—when you say, "We will be like the nations, like the families of the lands." As I live—declares the Lord God—I will reign over you with a strong hand, and with an outstretched arm, and with overflowing fury.[324]

The Jewish People cannot escape antisemitism by trying to be like everyone else: Jew-hatred singles them out even when they want to blend in. God works through history, and Jew-hatred is a painfully effective tool, as the Talmud relates:

> Greater was the effect of the king (Ahashverosh) removing his signet ring (empowering Haman to decree genocide on the Jews) than the effect of the forty-eight prophets and the seven prophetesses

who had prophesied to Israel (to improve their ways)—because the rebuke from the prophets did not get the Jewish People to repent, whereas the "removal of the signet ring" succeeded in helping them repent for the good.[325]

Antisemitism serves as a reminder of their Jewish identity and ensures that the Jews survive.

Rabbi Kook explained this idea in a public speech in Jerusalem's Old City in 1933, the same year Hitler came to power. Speaking from the pulpit on Rosh Hashanah, the day Jews blow the *Shofar* (ram's horn) to help wake up spiritually to improve their ways, he suddenly broke down, sibbing. After a few minutes of stunned silence, he composed himself, quoted from the prophet Isaiah[326], and explained that when the Jews are not fulfilling their role in history as they should, a different type of Shofar will blow to wake them up. He explained that there are levels of Shofar, and the one he feared was coming won't be blown in prayer services but rather will be the most painful, the Shofar of affliction, when the antisemites are called to blow it to wake the Jews: "Whoever failed to hear the calls of the first two Shofars will be forced to listen to the call of this last Shofar."[327]

Antisemitism forces Jews to remember that they are a unique people. The experience of being disliked often confronts even the most assimilated with the enigma that is antisemitism. This is the Shofar blow that shocked me on that fateful day in high school, as I wondered, *Why are they picking on me?* I had thought we were all the same, but they let me know that I was not them. I was a Jew.

Anne Frank heard the Shofar in 1944:

> Who has made us Jews different from all other people? Who has allowed us to suffer so terribly until now? It is God Who has made us as we are,

but it will be God, too, Who will raise us up again...
We can never become just Netherlanders, or just
English, or representatives of any other country for
that matter. We will always remain Jews, but we
want to, too.[328]

And this was the Shofar that Hamas blew for Israelis and Jews
the world over on and after October 7, 2023, as so many Jew-
haters around the world mobilized in support of genocidal
terrorists. I have heard dozens of stories of how Jews in schools
and organizations around the world have come together, often
for the first time, in solidarity and brotherhood, since Jew-hatred
exploded. From Google to the Writers Guild and from the YPO
leadership community to college campuses, Israeli and diaspora
Jews have been forced to ask why; this book is meant to answer the
question and, with a deepened sense of purpose, help strengthen
our brotherhood.

Antisemitism is both a blessing and a curse. It can be a response
to both Jewish success and failure. It is a sign that our message is
changing the world and also that we cannot step away from it.

Summarizing the Jewish
Why and *How*

This has been a brief overview of how the Jews see the world.

Approximately 3,800 years ago, Abraham searched; what he found
changed the world. Abraham chose to become moral and holy,
to bring light into the human heart, and to play a special role in
sanctifying God's name in the world.

From Abraham's family, God established a people whose purpose
was to bring blessing to all humanity. That blessing was the

knowledge of the beauty and opportunity of a spiritual life even as we live in a physical world.

The Jewish People established a vision for humanity: that history has meaning, that our lives and our world have a purpose, to live with love, mutual respect, human rights, with a goal for all of humanity to unite in spirituality, brotherhood, and peace.

The Jews were given some divine assistance to help them accomplish their mission:

- **The Torah:** A divine guide for living.

- **The Mitzvot:** Also known as commandments[329] these are powerful spiritual connecting forces – between man and God and also man to man.

- **The Land of Israel:**[330] The ideal environment for the Jewish People to fulfill their mission and help the world while plugged into their spiritual source.[331]

And when all of that is still not quite enough, they are strengthened, purified, and protected by exile and antisemitism.

With this awareness of how Jews define their mission, let's circle back and see an astonishing picture.

Back to Hitler and Jew-Hatred

Since man is made of both body and soul and has free will, the fault line of every human life and all human history is the choices around that struggle: Will man lean into his humanitarian, higher, spiritual side, or will he tilt to his baser, animal side?

Hitler somehow understood most of this, made the wrong choices, and was terrified because his ideology was losing the battle for hearts and minds against the Jewish vision. He grasped the nature of the Jewish People and set himself against them as their implacable foe. This was what he meant when he said he was a "rational antisemite" and why, after centuries of persecution had only resulted in continued Jewish existence and increasing impact, he decided the world needed a "final solution to the Jewish problem."

God had told Abraham that he was His messenger, and to be ready for millennia of resistance to his message.[332] The resistance is Jew-hatred. It is antisemitism, anti-Zionism, JewPhobia—whatever name you want to call it. The antisemitic Nazi worldview was a mirror image of the Jewish worldview.[333] This is remarkable. And relevant.

The Path to Empowerment

Understanding the deep roots of Jewish resilience and the relentless opposition they have faced is not just a historical exercise; it's a vital foundation for moving forward. Recognizing the philosophical and spiritual underpinnings of the Jewish mission illuminates the path to personal and collective empowerment. As we transition to Part 2, we will take these insights and apply them to foster a stronger sense of identity, and moral clarity, ensuring that the lessons of history guide our actions and inspire our future.

Part Two

From Understanding to Action

7

Universal Lessons

I will bring them to My sacred mount
And let them rejoice in My house of prayer.
For My House shall be called
A house of prayer for all peoples.
–Isaiah 56:7

AT THE HEART of our exploration is the understanding that the Jewish journey reveals a profound truth: the most critical battles are played out not only in history but also within every human heart. The fierce struggle is between our animal- and God-like sides. In this internal war, every human being is a soldier whose choices are meaningful and impactful, both personally and collectively.

The story of the Jews is about the struggle of all human beings to grapple with the human condition, reminding everyone of the importance of choosing between good and bad, light and darkness, and the spiritual and the material. This narrative underscores the tremendous potential inherent in life itself when we embrace the challenge of being human, and it highlights the positive impact our choices can have on ourselves and our world.

This enduring legacy, memorialized in the world's eternal bestselling book, still speaks to us today. The Jewish mission—rooted in millennia of spiritual pursuit, moral wrestling, and relentless courage—contains valuable lessons for every individual, regardless of background or belief. The universal truths and wisdom in Judaism can help us understand the complexity of our lives.

Beginning with Abraham, the Body–Soul, Power–Peace, Chance–God fault line of human life was defined. Which side will we be on? On the personal level, we can choose compassion, love, and how we relate to our fellow human beings. On a broader level, leaders and nations will either improve human rights and increase peace or behave brutally, creating more trauma and war.

Developing oneself into a more refined, good, spiritual, and giving person is the most basic lesson of Judaism, and it is universal. Everyone can do better; everyone can grow. This is our life purpose. And while there are vast practical insights in Judaism to help, the Jewish People claim no monopoly on wisdom. People can learn valuable lessons from many different cultures and religions.

Another relevant area is standing up for truth, moral clarity, and against suffering. In the introduction, I mentioned how the Jews are likened proverbially to the canary in the mine shaft. With their heightened sensitivity to carbon monoxide, canaries were used in mines to warn miners of toxic conditions. When applied to Jews, the phrase "canary in the coal mine" suggests that threats to Jews serve as a broader warning to society that a much greater danger is approaching. It is not entirely a mystical warning—although it's worth noting with a touch of irony that Jews are usually the first victims—but also a reflection of where a society and its values are holding—and heading. The Jewish condition is usually an accurate barometric reading of how a civilization is doing. Historically, when Jews have been allowed to live freely with few economic or other restrictions, the host society has also been open, free, and successful. The opposite is also true.

This makes our story very relevant to all people. It means that antisemitism can and will affect everyone, not just the Jews. When antisemitism is exploding in the world, everyone should start worrying. This truth was profoundly seen in World War II, and poetically articulated by the prominent German Lutheran pastor Martin Niemöller in 1945:

> First they came for the socialists, and I did not speak out—because I was not a socialist. Then they came for the trade unionists, and I did not speak out—because I was not a trade unionist. Then they came for the Jews, and I did not speak out—because I was not a Jew. Then they came for me—and there was no one left to speak for me.[335]

In the 1990s, the world watched with indifference as the Palestinians initiated the worst campaign of Islamic suicide bombing ever seen, with more than 100 buses and cafes blown up in a three-year period alone, murdering more than 1,000 civilians. Then came 9/11. Suddenly, the world was paying attention.

The idea that ancient hatred of Jews is an early warning sign was true not only during the rise of Nazism and Communism; it's still the case now in Europe, North America, and of course the Middle East, where a pandemic of hate is raging. After October 7, 2023, Jewish students in America and elsewhere are being harassed and abandoned by campuses. Americans should be concerned—not just for the Jews, but for themselves, because when Jews are unsafe, it means that freedom and core liberal values are being undermined—for everyone.

"Globalize the Intifada"

In radical Islamic thinking, Israel is only the "Little Satan," while the US is the "Big Satan."[336] This is the clear intent behind the cry heard at protests on campuses and cities worldwide: "Globalize the Intifada." It signifies that violent Islamic Jihad aims to spread to the US and the West. The activists, forming an unlikely alliance of radical Islamic and far-left agitators, professors, and students, are not just calling for Israel to stop defending itself; they are advocating for an uprising to create fundamental changes in the US. Regardless of whether their goals align more with Islamic sharia or Communist values, they are united in their disdain for the US, as evidenced by the burning of American flags[337] and chants of "Death to America."

If the radical Islamic Republic of Iran successfully builds a nuclear weapon—and they are on the brink of achieving this—the Jews are not the only people who will be threatened. Iran funds and trains proxy armies and militias abroad and is the world's largest supporter of terror—they can attack almost anywhere. The UN and government leaders watch and talk—or, more accurately, blabber. However, the threat is not lost on Arab leaders as much as it is on Westerners: The approaching Shii Iranian nuke is such a threat to Sunni Muslims that it has already led several Arab states to normalize or make peace with Israel. They know better than the college professors that Iran won't hesitate to attack them, or Europe, or the US.[338] As the ancient proverb goes, "The enemy of my enemy is my friend."

Hamas, the Muslim Brotherhood, and other radical Islamists hate the Jews, but when they gain power, as we have seen in several regions,[339] it is very bad news not just for Jews but for women, gays, and people of any other religion. It is very bad for all human rights and freedom.

The bottom line is that Jew-hatred is not only a Jewish problem; it's an American and Western problem, and we need to fight it together.

This means we need to strive for moral clarity in the face of evil. Sadly, in 2024, when pushed to choose sides once again in this epic human battle, many otherwise progressive people aligned with the death cult of the radical Islamists, just as so many Germans chose Nazism instead of respecting the sanctity of life.

Clarity: Intellectual and Moral

But perhaps I am being too harsh and not judging favorably. Perhaps the social activists today are legitimately protesting for Palestinian self-determination and against a colonialist occupier fighting an immoral war, or they are just against war and concerned for the loss of life? How can we know if their intentions are pure?

Admittedly, the Israel-Arab conflict, and the Hamas war, are complex and confusing. While I am sure that some protestors are moved by honorable motivations, allow me to add some moral clarity by revealing the underlying bias of Jew-hatred that is hidden behind the movement.

We have noted that antisemitism morphs, sometimes appearing in the form of religious concerns (we killed Jesus), while other times it's about science (we are the lowest race), or economics (we are too rich). Could much of today's anti-Israel fervor be Jew-hatred in disguise, this time clothed in the garments of 'human rights' and 'justice'? I would suggest that for anyone with a nose, the activism does not pass the smell test, and when people say 'I am not antisemitic, I am just against genocide' it rings hollow.

The first clue that Jew-hatred was alive and well in the global protest movement was evident when, within 24 hours of 1,200 Jews being raped and murdered, support began pouring out for the genocidal terrorists globally.   As journalist Hadley Freeman wrote, "There were anti-Israel protests...before Israel had responded. That's all you need to know."[340] Six months later, this support had grown into the largest, most passionate—and best-funded—social justice protest movement since Vietnam.[341]

This was hard to understand and counter-intuitive: Why was there such a strong reaction in support of the people that had carried out the cruel terror attack and against the people who had been slaughtered? How was there so much support for the Palestinians and against Israel when Hamas committed so many war crimes and were using their entire population as human shields by establishing all of their military infrastructure under and inside civilian neighborhoods, schools, mosques, and hospitals?

How can we determine if this was a case of social justice warriors fighting for peace, justice, and human rights, or a well-organized and funded motley group of Islamists and progressives motivated by something less holy?

Let's explore and analyze what could have been igniting the passions of the demonstrators worldwide.

Question: Why All the Support for Hamas?

Concern for Arab/Muslim Lives

Were these protestors upset because of the death of Arabs or Muslims? If so, why did they mobilize only now, and not when 2 million were killed and continue to be killed in Sudan, or when Syria's Asad massacred 500,000 of his own (some with gas), or when Saddam killed more than a million? Where were the marches when hundreds of thousands of Muslims were killed in Yemen, Pakistan, and Afghanistan by their own? That the justice antennae were only activated when Israel's war caused some 25,000 deaths,[342] at least half of whom were terrorists, is suspicious.

Concern about War

Maybe it was simply that the horrors of war got them so upset? If so, then why did Russia's war against Ukraine, with an estimated 500,000 casualties since 2022, not evoke an international protest wave and campus encampments as the Israeli–Hamas war did? Sudan? Yemen, Syria, Ethiopia, Nigeria, Haiti? No. No. And no.

Concern for an Unjust War

Maybe it was because Israel's war was morally unjustified, while Russia's was not? Maybe Israelis are "colonialist occupiers" and the Russians are not? Ummm, no. Russia invaded the independent Ukraine. Israel returned to its ancient homeland, they had not been in Gaza since 2005, and the war was a response to a brutal and massive pogrom in an effort to prevent another one. As NYU Professor Scott Galloway said on MSNBC in April 2024, if Mexico freely elected Jihadi leaders and then attacked the US and killed 35,000 Americans, and on the way home back took a few thousand hostages, what would the US do? "We all know that Mexico would be a parking lot."[343]

Concern for Innocents

Maybe the passion was stoked by a sense of injustice and concern about persecution of innocents? Or maybe the constant global attention was because so many civilians are involved? Hmmm, no. China has incarcerated more than a million Muslim Uyghurs in concentration camps and systematically abuses their human rights, and yet the campuses hardly raise a peep, and the media, in relative terms, almost completely ignore them. It has certainly not produced a global resistance movement. When the US was fighting ISIS in Mosul, there was no parallel obsession with the number of civilian casualties.[344]

Concern for Palestinians

Maybe it is the global community's unique sympathy for the Palestinians? After all, they have been given more humanitarian aid money per capita than any other group on the planet over the past few decades and have special privileged refugee status that ensures the money keeps flowing.[345] But if this is the core motivation, why did the world not accept them into their countries as refugees and save them from a war zone? Why, when Russia invades Ukraine in 2022, do 40 nations welcome 7 million refugees in humane generosity to provide safety. When war broke out in Syria, 6 million were accepted by dozens of countries between 2011 and 2016. But now in 2023–4 the world refuses to accept Palestinian refugees?

In 2022 alone, 108.4 million people worldwide were forcibly displaced as a result of persecution, conflict, violence, and human rights.[346] But in the Hamas war, as Gazans were pleading to be let out, the global community rose as one, seemingly discovering a new moral principle, exemplified by Secretary of State Antony Blinken's strange slogan, "No forcible displacement."[347] After six months, only a few hundred Palestinians had been allowed to escape the war zone.[348]

Furthermore, there was no global outrage expressed for Palestinians when Jordan massacred thousands in Black September 1970, when Kuwait expelled 350,000 of them in 1990,[349] when 125,000 had been displaced by the Syrian civil war since 2011,[350] or when Hamas (and the Palestinian Authority) imposed sharia law and took away the Palestinian's human rights for almost 20 years.[351]

Indeed, the entire Palestinian cause became cause célèbre only after 1967 when Israel regained the West Bank and Gaza. There was no concern—and certainly no global movement—on behalf of the Palestinians to have a state of their own so long as Egypt and Jordan were controlling these territories. Only when Israel won the territories did the world start caring.

Concern for Shared Values

Maybe international solidarity with Hamas and the Palestinians is strong because of shared values between Hamas and some Western liberals. However, Hamas explicitly names genocide—the destruction of the entire State of Israel—as its primary goal (not, say, the welfare of its people) in its official charter,[352] embedding this aim deeply into its culture.[353] It is an internationally recognized terror organization governed by sharia law, which opposes most progressive values, such as gay and women's rights. They systematically raped, violated, and murdered innocents on October 7 and openly said that they will do it again if given the chance.

Yet, we see phenomena like Queers for Palestine, where LGBTQ+ activists march in support of Gaza on campuses, hand in hand with Hamas supporters, despite the fact that their lifestyle would likely result in the death penalty if they visited Gaza. Women's rights groups remain silent in the face of systematic rape, and progressives rally behind

Figure 8. Protester wearing a black mask, and a Palestinian flag as a cape at NYC Israel Day Parade on June 2, 2024 with a "Kill Hostages Now" sign. FNTV.

one of the planet's most illiberal and oppressive cultures.[354] This is almost as morally absurd as a movement of "Cows for McDonalds."

Hamas's main patron is Iran, the world's largest supporter of global terror, along with allies like Russia, Turkey, Qatar, and North Korea. In contrast, Israel is a liberal democracy and a close ally of the United States. When the leader of The Islamic Republic of Iran, Ayatollah Ali Khamanei, writes a letter of solidarity and produces a YouTube video[355] praising campus activists for being "on the right side of history" and for creating a new "branch of the Resistance Front," it is a clear signal to question which side you are aligning with.[356]

Only One Answer Remains

If none of these reasons explain why the Hamas war garnered so much political and media attention and sparked a global protest movement, then what does? What could be unique about the Hamas war that ignited such widespread passion? If it wasn't due to the scope or nature of the conflict, a deep concern for Palestinians, or shared values, then what else could be the common denominator?

Only one answer remains: the Jews.

Answer: Antisemitism

As the *Wall Street Journal*'s editorial board observed, "Only when it can damage Israel does it become the liberal position to close the borders and keep refugees penned in a war zone."[357] This starkly highlights that it wasn't just Hamas cynically forcing their own people to remain in danger as human shields. The global community also conspired to lock them in, leading to the deaths of *innocents*[358] and creating a humanitarian crisis--subsequently blamed on the Jewish State.

Israel defends itself using the most careful tactics ever seen in modern warfare, even as they face an enemy that commits more crimes against humanity than perhaps ever seen in modern times.[359] Despite these efforts, Israel is accused of committing genocide. John Spencer, chair of urban warfare studies at the Modern War Institute at West Point, has repeatedly highlighted the unprecedented efforts the IDF makes to protect civilians.[360] And yet, students protest, professors lead demonstrations, schools close, the UN condemns, the ICC investigates, and the zeal for "justice" boils over—when Jews are involved. Even ISIS beheading its way across the Middle East did not generate anywhere near the level of opposition from progressive activists.

Make no mistake: The double standards reveal the Jew hatred.[361] The strongest social justice protest movement since Vietnam proves it.[362] If you still don't see it, the calls to kill Jews and eliminate Israel[363] often heard at these "pro-Palestinian" rallies should tip you off.[364]

Will We Be Silent Again?

During World War II, much of the world lacked moral clarity, turning a blind eye—and many non-Germans assisted—as six million European Jews were slaughtered. Today, Israel fights a relentless war against forces that threaten not only the Jewish People but also American and Western civilization. Radical Islamists openly declare that their primary enemy is the US, not Israel. Yet, Israel is condemned by the international community. Remaining silent now would be another colossal failure of our collective moral duty.

As Elie Wiesel said at his 1986 Nobel Peace Prize acceptance speech:

> We must always take sides. Neutrality helps the oppressor, never the victim. Silence encourages the tormentor, never the tormented. Sometimes we must interfere. When human lives are endangered, when human dignity is in jeopardy, national borders

and sensitivities become irrelevant. Wherever men or women are persecuted because of their race, religion, or political views, that place must—at that moment—become the center of the universe.[365]

In June 1961, the State of Israel put Adolph Eichmann on trial for being one of the chief Nazi architects of the Holocaust's death machine. Yehiel De-Nur, who was one of the few survivors who encountered Eichmann during the war, was called to testify. He began by describing "planet Auschwitz," a place where:

> The time there is not the same as it is here, on Earth...And the inhabitants of this planet had no names. They had no parents and no children. They did not wear (clothes) the way they wear here. They were not born there and did not give birth... They did not live according to the laws of the world here...

And then, De-Nur collapsed. He never finished his testimony.

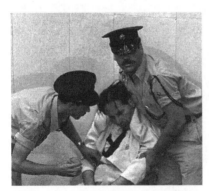

Figure 9. Yehiel De-Nur collapses
Courtesy of the Israel Govt. Press Office.

It took six months in the hospital before he was able to stand again.

A few years later, when asked whether it was fear or horrific memories that overwhelmed him at that moment in front of Eichmann again, he replied that it was none of the above, but the realization that Eichmann was an ordinary man:

> Then it was clear to me that Auschwitz is not another planet as I thought before. Auschwitz was not created by the devil, nor by God, but by man... Hitler was not a devil. You could enter a

kindergarten, among fifty children there was one child named Adolf Hitler. He was a man…

De-Nur understood the terrifying truth that regular human beings can choose to be evil: Hitler was human, like everyone else. Man can become an animal or reach the heavens.

We Can Choose to Make a Difference

Although our world certainly has much room for improvement, it continues to make progress. It is within the gap between the world as it is now and where it needs to be that we can all make a difference. This is the Jewish message to every human being: we are spiritual beings in a physical body and world, and as souls, we can choose life, make a difference, and elevate the material to achieve self-transformation. By fixing ourselves,[366] we can also be a light to the world.

Russian Red Army war correspondent Vasilii Grossman witnessed the higher side of humanity when he saw the liberation of the Treblinka death camp in 1944. After hearing numerous stories of spiritual resistance, he wrote:

> Great is the power of humanity; humanity does not die until humanity dies…And the beast who slays the man remains a beast. In this immortal spiritual strength of human beings is a solemn martyrdom, the triumph of the dying man over the living beast. Therein, during the darkest days of 1942 lay the dawn of reason's victory over bestial madness, of good over evil, light over darkness…an awesome dawn breaking over a field of blood and tears…
>
> The beasts and the philosophy of the beasts foreshadowed the end of Europe, the end of the world; but people remained people.[367]

The Jewish quest to harness human potential lies in the revelation that choices are real and change is possible. It's an idea that remains deeply controversial thousands of years later, as genetic research, evolutionary psychology, mass movements, and the fatalism of an impersonal universe chip away at our sense of personhood, identity, and control over our lives.

What Judaism implores of us all is to live consciously of our choices, because these choices can change everything. That ethos, a quintessentially Jewish one, now permeates the civilization that we live in. Bringing choice into the world is inherently disruptive. It endows life with meaning and purpose, creates conflict, unearths the past, forces us to confront the future, and tells us that we do not just exist--we have the ability and responsibility to shape ourselves and our world.

We Can All Be Lights

The Jewish story is meant to inspire everyone. Just as "let my people go" became a rallying call for every oppressed group, "choose life" calls us to realize our potential. The Jewish journey from slavery to freedom, from darkness to light, is not a solitary path but a shared voyage toward universal peace, respect, and divine awareness. The Jewish story serves as a metaphor for the human family, illustrating both man's inhumanity to man and our inspiring resilience. As we strive for a brighter future, let's all choose life.

8

The Messenger's Choice—Turning Adversity Into Strength

"What is your name?" He replied, "Jacob."
Said he, "Your name shall no longer be Jacob,
but Israel, for you have striven with beings
divine and human, and have prevailed."
–Genesis 32:27-28

And there we saw the Nephilim (giants)...and we were
in our eyes like grasshoppers; and so we were in their eyes.
–Numbers, 13:33

ALTHOUGH THE JEWISH mission and antisemitism present a challenge to everybody, Jew-hatred specifically confronts Jews in a unique way, impacting both our individual Jewish identity and collective self-esteem. To expect otherwise would be to expect something beyond normal human capacity, and Jews are nothing if not very human. So let's acknowledge and understand it. But let's also do something about it. Put another way, let's ask whether Jews themselves have become somewhat afraid of the big, bad Jew.

The Challenge to Jewish Identity

That the Jewish People are sometimes worn out and discouraged is understandable. The scope of Jewish pain is so deep and beyond description that the continued commitment of the Jewish people is remarkable. They've endured millennia of relentless hatred, bullying, oppression, crusades, pogroms, and the Holocaust, producing multigenerational trauma that is profound and often beyond description. The toll on the Jewish psyche is immense, as Jew-haters have been sought to solve the "Jewish problem" in every generation, leading to deep and lasting scars.

Rabbi Lord Sacks poignantly writes of the consequences of antisemitism and the Holocaust, "Collective traumas of this magnitude take several generations to play themselves out, and we still live with their aftershocks. Like Jacob after his wrestling match with the angel, we limp."[368] In clinical terms, it is accurate to say that the Jewish People suffer from multigenerational PTSD.

So, how do we respond to these very profound experiences and pressures? How do we retain our sense of self and define our identity?

There are, broadly speaking, two approaches to these questions.

Approach #1: Defense

When Jews encounter antisemitism, they can feel inferior, buying into the charges against them that they are, in some way, the problem. In response to being disliked, Jews try to adapt to the accusations against them and hope for acceptance. They appeal to their detractors to stop hating them, saying, "We are not what you accuse us of; we are just like you, and everyone should be nice.

In the past couple of centuries, the Jewish People have been playing defense.

250 Years of Defense

Many Jews cope with antisemitism by trying to "fit in." They undergo social and intellectual "makeovers" to change themselves into the opposite of what the antisemites claim to hate about Jews. Starting in the early 1800s, the objection to the Jews was that they were too different. Convinced that by becoming like everyone else they would neutralize the detractors, Jews made an effort to become less Jewish.

Most German (and Austrian and Hungarian) Jews were convinced that if they demonstrated national loyalty and contributed to society, the hate would disappear. They reacted to rising antisemitism by discarding much of Judaism and disavowing Israel as their homeland. But even after all the Jews' contributions to Germany, the nation they adored still sent them to the concentration and death camps. Siegfried Marcus's invention of the first gas-powered car, Heinrich Hertz's vision birthing everything from radio to radar, Einstein's Theory of Relativity, and Casmir Funk's discovery of vitamins did not stave off the Holocaust.

I always recall, with trembling, being told by a survivor that some German Jews who had served with distinction for the "Fatherland" in World War I went to the gas chambers proudly wearing their uniforms, medals and all. Up until the very end, they were convinced they were more German than Jew and it could not happen to them.

The Enlightenment Jews and the Reform movement they initiated attempted to fit in by discarding the core Torah idea of Jewish Peoplehood. They reasoned that if Jews were only a religion, then they would simply be Germans, French, or "of the Mosaic persuasion," and the host nations would accept them. However, this approach failed dramatically. The father of modern Zionism, Theordor Herzl, declared, "We have honestly striven everywhere to merge ourselves in the social life of surrounding communities, and to preserve only the faith of our fathers. It has not been permitted to us."[369]

Herzl and the early Zionist ideologues took the opposite approach: They believed that by becoming a secular Jewish nation with Judaism neutered, they would be like all other nations and then be accepted.[370] This solution to the "Jewish problem" has also failed, as the Jewish State became the lightning rod for new antisemitism.

Jews can attempt to change themselves, but so can antisemites. As Rabbi Sacks has said, "Jew-hatred is usually justified by what a culture holds most dear." During the Middle Ages, it was religion, and Jews were charged with killing God. In the modern period, it was science, and Jews were deemed by science to be an inferior race. Today, post-Enlightenment and post-Hiroshima, neither religion nor science are the most prestigious sources of authority. Post-Holocaust, the highest values are human rights, so the Jewish State is portrayed as the worst violator.[371]

On campuses today and in refined societies, Jewish students and others are accused of the crime of being Zionists. The recent abandonment of Israel by many diaspora Jews is perhaps subconsciously motivated by the hope that by positioning themselves as disconnected or pro-Palestinian, they can fit into a progressive society that has declared Zionism unacceptable.[372] Many young Jews have become passionate opponents of Israel—even leaders, as if by condemning Israel they will eliminate the cause of their insecurity and alienation.[373]

This goes together with the abandonment of Judaism and everything that makes Jews exceptional. The new "*Tikkun Olam*" (repairing the world) movements do not reflect the deep Jewish idea whose name they adopted[374] and have become synonymous with progressive social justice. In striving so hard to fit in, they have inadvertently dispensed with the need for Jews. If Jews only exist to advocate for social justice, wouldn't the world be better off if Jews traded their tribal identity for membership in the global, activist community?

Such a logical conclusion of this popular, modern definition of Jewishness was articulated clearly by Pulitzer Prize winner Michael Chabon when he gave the convocation at the 2018 Reform Rabbis graduation. Speaking to the future Reform leaders, he encouraged them to embrace universalism over Jewish particularism, to encourage their flock to "marry into the tribe that sees nations and borders as antiquated canards and ethnicity as a construct prone, like all constructs, to endless reconfiguration," even if it meant the end of the Jews.[375]

Without knowing the nature of antisemitism, Jews can become confused by insecurity, fear, and shame. Jews who have lost touch with their mission might think that they are the problem because they are hated, rather than understanding that they are hated because they hold the answer.

The phenomenon of Jews turning themselves into pretzels was observed by the historian Bernard Lewis in *Semites & Anti-Semites*, "the neurotic reaction which one finds among some Jews to the impact of antisemitism by accepting, sharing, expressing and even exaggerating the basic assumptions of the antisemite".[376]

As opposed to Chabon, the political commentator Daniel Greenfield has characterized this defensive Jewish response as the real ghetto mentality:

> The Ghetto Jew is the Jew who has not found a Jewish identity. He has let his enemies define him. His efforts go to fight a losing battle because he has

allowed the enemy inside his head. He has failed
to build a positive Jewish identity...He is other-
directed. He cares little what Jews think of Jews.
What interests him is what everyone else thinks of
Jews. He will enthusiastically fight for the causes
of others, rather than for his own, to avoid any
accusations of selfishness...In doing so he thinks
that he is helping Jews, because to him the Jews can
only be helped by changing how others see them...
For all his sophistication, erudition and education,
he is an empty house with no one living inside.[377]

This is also the story of Israel's far-left peace activists. They were
unable to see the deep hatred of the other side. They assumed
that it was primarily Jewish avarice preventing peace, and not
the intransigence and Jew-hatred of Hamas and much of the
Palestinian population.

They were certain, before October 7, that the settlements were
the main stumbling block preventing peace with the Palestinians
and causing anti-Zionism to rage[378]. Then came October 7 and
everything changed. Batia Holin, a survivor of Kibbutz Kfar Azza,
lost her faith in that narrative: "They not only killed friends of
mine, they killed my beliefs." Amit Siman-Tov-Vahaba, who lost
her entire family in the attack, shared, "My deepest beliefs were
turned upside down. I (had) thought the Gaza Strip was full of
people who looked like us (and wanted to live in peace)..."[379]

Amazingly, the Kibbutz Nir Oz, which had a quarter of its
population murdered or kidnapped on October 7, had planned to
participate in a protest rally on that very day with the slogan that
peace cannot be achieved because of Jewish settlements.[380] They
did not make it to the rally. The pogrom blasted a hole in their
mistaken assumptions, and they were forced to come to terms with
Jew-hatred. They had made the classic Jewish mistake of falling for
the excuse instead of discerning the reason behind the hate.

Faced with the aftermath of October 7 and the global surge in antisemitism, Jews on defense can only stare into the abyss and wonder. Yet, this was not the first time Jews have been shocked out of their misconception about how the world views them. Some 2,500 years ago, the Jews of Shushan (Purim) were confused when the genocide decree was announced. When Hitler came to power and forced the Jews to wear a yellow Star of David on their arms,

Figure 10. Close up of sign in Nir Oz for a settlements protest on October 7, 2023.

the German-Jewish community, who had mistakenly believed they had won acceptance, were stunned and disheartened.

Similarly, 150 years ago, Herzl and the Jews of Western Europe were shaken to their core by the Dreyfus Affair. When France descended into antisemitic hysteria, Herzl described the shared dismay:

> ...the most profoundly affected were the Jews themselves. The confidence of Jews in the liberal order was severely shaken. That such an affair could occur in France, the cradle of modern democracy, stunned many. The fact that a public—not just the riffraff—schooled for over a century in the principles of "liberty, equality, and fraternity"—could still contemptuously regard Dreyfus, an utterly assimilated Jew, as an outsider seemed to prove that assimilation was no defense against antisemitism.[381]

In 2024, I have heard the exact same sentiments expressed by countless Jewish friends – they just substituted 'France' with 'USA', or 'Canada', or 'Europe' (again). In high schools, on college campuses, and in multicultural offices, Jews today often feel lost in environments where their educated peers, professors, and social justice organizations dropped all of their lofty principles when it came to the Jews and Israel. From high schools to NYU to Google offices, I have heard many horror stories of Jews feeling abandoned and unsafe in their institutions and corporations, despite all the DEI programs and sensitivity to microaggressions against every other group.

It is certainly distressing when you are on campus and most of the student body, as well as the professors, condemn Israel and directly or indirectly accuse you, a Jewish bystander, of being guilty of something very serious, something you felt very little connection to in the past. What does Israel have to do with you, you may wonder?

It is certainly distressing when comedian Dave Chapelle says to millions on *Saturday Night Live* that the "delusion that Jews run show business" is "not a crazy thing to think," but "it's a crazy thing to say out loud." He continued with a deep insight, "You know, the rules of perception. If they're Black, then it's a gang. If they're Italian, it's a mob. If they're Jewish, it's a coincidence and you should never speak about it."[382] Dave was correct in observing both Jewish influence as well as Jewish discomfort at acknowledging it. The answer, Dave, is that Jewish success is real, but it's not a conspiracy and it's not a coincidence. We Jews should talk about it; we should be proud of our talents and accomplishments. This book is talking about it.

The antisemites are reminding you that you are, in the core of your being and not just as a cultural curiosity, a part of the Jewish People.

While there are myriad reasons why many Jews do not feel strongly connected to their people or Judaism today, years of hate creates great discomfort around being Jewish, and it can be observed in quantifiable ways: growing assimilation and intermarriage rates, lower observance rates, lack of philanthropy prioritization for

Jewish causes, waning involvement in the Jewish community, and illiteracy (in Judaism and Israel studies).

In 2013, a Pew research survey[383] asked American Jews what it means to be Jewish:

- 73% answered remembering the Holocaust.

- 69% replied that being Jewish meant leading an ethical life.

- 56% thought it was working for justice and equality.

- 42% thought that being Jewish meant having a good sense of humor.

While many of these areas can definitely be considered part of the Jewish heritage, most are not unique to Jews, and less than 30% referenced anything about *being* or *acting* Jewish in any distinct way.

Author Charles Murray also observed the phenomena of weak Jewish self-esteem when he did research on outsized Jewish success and influence. "I have personal experience with the reluctance of Jews to talk about Jewish accomplishment..." While other peoples naturally embrace their legacy accomplishments, he noticed a distinct aversion of Jews to discuss what Murray called for, "...a systematic discussion of one of the most obvious topics of all: the extravagant overrepresentation of Jews, relative to their numbers, in the top ranks of the arts, sciences, law, medicine, finance, entrepreneurship, and the media."[384] Murray concluded, in response to Jewish hesitancy to self-appreciate, "And so this Scots-Irish Gentile from Iowa hereby undertakes to tell the story."

What, many Jews wonder, do they have to be proud of? Like the Fourth Son in the Passover Seder, the "one who does not know how to ask questions," they don't even know what they don't know. Despite their people's unparalleled legacy of 3,000+ years of outsized positive global impact, despite being part of an incredibly sophisticated and rich intellectual and spiritual heritage, many Jews have lost a basic understanding of what being Jewish is about. I believe that the continuous assault on Jews, combined with the allure of assimilation, has led to a crushing erosion of Jewish self-confidence and self-awareness. Under the agonizing repressiveness of thousands of years of persecution, Jews have occasionally lost sight of their empowering legacy.

It is a sad irony that Hitler understood the Jewish People's unique contributions and mission; philosemites admire their positive influence on human affairs; but many Jews today seem to be in the dark.

The Messenger Who Forgot His Message

When I was a college student in Toronto, Nobel laureate Elie Wiesel visited. I heard him compare the Jewish People to a messenger that got hit on the head. When the messenger woke up, he couldn't remember four things:

1. Who sent him

2. To whom he was sent

3. What the content of the message was

4. That he was, in fact, a messenger

This national memory loss, this diminishment of Jewish moral self-confidence, is, in fact, the true victory of the antisemite. It is why philosopher Emil Fackenheim famously declared the concept of the "614th commandment" as the moral imperative for Jews not to give Hitler a "posthumous victory" by assimilating.[385]

Perhaps it's time we write a new ending to our story.

The process of recovery and personal growth can only begin by acknowledging that, in many ways, we have lost our way and we need help.[386] As Leonard Cohen poetically warned Montreal's Jewish leadership in a 1963 address:

> Now, before we begin we must face that despair that none of us dares articulate: that we no longer feel we are holy. There will be no psalms, there will be no light, there will be no illumination until we can confess the position into which we have decayed.[387]

He added:

> This is the declaration that I wait to hear going out of synagogues, and from the lips of cultural Jews and ethical Jews. This is the confession without which we cannot begin to raise our eyes: the absence of God in our midsts. And I am laboring under the misapprehension that the Jewish People represent that testimony on the earth[388], and that without that testimony informing its actions, Jewish survival is nominal and no more important to me than Armenian survival or Greek survival. The absence of God in our midsts is a deep, rotten cavity that has killed the nerve of the people.

But this recognition of our current state can be the first step toward renewal and strength. Just as our ancestors have done throughout history, we can rise and reclaim our connection—with ourselves and with God—so we can move forward with resilience and embrace our sacred mission.

Approach #2: Resilience and Grit Judaism

In response to the Nazi yellow star, German–Jewish World War I veteran Robert Weltsch published an inspiring message to his brethren, entitled "Wear It With Pride":

> April 1, 1933, could be the day of Jewish awakening and rebirth if the Jews desire it, if they show maturity and greatness within them, and if they are not as misrepresented by their opponents.
>
> Under attack, the Jews must acknowledge themselves. It is not true that the Jews betrayed Germany. If they betrayed anyone, it was themselves, the Jews.
>
> Because the Jew did not display his Judaism with pride, because he tried to avoid the Jewish issue, he must bear part of the blame for the degradation of the Jews.[389]

Since October 7, a choice has been forced upon us by Hamas and the global community, just as Germany challenged the Jews 100 years ago. There is again a unique opportunity to rekindle the Jewish spirit, to rediscover our self-worth that transcends the scars of the past and embraces a proud heritage. The choice is not easy, but it is simple: to embrace ourselves, our history, peoplehood, and mission—or to deny.

This gritty approach is expressed humorously in the old Jewish joke about two elderly Jews riding a train in 1930s Germany. One of them is reading a Jewish paper while the other is eagerly turning the pages of *Der Sturmer*, Streicher's violently antisemitic Nazi rag:

> "How can you read that filth?" the first Jew asks.
>
> "Simple," his friend replies. "In your paper, Jews are being beaten, robbed, and deported. But in the Nazi paper, it's all good news. I just found out that the Jews control the entire world!"

The deepest victory over Hitler and antisemitism comes when the Jews stop defining themselves by this hatred and instead embrace what makes us strong, what makes us great, and what our mission is. Our real education begins not when we escape antisemitism, but when we confront it.[390]

Antisemitism, seen from this perspective, actually acknowledges Jewish impact and exposes the failings of the antisemites themselves. Embracing our Jewish identity starts with understanding why we have been targets of hate, but it flourishes only with a deep understanding of who we truly are.

Learning this secret unlocks our potential—not just as a people, but as individuals. The real power of the Jewish people is not about controlling governments or manipulating economies, as our detractors falsely claim. It is about each of us striving to become the best version of ourselves.

As the Torah says, we are a "stiff-necked people." This can mean that we are slow to learn our lessons, but it also signifies a positive trait: the stubbornness of conviction, combined with resilience and clarity of purpose. We can either be stunned, confused, and paralyzed in the face of resurfacing Jew-hatred, or we can recognize that it arises because of the good we represent. With this understanding, we can stand tall - with pride, moral clarity, and conviction.

To be Jewish is to be a messenger carrying mystical knowledge across thousands of years. Even when we forget the message, we are hunted for that knowledge. Leaving behind the secret doesn't leave behind antisemitism. Jewish history has two sides: Jewish greatness shines through even the darkest of times one side, while the hatred of antisemites casts a dull shadow on the other. When Jews look into the eyes of antisemites, they may feel weak, but antisemites are actually acknowledging Jewish greatness.

Jews with grit and resilience understand that antisemitism is not caused by their own actions, but by the antisemites' issues. They see antisemitism as a vindication of Jewish impact not an indictment. For these resilient Jews on the offense, antisemitism is a metric of Jewish success. For them, the endurance of antisemitism throughout history highlights the incredible journey of the Jewish People through time and space as well as intellectual and spiritual landscapes.

Embracing this perspective, Jews can celebrate their unique heritage, love themselves, and, when necessary, stand up and fight.[391] Today, many Israeli Jews have taken this new attitude, and it is encouraging for our future. These young Israelis have no doubts about the justice of their fight against Hamas and those bent on their destruction.[392] They recognize the deep antisemitic bias of much of the international community and institutions like the UN—and, frankly, it does not bother them too much. They know who they are, and they are proud to be Jewish.

Why Be Jewish?
The Case for Jews to Embrace Themselves

The Second Reveal of October 7: Family

I started this book by discussing October 7 and its aftermath, which has been a horror for Jews, but I've come to realize that it also revealed something very positive. Forced to confront a painful new reality, Jews responded with deep awareness of being family. From all over the world and from very different backgrounds, Jews touched an intuitive inner sense that many did not even know that they had and discovered a profound sense of connection with their people. Overnight, in the face of evil and the world's unmistakable double standards against the Jewish People, Jewish identity increased.

The Jewish community rallied together in an overwhelming

expression of shock, unity, and generosity. Jews gathered in Israel and all over the world with love and energy to volunteer, organize, and provide for those in need in Israel, whether it be emotional or material support. While it is sad that it took bloodshed and suffering to generate such Jewish brotherhood, it has been a beautiful development.

This return home was not new. The Jewish People's enduring commitment to both our covenantal kinship[393] and our mission inspired our forebears, nourished them, and made them amazingly resilient. That is why you are here as a Jew today. This resilience is strongest not among those who fit in, but those who don't.

It is gritty Jews who carry on after a civilization collapses rather than sifting through the ashes and mourning the German culture of the Weimar era, the flowering of Spain's golden age, or the glory days among the gardens and temples of Greece and Rome. These are the Jews who keep going because they remember who they are, why they are here, and what their mission is.

The Jewish mission is not limited to any single culture or time period; it is for all of humanity and transcends civilizations. That is why Jews have the strength to journey across civilizations. French philosopher Jean Jacques Rousseau wondered at Jewish toughness:

> What must be the strength of legislation capable of working such wonders, capable of braving conquests, dispersions, revolutions, exiles, capable of surviving the customs, laws, empire of all the nations, and which finally promises them, by these trials, that it is going to continue to sustain them all, to conquer the vicissitudes of all things, human, and to last as long as the world?[394]

Jews endure because they have always been animated by a grand mission that is about a deep, spiritual *tikkun olam* and being a light to the nations that includes but goes beyond the social justice, technology, or politics of any particular time or place. Civilizations rise and fall, mores and movements change, and the Jewish mission keeps its vision fixed on the eternal.

The Jewish People are arguably the most persecuted and hence the least privileged nation on the planet. But we are privileged to have a special destiny and so have never mired ourselves in victimhood. Our strength is derived from remaining steadfast in our identity as privileged to be alive, as members of a great family, and for being granted an opportunity and responsibility to play a meaningful role in history.

The scope of our mission is almost unimaginable, and so are the challenges we have undergone. The existence of the Jews after all these thousands of years is a miracle, but it is a miracle born of a higher plan and purpose.

Many people will bristle at some of these ideas, but this is the Jewish legacy and mission—a worldview that our ancestors understood, owned, lived, and died for—for more than 120 generations. It continues to animate Jewish life today.

The Jewish mission has been forgotten by many today, and as bitter a pill it may be for some to swallow, it is even more loathed by the Hitlers, Hamans, and Hamas terrorists who recognize it as a threat. That's the bitter truth that we learned, not only under Communism or Nazism, or the ugly moments of history going back to Babylon, Persia, and Rome, but now also in our comfortable cities and campuses in America and Europe.

We are left with the astonishing yet indisputable reality that antisemites cannot defeat us and, as a people, we cannot disappear. And so we are here, *Am Yisrael Chai*—the Jewish People live. We may as well own it.

This revolution is our story. The struggle is all humanity's story. It is the playing field of every human life, the drama of human existence.

The civilizational gifts of the Jews come in two varieties: There are the gifts of science, innovation, social change, and culture; and there are the spiritual gifts that have transformed the world.

The intellectual, technological, and scientific impact of the Jews is truly remarkable, but these are all really just the fumes of the deeper impact that began more than 3,300 years ago. Rav Kook clarified that the greatest Jewish gifts are those of the spirit: the knowledge of God, wisdom, and moral truths that transcend technology and politics: "Israel also has a richness of physical and technological resources, in line with other nations, but the knowledge of God is our specialty."[395]

Judaism's ultimate vision of *Tikkun Olam* is the perfection of the world that comes when all people connect to their souls and to God, violence and oppression end, war ceases, and a world of love and peace becomes possible.

Our story has been the hidden Jewish mission of building a spiritual empire in exile that was not seen but it could not be broken. And now, in the closing chapters of our story, the Jewish People are meant to return to their Land and create a holy national home based on that spiritual mission.

We are just getting started on this, and admittedly have made mistakes and have a long way to go, but the vision is clear: through the vehicle of a nation-state, with morality imbued in all of its national structures (government, legal system, economic model, army, social structures, and so on), our society will serve humanity as a symbol of love, peace, and spirituality.[396]

Clarifying the Call to Action

Being Jewish is not just about feeling proud of a country or celebrating a family member's achievements. It's more than a religion; it's a family and a way of life that encompasses peoplehood, nationhood, morality, ethics, spirituality, and purpose. It's who we are.

There are many ways to express a deep connection with being Jewish—through learning Torah, commitment to Israel, doing mitzvot (commandments), believing in or struggling with God, community involvement, and many other ways we will explore in the next chapter. It's not an all-or-nothing proposition. To be clear, I am not suggesting that everyone has to adopt all of these things to take their place among our people. Each person can find their unique way to connect and grow within our shared heritage.

As author Ze'ev Maghen writes in his classic, *John Lennon and The Jews*:

> Being a connected Jew has always meant being on fire. Sometimes we simmer softly over a low flame, other times we are all but consumed by a roaring conflagration. But we always burn. How could it be otherwise?...Each generation imbibes thirstily from its predecessor, drinking down the bitter with the sweet—we have accumulated over the ages fuel reserves so vast they make those of Saudi Arabia look like a grease stain. Each century that elapses in our fathomless history, every event we experience, ordeal we endure...feed(s) our *ner tamid*, the eternal flame of Jewish Passion in the present.[397]

The Jewish People inform who we are as individuals. It is part of who we are, so let's allow it to be expressed. Hitler was right when he declared that in Jews we see the idea of spiritual epigenetics: "... the Jewish spirit is a product of the Jewish person."[398] He speculated that, "Probably many Jews are not aware of the destructive power they represent."[399] Rav Kook expresses the same idea but positively, that Jewish spirit thirsts to improve the world, because "This spirit of idealism, to bring goodness and perfection to the world...is embodied in the inner soul of Israel."[400]

Choices: To Be or Not to Be

Abraham was the first to choose the mission. His journey established the Jewish People by leaving his homeland and going to a land he had never seen before, toward a life he did not know. That's the Jewish journey. By venturing into the unknown, the original patriarch discovered who he really was. By continuing the journey--one of personal, national, and universal discovery, and actualization--we discover who we are.

As a Jew, you face a choice: adopt a defensive stance or embrace resilience and grit. It is not an easy choice. There is deep social pressure against going all in, and added to that is the weak Jewish education that most of us received. If there's no compelling reason to be Jewish, if it's just an accident of birth, a quaint cultural happenstance of a last name that ends in "Berg" or "Stein," why should you care?

These questions deeply affect every young Jew today, whether they are conscious of the pull or not. As Maghen eloquently describes:

> Why bother? Everything logical, indeed, every major ideology comprising the modern, Western world-view, would appear to be solidly stacked up against such a foolhardy stance (being a committed Jew). Hell, *inertia itself* is beating us, with both hands tied behind its back: like their gentile counterparts,

most young Jewish people of this relatively placid and malleable generation (the sixties it ain't) are more or less going with the increasingly coordinated and egregiously conformist global flow, streaming away from everything the Jewish People once were, away from everything we could yet be together.[401]

Why Be Jewish? Let Go

The answer to "why be Jewish?" is very deep, and reaching it is not easy. In Chapter 6, we spoke of Purim, the holiday celebrating the Jewish victory over our arch-nemesis, as the holiday where everything is turned upside down. The deeper spiritual opportunity of Purim is achieved when Jews fulfill the commandment to become so drunk that they lose sense of some cognitive faculties until they no longer see the difference between "cursed is Haman" and "blessed is Mordechai."

The insight is that sometimes getting drunk can help us get clarity by letting go of the ego and quieting the mind, which often tends to overanalyze. One day a year, we uplift ourselves spiritually using the power of wine. The famous Rabbi, the Maharal of Prague, explains the idea of being a Jewish drunk (they are usually seen stumbling around and telling everyone how much they love them): that by going beyond, we connect with our souls and see the world from that vantage point.[402]

From the soul's point of view, we can learn from the antisemites. The line between evil Haman and blessed Mordechai gets blurred: from the evil we see our goodness; from the hatred we see our power to love; from the drive to kill Jews, we see that we are different. We can embrace our identity as Jews; we can connect to ourselves. We can realize on a deeper level the beauty of being a member of a people so special that evil always chooses us.

I hope that this book can help you reach that level of soul clarity without getting drunk, but, rather, by using your intellect and listening to your soul.

Our self-actualization comes down to our choices. For Jews with a strong Torah education, much of what I have written here might be clarifying and familiar. For those without a strong foundation in Jewish philosophy, this information may come as a surprise. You may have learned something about yourself that you didn't know, but that perhaps the antisemite does. Part of you may not want to know this, but it's important to understand: Jew-haters sense something in you that you may not. As the Maharal writes, the fundamental cause of Jew-hatred is that they sense that something different in your core being.[403]

We can die in a land of physical or spiritual exile or be reborn in the promised land of our ancestors and our descendants. Let's stop defining ourselves by the haters;[404] let's stop defensively reacting with "never again" and focusing on mere survival, and instead learn about and love what makes us strong, what makes us great, and what our unique particular-universal mission is.[405]

Today is an opportunity to step out of the shadows, get off the fence, and to step into your role as messenger with courage and conviction. I promise that, in doing so, you can help heal the wounds of our collective past and chart a course toward a personal, Jewish, and human future brimming with hope, unity, and purpose.

I invite you to embrace your identity fully and joyously and to unlock the profound sense of meaning, purpose, and pleasure that comes with understanding your unique place in the world.

9

Clarity and Connection in the Face of Jew-Hatred

But Ruth replied, "Do not urge me to leave you, to turn back and not follow you. For wherever you go, I will go; wherever you lodge, I will lodge; your people shall be my people, and your God my God."
– Ruth 1:16

Moses said to …(his) father-in-law, "We are setting out for the place of which God has said, 'I will give it to you.' Come with us…"
– Numbers 10:29

IN THIS FINAL chapter of our journey, let's shift our focus to taking deliberate action. We can learn to not only endure but thrive amidst the challenges of prejudice and discrimination.

Let me again quote the poet Leonard Cohen as he expresses in his song "Anthem" the idea that we can navigate through and even grow from turbulence and pain:

Ring the bells that still can ring
Forget your perfect offering

There is a crack, a crack in everything
That's how the light gets in.

We can all act and let more light in; and when we do, we will shine.

As this book has shown, antisemitism is a moral and spiritual phenomenon. Therefore, in addition to the imperatives of protecting ourselves so we can stay alive when faced with terrorists and acting to defeat our enemies physically, we must also provide a moral and spiritual response.

The horrific attacks and the explosion of Jew-hatred around the world has revealed an enduring desire to annihilate Jews; this is not something that will go away by ignoring it. We need to understand this and respond accordingly. We must choose to not revert to the mindset of October 6 but instead embrace the positive potential of our new reality.

If so many hate me for being Jewish, I will respond by proudly embracing my Jewish identity. If there is meaning in the hatred, as we have shown, I will find meaning in embracing my Jewishness. And for non-Jews, in the face of moral confusion and indifference, I will stand up against prejudice and Jew-hatred. I will speak truth to power.

There is a Torah idea, alluded to in the name of one of Rabbi Sacks' books,[406] that every Jew is a letter in the Torah scroll. The meaning, he says, is that each of us has a role to play, a unique difference to make: "Judaism is not a theory, a system, a set of speculative propositions, an 'ism.' It is a call, and it bears our name."[407] That is the essence of this book's take-away—you can discover your place, your passion, and where your talents and interests align with your unique mission.

Finding your particular place, your *yiud* as it is called in Torah thought,[408] can take time; in fact, it is a lifetime process and requires patience. The idea can seem daunting, and admittedly, this book may have inadvertently set a very high bar. So, let's bring it down to earth by providing some real examples of individuals (most of whom I know personally) who have responded to hate with inspirational positivity and a deep connection to the Jewish People. These role models can help give a better idea of what "owning being Jewish" looks like.

First, an important definition. This book is about what it means to be Jewish. Even in the context of what I have written, that can mean many things, so let me clarify what I am trying to say.

The *Midrash* says that the Jews were redeemed from Egyptian slavery on the merit that they did not change their Jewish names, their unique clothing, or their language.[409] The situation being described by this statement is clear: at that point, they were not very 'religious'. In fact, we know that they were quite assimilated and, like the Egyptians, even worshiped idols. But the meaning is that these Jews had a very strong Jewish self-identity—it was their main identity—and it was expressed for all to see, even if they didn't 'do it all'.

So, let me be clear: 'embracing your Jewish identity' is very broad. It can mean learning Torah and/or becoming more religiously observant; it can mean standing up for Israel or making *aliyah* (moving to the homeland); it can mean community involvement, philanthropy, and of course, being a more giving person and helping those in need. The list can go on and on, of course, but my point is that there are different ways to express yourself as a Jew.

At the same time, being Jewish has real meaning and definitions. Judaism is not only about social activism, or fitting it into a box according to current cultural trends or your whims. While social justice is indeed a fundamental part of our identity and philosophy, Judaism encompasses much more. The key is to keep growing: learn more, gain wisdom from the Torah, and understand what is truly valuable and correct in life. Listen to your soul and identify your internal intent—*kavana*, as it is called in Judaism. Ask yourself which direction you are headed and whether you are deepening your connection.

What do Jewish Moral and Spiritual Responses Look Like?

Compassion for Family

Let's accept completely that we are one people, one family, with one heart. On October 7, this feeling was palpable to Israelis and to Jews around the world: the hostages; the victims of barbaric torture, rape, and murder; the soldiers who fought and those that gave their lives; the families of those murdered; the evacuees; the students on hostile campuses—we were united. We can try to feel the pain, have compassion, and act with commitment to family— respect others, avoid divisive and damaging speech, and support one another—because we are in this "together consciousness," even if we disagree on strategy, approaches, or worldviews.

Connecting to Our National Purpose

Hamas united us, but it should not be our enemies that keep us together. Nor is unity by force sufficient for our fulfillment as a people. The emerging cracks in our unity, especially in Israel, threaten to return us to October 6th. We need to strengthen our national unity by deepening our understanding of and commitment to our shared values, destiny, and purpose.

Judaism is a religion in some ways, but it is much more than that. We have a national mission to be a Light to the Nations: "I ...have summoned you, and I have grasped you by the hand; I created you, and appointed you a covenant people, a light of nations."[410] As this book has laid out, this is not about elitism; it is a responsibility.

Learning Torah

One effective way to connect is to find out more about what it all means: read about Jewish history,[411] study the Arab–Israeli conflict,[412] and, most important, learn Torah,[413] the source of it all. To illustrate why learning is so critical, here is a story I heard from one of my Rabbis, Shalom Schwartz[414]:

> Shalom: When I was a young rabbi in Toronto, Canada, I was sitting with a group of young Jews with whom I played a weekly pick-up hockey game. One turned to me and said, "I want you to know that I am very proud to be a Jew."
>
> "Really, Mike? Tell me more: What are you proud of?"
>
> He answered, "I grew up in a small town in Eastern Canada, and every day I had to fight my way to school because I was a Jew."
>
> "Wow, that must have been difficult," I responded. "But tell me: What is it that you are proud of in being a Jew?"
>
> He answered, "Every day I had to fight my way to school because I was a Jew; I am proud to be a Jew."
>
> "I appreciate that it must have been very challenging, but what exactly are you proud of in being a Jew?"
>
> He answered, "Every day, I had to fight …"

After a few rounds like that, Shalom realized that it was not going to get any deeper. And that's okay, because Mike felt deeply connected. But ideally, people should invest their Jewish identity with meaning and the richness that it offers by deepening their understanding. And for that, the best place to connect is the Torah.

Antisemites want to erase the Jews because of what we represent, so let's strengthen and affirm our understanding of our core values so that we can live them fully.

Israel

The Torah asserts that for the Jews to fully complete their mission of being a Light, we need to have our own independent, sovereign nation. Only a nation can effectively demonstrate the reality of a society that embodies the Torah's core values and applies them in every dimension of its functioning.

The Jewish vision—and we are aware that, as of now, we are still far from this—is creating a society with a dynamic energy born of unity with respect for diversity amongst different sectors, commitment to individual freedom, responsibility to man and God, while balancing compassion and justice. For 2,000 years, we held on to this vision and believed that somehow, someday, we would be back in our Land and could try to fulfill it.

Today, with an ingathering of Jewish exiles from the four corners of the world well in progress, the opportunity is in front of us. A commitment to help and build Israel, or even to make *aliyah*, is an incredible Jewish response.

I hope this has helped you create a clearer picture of what *owning it* looks like in theory. And now I will share some real and inspirational stories of it being lived in practice.

Stories of Jewish
Moral & Spiritual Responses

The following accounts of moral and spiritual responses, told by people who experienced anti-Jewish hate, including from the events of October 7, and responded by facing it head-on, can help inspire us and strengthen our moral self-confidence so we can turn the label of "the big, bad Jew" into a badge of honor. When you come up with your own unique response, you can not only defend against external negativity; you can actively shape yourself and your world into a more beautiful place.

Bucky

On October 7, I was praying at the morning Simchat Torah celebrations. With me were three siblings who grew up with my kids and who lived just down the street from us. At the time, they did not know that their brother, David, was at the Nova festival. He was killed that day. But before his fate was determined, along with 360 other young party-goers, David's friends, Gidon and Bucky, were alerted to his danger when they received a text message from him:

Pray for me.

and then another:

Something terrible has happened.

Determined to save him, Gidon and Bucky, along with David's cousin Ezra, a combat medic, set off towards the south. They stopped only to pick up a gun and bulletproof vests from a friend. The area had become a war zone, and they never made it to the party grounds in time to help David. Instead, they joined medics at a field hospital in the area of Sderot, spending the day treating wounded people who had come from the festival. "We didn't really understand that there was a war breaking out," Hazony told *The Times of Israel*. "We thought it was just a terrorist attack at a party." Despite their devastation, they responded with action.

That Sunday night, October 8th, only hours after returning from the south, Bucky created a WhatsApp group called *Let's Do Something* and added some of David's closest friends. Within 24 hours, they had a plane full of aid on the way to Israel.

That night they founded their organization, *Let's Do Something*. Within a week, they had raised $500,000 and brought several planeloads of aid. In less than 6 months, they brought over $25 million in equipment, including search-and-rescue gear and several ambulances. As the conflict developed, so did their organization:[415] They now work with the IDF to create support programs for soldiers, collaborate with communities across Israel to get aid to those affected by October 7th, and use their story to inspire pro-Israel engagement, with videos already garnering over 30 million views.[416]

Sapir

Sapir was kidnapped from kibbutz Nir Oz on October 7 and was held in Hamas captivity for 55 days. As of this writing, her boyfriend Sacha is still captive; all of his family was either killed or are still being held. Sapir was not religious but said that during her captivity, she felt God's presence and angels protecting her. She believed she was there for a reason, to use her abilities to take care of other female captives who needed her support. Trusting in God gave her meaning and strength.

During her captivity, Sapir's mother organized daily Torah classes for women in her home, dedicating three hours each day. Her mother remained positive, encouraging everyone to send positive energy to Sapir to give her strength.

When Sapir was released, she was smiling. People asked her how she could smile after enduring such horrible conditions, and she replied, "Even in the worst of times, you can choose to be happy, and that is what I did."

Upon learning how many people prayed for her and took action to become better people in her merit, she understood where the protecting angels came from.

Sapir shared that when the terrorist first broke through her door, her first thought was, *God, I will start to keep Shabbat*. Although she was not observant, and doesn't know why that came to her, she made the commitment and has kept it ever since: "Now, on Shabbat, I put everything on the side, and I feel free, and I feel peace in my body and my mind. This gives me a lot of energy to start the new week."

Her time in captivity within Gaza also changed her in another way: she became less self-focused and more giving. All of her time is now focused on others—volunteering, speaking, and helping to give people power to others by encouraging people to also become givers.

What does she want now? "In one of the tunnels where I was held, one of the terrorists forced me to watch TV. The program was showing a rally in Tel Aviv in support of the hostages. The terrorist said to her, 'Look, when the Jews are together like this, they are very, very strong.' That is amazing, that they know this. This is my hope, that one day all the Jewish People will be united, and not like we were before October 7."

Sapir has traveled the world speaking to groups about her experiences, because, she says, "I want the whole Jewish People to feel connected and feel the same feelings we felt on that day [October 7]."[417]

As Sapir suffered in captivity, the IDF began the job of destroying Hamas so that they could not repeat what they told Sapir was their plan, to do it "again and again."

The IDF has many brave soldiers, including young people who have left the comfort of the Diaspora and moved to Israel to fight for their people.

Ben

Ben was not raised religious in his native South Africa, but his bar mitzvah trip to Israel had a profound impact on him. Connecting deeply to the land and the people, he decided then and there that when he grew up, he would return and serve in the IDF to connect with his Jewish roots and help his people.

At 22, as Hamas rockets rained down on Israel, Ben decided it was time to stand up and do his part. He moved to Israel, knowing no one in his new homeland, and signed up for the full three years of army service. He served in Gaza during the Hamas war as part of a team rescuing injured soldiers. But his most dramatic experience wasn't on the battlefield.

While on leave, Ben posted some photos on Instagram. His account was hacked by anonymous pro-Palestinian groups who posted his photos and articles labeling him as a "genocidal war criminal." He received death threats. Then his parents' company's Instagram account was linked and targeted; they faced threats, bad reviews, and calls for a boycott. After numerous threats to his parents and sisters, the family had to shut down all their social media.

A few weeks later, a journalist asked Ben to comment. Hoping to correct the record, he spoke, but the news site portrayed him as a villain when presenting the story. Major South African media picked up the story, depicting him as a baby killer and the face of the "evil IDF soldier". They targeted him for prosecution; the police opened a file and planned on asking Israel to extradite him.

The final blow came when the antisemitic South African government decided to prosecute any South African who served in IDF. Ben was placed on the prosecution list, meaning he couldn't return to his hometown to visit his family—not now and maybe not ever. Despite everything, Ben has no regrets about his move to Israel. "Absolutely not," he says. "It was the best decision of my life. I am stronger now from experiencing harsh Jew-hatred, so I know what we are fighting for, and we need to fight harder. History repeats itself, like in Germany, and we can't stand by."

Ben learned the hard way that Jews are fighting battles on two fronts—one in Gaza and another in the media.

That Guy

For the second war—the battle over hearts and minds--we need people to stand up and defy the mainstream, popular attitudes, just as Abraham did so many years ago. Here is a beautiful story of defiance that I read in an excerpt from the upcoming book *Moral Ambition* by Rutger Bregman:

> There's a famous photograph from 1936 of German dockworkers giving the Hitler salute. If you look closely, you can see that just one person in the entire crowd is not participating. While more than a hundred people extend their hands to the Führer, he stands alone, steady and serene, with his arms crossed.
>
> 1936 photo, in which a man alleged to be August

Landmesser is conspicuously not giving the Nazi salute.[418]

Who was this man? And where did he find his courage? For years, the photo lay in a dusty archive, until one day a German historian stumbled upon it. On 15 November 1995, he placed an appeal in the *Hamburger Abendblatt*, asking whether there might be anyone who recognized the man. That same week, a reader responded that it had to be her father, August Landmesser.

The image of the dockworker went around the world. August Landmesser ended up on millions of buttons and postcards, T-shirts, and posters. The photo was hung in dorms, pubs, and offices, and still every so often the image goes viral, often with the same comment: BE THAT GUY!

After all these years, the-man-who-didn't-salute

Figure 11. Photo of 'That Guy'. A 1936 photo in which a man alleged to be August Landmesser is conspicuously not giving the Nazi salute.[418]

still seems to stare at us: What would *you* have done in my case? Would you have been just as brave, or would you have joined the crowd? We hope for the former, but fear the latter. "Looking back from our vantage point," writes the journalist and historian Isabel Wilkerson, "he is the only person in the entire scene who is on the right side of history. Everyone around him is tragically, fatefully, categorically wrong."[419]

Next, I share stories of two amazing non-Jews, a man and a woman, who stepped up to BE THAT GUY!

Douglas

British author and political commentator Douglas Murray stands as a model for his courage and moral clarity. He is not Jewish, but since October 7, he has been shining a floodlight into our world.

Murray has been to numerous war zones as a journalist, but he was deeply shocked by what he saw in Israel's south: "If I could put that into a word, I think it is the 'glee' with which the terrorists attacked. I've seen quite a lot of human savagery, but gleeful savagery is unusual."

He has been speaking around the clock on every available media, combating a tsunami of anti-Israel haters, and helping people globally gain moral clarity. At one event, he remarked, "My political awareness began when I was at Oxford University." He continued, "The Second Intifada was happening at the time, and then 9/11 happened and I noticed that everybody who was very against Israel was also very against America and Britain, almost without exception, and the strongest condemnation was always against Israel. I was brought up to know the difference between right and wrong, and when I became a writer and first started coming to Israel, I saw a jarring disconnect between what I saw for myself was happening and what was reported. Fairness is a clear concept for me. I admire Israel as a country and I admire its people, and they are horribly and unfairly treated. I call it out and I regard doing so as a duty and pleasure."[420]

Here is one example of his brilliance at calling attention to the double standards against Jews that are often taken for granted: He noted that we have all seen and heard of the posters of Jews still in Hamas captivity that have been torn down all around the world. To compare, he asked us to consider this: If someone had torn down a poster of a missing dog, where someone was asking for help to find their dog, would we not all ask what is wrong with our society? Why are we producing people so pathological? And we would probably want to know that people have consequences for such behavior. But when there are posters of captive Jews, including babies, children, and women, they are torn down in every major city in the world outside of Israel. Why is there no sympathy for the Jews?[421]

Murray is ingenious, articulate, and fast. I would call him a black-belt debater, and I am happy I don't have to go head-to-head with him. Not everyone is as clever—or even as brave—as Murray, but we can all stand up in some way. We can all rise.

Rawan

On October 7, Rawan was sitting in her flat, studying for a paper at the University of Heidelberg, when she heard the awful news. The next day, when she saw the world erupt against Israel, she decided to become an active spokesperson for Israel and the Jewish People. What makes her story unique is that Rawan is an Arab who grew up as a Muslim in Syria and Lebanon; she wanted to speak in her native tongue to Arabs and Muslims around the world.

Since 2015, Rawan has lived with a sense of urgency in Germany. She understood that the influx of Syrian refugees would inevitably jeopardize the ongoing reconciliation process between Germany and the Jews unless authorities had a plan to cure a million newcomers of antisemitism.

As a Syrian-Lebanese raised in the Middle East and taught that all Jews deserve to die, Rawan calls herself a "recovering antisemite." She was particularly alert to the risk of increased antisemitism. After the signing of the Abraham Accords, she took part in the first Arab delegation to the *International March of the Living* and became involved in educational programs informing Arabs about the Holocaust. Her driving force until October 7 was optimistic, "If there is a German embassy in Israel and an Israeli embassy in Germany, everything is possible, even peace in the Middle East." After the massacre, she had to adjust her expectations: "Never have I imagined that an entity worse than ISIS existed," she said.

Figure 12. Rawan as part of the Sharaka delegation visiting remnants of the Nazi concentration camps in March 2022.

Watching the world justify the attack before Israel even counted the bodies transformed her into an activist identifying publicly as a Zionist who advocates the eradication of Hamas. She started the *Arabs Ask* channel on social media, now reaching hundreds of thousands each month. She also decided to share publicly her budding relationship with Judaism, which, prior to October 7, was a private matter. Additionally, she narrated my film, *Tragic Awakening: A New Look at the Oldest Hatred* (available at *tragicawakening.com*),[422] and is telling the world: "May my fate be that of the Jews."

Oren

Another great spokesperson for the Jewish People is Oren, a man I met in the most unexpected place: the Majdanek concentration camp in 2006. When I met him, he didn't even notice me. I was filming for a movie we were producing, and he was on the ground, crying uncontrollably. I have never seen someone cry so hard and for so long.

Oren was born in Israel, but he had become very disconnected from his people. A student of history, he had taken a five-month trip on the footpaths of World War II, traveling from Normandy through Poland to Stalingrad. He had seen many difficult places and always held it together, but when he saw the pile of seven tons of ground-up human bones and ashes at the memorial in Majdanek, he collapsed. As one observer said, "Nothing says mass murder quite as effectively as a giant pile of human ash." That finished Oren off.

"All of the pain of an entire world that burned, a whole world of Jews that disappeared—I lost it. It was the big picture that got me; Jews of every form and type, religious and not, right wing and left—all gone and turned to dust. We tend to look at the death part of the death camps, but in that moment I saw the entire world of Jewish life in Europe that was gone."

His main takeaway from the trip was that there is good and evil in the world, and he understood that he needed to do his part to fight the evil. Upon his return to Israel, he became a tour guide but wanted to make Israel accessible to everyone, even people who could not afford a private guide. This led to making short videos on YouTube (@Travelingisraelinfo) explaining how-to's for Israel travel, and also to tell the deeper stories beneath the surface. Slowly, he realized that Israel was in a global war for hearts and minds and that he needed to become a soldier in that army. In 2019, he started to take it seriously and began producing videos explaining Israel, the issues it faces, and the conflict. Since October, he has focused almost exclusively on current events. He has become a major YouTube star because his videos present Israel's case in a clear and balanced way, always with fascinating angles. He produces several short educational pieces each month and routinely gets five million views a month.

Maybe you don't have the same gift of the gab that those three brilliant people have, but sometimes the fight comes to you, and if you are strong enough, you can step up. That is what happened in the past few years when the intifada came to campus. Next are the stories of three students who met antisemitism head-on at U.S. campuses.

Blake

Blake arrived at George Washington University in 2018 with big plans. "I landed on campus identified as a progressive activist, ready to spend my weekends marching the streets of DC against the Trump administration, against Brett Kavanaugh, against the evils of capitalism and corruption. Of course, I had heard rumors of anti-Israel activism that occasionally 'crossed a line,' but these stories came from them. You know ... The AIPAC Jews, the Trump Jews, the right-wingers."

But as freshman year went on, he encountered blatant antisemitism time and again from his progressive peers. When he heard that a pride event in DC had banned Star of David and rainbow flags, he and others showed up anyway, flags in hand, only to be blocked from entering by the march organizers. The unspoken message was clear: you can be a liberal who happens to be a Jew, but you can't be openly proud of being a Jew or feel any connection to the State of Israel.

Many would have altered their path to fit in, but not Blake. He wrote an important piece in *The New York Times* describing the bigotry he faced on campus and became something of a celebrity. This earned him a place in my 2023 film on campus Jew-hatred.[423] He was shocked as friends, both in real life and on social media, distanced themselves, and not one professor reached out to discuss the article. His unforgivable mistake had been being openly proud of being Jewish and calling out the Jew-hate.

Following the NYT article, harassed Jews from all over the country reached out to him for support and advice. "I have sat in front of my computer fielding these sorts of missives almost every night since November 2019 (when the *Times* published). After years of this, I want to put it to you as plainly as possible: What we are seeing on our college campuses is not criticism of Israel. It is not even hatred of Israel or Zionism. It is unmitigated, often unprovoked rage at Jewishness. 'Anti-Zionism' on college campuses is not a political disagreement confined to the boundaries of academic discussion in the classroom. It is an obsession. It is an insistence on making Jews feel uncomfortable—or worse—wherever, whenever, under whatever conditions."

After losing a great deal of friends and even relationships with his professors due to his unwavering support for Israel, he compared the experience to how Jews throughout history have been promised acceptance and freedom at the expense of a primary marker of their Jewish identity. After spending considerable time reading and learning more about Jewish history and Israel, Blake no longer felt at home in America. To fully express his increasingly important Jewish identity, he realized he needed to either become more religious or make *aliyah* to Israel. Not knowing much about Judaism as a faith, he moved to Tel Aviv in 2022, where he is now a successful journalist, continuing his proud, pro-Jewish and pro-Israel work.

Max

Max started his Harvard journey in 2016 as a proud Jew but with very little knowledge of his heritage or Israel. He came to a couple of Israel events and was mildly surprised to encounter anti-Israel protests on campus that disrupted events. Things changed when Max met more observant Jews and Israelis; their passion and dedication sparked his interest in Israel and Torah learning. As he delved deeper, he saw the need for a broader conversation about Israel on campus, beyond politics, so he organized the Israel Summit in April 2018. His goal was simple: to show a bigger picture of Israel and reach beyond the usual audience. After raising an impressive $200,000, the summit was a hit, attracting 500 people. Max teamed up with my non-profit media educational company, OpenDor Media, to make a video about the event that educated more than a million people.

The summit's success inspired others, and Max helped take his initiative to other campuses in 2019. Even after he graduated, the summit continued under Hillel International; it has raised more than $2 million and reached thousands across many states.

After Harvard, Max started a career in a large private equity company, spending two years in New York and the past two in Israel. He's helped invest hundreds of millions in Israeli companies, deepening his connection to the country, which has become his home.

Personally, Max has grown, too. He's been studying Torah and observing Shabbat for three years now. His activism continues as well, helping to run a Shabbat program that organized dinners for 10,000 people across 42 states, and supporting families of fallen soldiers.

Looking back, Max faced challenges as a Jewish student at Harvard, but he's grateful for the journey it started, because it is where his Jewish values and career path met, guiding him to grow personally and professionally.

One of the people Max raised money from was a family friend named Marc, who is the CEO of one of the largest hedge funds in the world. His Jewish response story is also amazing. Read on.

Marc

Marc, a supporter of mine and an emeritus board member at OpenDor Media, is known for his strategic thinking and big-picture perspective. When the anti-Israel conference called Palestine Writes Literature Festival was held at his alma mater, Penn, hosting many known antisemites, Marc sprang into action.

As one of Penn's largest donors and Chairman of the Wharton Business School, his voice did carry significant weight. Marc stated that the central issue was not free speech, but Penn's leadership failing to forcefully condemn the festival.[424] In an interview on MSNBC, he clarified, "Microaggressions are condemned with extreme moral outrage; and yet violence, particularly violence against Jews, antisemitism, seems to have found a place of tolerance on the campus."[425] Two weeks later came October 7.

As anti-Israel rallies grew at Penn and the university leadership failed to call out the blatant antisemitic and anti-American rhetoric at the protests, Marc started a campaign among alumni, calling for the leaders of the University of Pennsylvania to resign and donors to close their checkbooks. He believes strongly that donors should play a role in holding schools accountable for bias and racism of any kind. He understood that the campuses were not just dealing with Jew-hatred: "I think we're fighting something else. We're fighting anti-Americanism. We're fighting anti-merit. We're fighting anti-power. We're fighting really for the soul of these institutions."[426] His leadership was effective: The school lost millions in donations, and soon after Penn's president's embarrassing testimony at Congress, where she was unable to clearly say that calls for genocide were harassment of Jews,[427] she resigned.

Upon reflection, Marc takes his activism in stride. "Why would I not call out philanthropic institutions that behave in an antisemitic fashion? Why would I give to organizations, cultural organizations or otherwise, who are making it difficult for Jews? This is just common sense."[428]

In a moment of great need, Marc stepped up as a leader and a role model; he used his position and influence to make a difference for the Jewish People and for America.

Queen Esther

Perhaps Marc was inspired to use his position to help the Jewish People by one of the greatest role models in Jewish history, Queen Esther, whose story we recall and celebrate each year on the holiday of Purim.

When Haman declared genocide on the Jews, Queen Esther, who had concealed her Jewish identity at the instruction of her cousin Mordechai, found herself in a pivotal position. Mordechai, learning of the decree, appealed to her to intercede with the King to rescind the evil edict.

Esther knew that entering the King's chamber without an invitation carried a death penalty, unless he extended his favor.

Understandably, she hesitated. Mordechai's response was powerful and timeless : "You cannot remain silent. Who knows? It might be that you were chosen to be queen just for this moment!"

For the sake of her people, Esther took the risk. She approached the King, and the rest, as they say, is history: The Jews survived, Haman was hanged, and then the Jewish People celebrated.

Esther's story teaches us that every talent, strength, and resource we possess is given for a purpose. Each of us is a letter in the scroll, with a unique role to play in this world.[429]

Esther requested that the scroll recounting her story, *Megillat Esther*, be written and shared across generations. She desired that every man, woman, and child, in every land, forever hear her timeless message. Queen Esther's legacy continues to resonate with us today.

Avital Sharansky

A modern-day heroine who modeled the queen's determination against a mighty empire is Avital Sharansky. She and her husband, Natan, were Soviet *refuseniks*, individuals who, after applying for visas to immigrate to Israel, were refused permission to leave. As a result, they often lost their jobs and faced various forms of mistreatment and discrimination from the authorities, coworkers, and neighbors.

During a time when the gates were closed to Jewish immigration and persecution against Jews was widespread, Avital was eventually granted an exit visa. Natan, however, was denied. The couple married in 1974, and one day later, with her visa expiring, Avital left Russia for Israel. In 1978, Natan was sentenced to 13 years of forced labor on trumped-up charges of high treason and espionage. He endured time in several notorious prisons and a Siberian "strict regimen colony."

Avital embarked on an international campaign to raise awareness of her husband's plight with the rallying cry, "Let My People Go." Despite being one of the most introverted people I have met speaking very little English at the time, her campaign became one of the most effective PR campaigns ever built by a human rights activist. She met with members of Congress, American presidents, and leaders around the world, making the cause of Soviet Jewry a household issue.

The pressure on the Soviets became so great that Natan was released in 1986 in a prisoner exchange and reunited with Avital in Israel, where more than 100,000 people celebrated with him at the Western Wall upon his arrival. Many observers said that Natan and Avital created the largest cracks in the Iron Curtain, demonstrating that the Soviet regime could be beaten by defiance, which eventually led to its collapse.

In 1988, Natan wrote *Fear No Evil*, a memoir of his time as a prisoner, and went on to become a great leader in Israel. He helped people understand the essence of freedom: "Freedom is when you can do and say things you believe in. In this respect, in prison I was much freer than those who interrogated me. During the interrogations, I really liked to tell anti-Soviet jokes about Brezhnev. The guards were almost bursting but could not laugh because of the consequences. And I would say to them, 'Well, you want to tell me that I'm in prison? You're in prison—you cannot laugh.' For me, freedom is very much related to identity, because we found the strength to fight for our identity only when we became a free people, and vice versa".[430]

During the campaign, when people asked Avital what they could do to help her husband, she replied in a matter than can inspire all of us in times of trouble , "I don't know, but if he was your brother, you wouldn't stop trying to figure out what to do...you wouldn't rest until he was released."

Aryeh, Misha, and Dina

The Sharanskys' defiance and strength galvanized millions of Jews around the world, like Aryeh, Misha, and Dina.

As a self-described "somewhat naïve and ignorant college student of 21," Aryeh flew to Russia with a group of other U.S. students for some interaction with Soviet academics, seeking to find common ground. Aryeh was a regular middle-class Jew from San Francisco, not particularly observant and had little knowledge or experience with antisemitic discrimination. It was 1984, in what he called the "bad old days" of the Soviet Union and the communist party. Through a series of coincidental and later orchestrated meetings with Jews, he met several Jewish *refuseniks*: "I discovered a tremendous Jewish self-confidence in the face of Jew-hatred, as these quiet heroes responded by embracing their Jewish identity," Aryeh said. For example, "There were the half-dozen or so Jewish men and women baking *matzot* for Passover in secret in the basement of a building next to the synagogue ("closed for repairs" for over 30 years already) in the center of Riga, Latvia, and there was Misha, the only young man helping to make up a minyan in the main synagogue of Leningrad on the night of Passover, with his long, brown beard and sparkling eyes."

Misha invited Aryeh back to his home for the *Seder*. Their festive meal consisted of weak barley soup with a very small portion of tough and chewy kosher meat, yet "...it was without question the most uplifting seder night [he] ever experienced, prior or following."

Misha and his wife, Dina, were not only *refuseniks*; they had become religiously observant and thus suffered a double infliction of discrimination. Aside from being fired from various jobs (as Misha refused to work on Shabbat), and having limited access to kosher meat, which restricted their diet, they were ostracized by many of their friends—including fellow Jews.

"Dina and Misha demonstrated a powerful and deep connection to our people, our history, and destiny, and an 'owning' of (and sacrifice for) their Jewishness, which I had never before encountered," Aryeh recalled. "Considering that I was soon to begin studies in Jerusalem to become a reform rabbi, their commitment inspired me to ask (and answer) two basic but life-changing questions: Why would a Jew endanger his/her welfare, job security, social standing, liberty, even their life, just to move to Israel? And why would they do so to become observant of Jewish tradition?"

Aryeh was incredibly moved, "Their stories, and those of thousands of others across the Soviet Union (and elsewhere, across time— including my ancestors who as crypto-Jews in Spain and Portugal risked their lives to preserve our Jewish identity until coming to England and the American colonies in the late 17th century) served as a shining light and guide to me." He learned from the exhilarating bravery of these regular people, as he said, "...whose spiritual, mental, physical, and emotional activism transformed themselves and others." And so he followed, and made *aliyah*, "... joining the Jewish People in this miraculous return to sovereignty in our land, accompanied also by a transition to traditional religious observance."

Defiance, faith, and maintaining human dignity was also a feature of Jewish response during the Holocaust.

Shmuel's Mom

One of my friends and supporters, Shmuel, shared with me the story of his remarkable Mother:

My mother grew up in Hungary and wanted to become an attorney. Being exceptionally brilliant, she graduated at the top of her high school class. However, when she applied to the university, she was told that the policy had changed from admitting very few Jewish students to not admitting any Jewish students at all. Undeterred, my mother decided to continue working in the family business and learn even more from her father and brothers. The family business was very successful. In 1944, Hitler decided to go after the Hungarian Jews and kill as many of them as possible.[431] Overnight, the Nazis took over all our factories and properties and sent my family to the concentration camps. Most of my family was murdered in Auschwitz. My mother managed to survive and return to Hungary as the admired leader of 1,000 women, whom she managed to save, support, and transport back to Hungary, on a special train she procured.

In the camps during these devastating times, she never lost her resolve and was able to lead wisely. She also never lost her belief in Judaism and hoped that God will destroy evil and help save His nation—she used her faith to give strength and hope to many others. These 1,000 women were partially composed of those interned with her in Auschwitz and others she "collected" on her way to freedom. These lost women were concentration camp inmates wandering in confusion and despair, not knowing what to do. She fed them, provided them with clothes and shelter, and led them all back to Budapest, Hungary after Auschwitz was liberated.

In the meantime, my father, who survived the abusive and cruel slave labor in the Forced Labor Camps of the Hungarian Army, returned to Hungary before my mother. Together with his friends, they established the "Joint" organization in Budapest to try and help the eventual survivors. They did not know who survived, but they were certain that there would be an influx of devastated people in their early days back to freedom.

When my mother got closer to Hungary, she sent a telex to the

Joint, alerting them that she was coming with so many traumatized women, so that they should try and prepare for their arrival. The person that got the message was my father, and he told his friends that the text "sounds like a message from my wife." This was how my parents were reunited after the war!

Having lost most of her family, friends, and wealth, she managed to restart her life. Once my parents heard that the state of Israel was established on the ancestral homeland of the Jewish People in the land of Israel, they decided to join the other citizens of Israel, moving there in 1949 to help rebuild the country. My father was one of the founders of the Ministry of Health and was involved in multiple community affairs, and my mother was instrumental in absorbing and helping the Jewish refugees from Europe and many Arab Countries.

As we know, Jew-hatred did not end when courageous people like Shmuel's mom came to Israel. The Jewish response continues to be one of hope, care, love, and life. Next, Sherri's story is one of the most tragic yet inspiring.

Sherri

Sherri and her husband, Rabbi Seth, led the Hillel on campus at the University of Maryland. Sherri was not particularly into the role of the Rabbi's wife—she had no Jewish education growing up and was more focused on being a feminist, a creative writer, and a mom. The couple decided to travel to Israel with their four kids during Seth's sabbatical from Hillel. She did not know that Seth made sure it was a one-way trip; unbeknownst to her, Seth quit his job before they left America, intending to stay with Sherri and the kids in Israel permanently.

Life was good until one day, during the second intifada in 2001, their oldest son, Koby, who was 13, was out for a walk with his friend Yosef., Both boys were brutally murdered by terrorists. They were among the 1,200 Israelis murdered by that wave of Palestinian terror and suicide bombings.

"My life was over," Sherri told me, "I wanted to die; it was just too painful." She found solace in spirituality, as the mondane world felt too trivial, and she lost interest in the small things. Sherri became deeply connected to God after Koby's murder. Learning Torah and saying Psalms were healing for her—she found her personal story reflected in the sacred words.

Listening to people talk about everyday matters was painful—she felt as if she was already living in the "world to come," and her comfort came from family and from connecting to the purity of Torah and prayer. Sherri's Torah learning sweetened her pain and tragedy—when she learned, she felt she was visiting the next world where Koby was—and it allowed her to experience that her "little life in this gigantic world is connected to something much greater."

Then came the birds. They kept falling from the sky in front of her, on her car, and one even hit her in the head. It was weird. She had dreams with birds, and then another dream where she spoke to God and asked Him how can He be a God of kindness. God answered that "He does the mitzvah of *shiluach haken*," an obscure commandment where one sends away the mother bird from her young on her nest. That answer was very confusing, but later that week, Sherri went to her regular Torah class and the teacher said, "Today, we will learn about *shiluach haken*."

She learned that it is a deeply mystical command and that the *Kabbala* (Jewish mystical texts) says that the highest place in *Gan Eden* (the world to come) is called the supernal bird's nest.[432] In that nest lives all the Jewish People who died al kiddush Hashem, sanctifying God's name as a result of being killed by Jew-haters just for being Jewish, like Koby. Sherri realized she was part of a much bigger story and that God was sending her messages.

Being connected to the Jewish community also gave Sherri tremendous strength and meaning. She and Seth established The Koby Mandell Foundation and Camp for Koby[433] to help other families who were victims of terror. She understood that after she died, the only meaningful actions would be spiritual, and that meaning in life was found by giving to others. Plus, she wanted to keep Koby's spirit alive.

"When we gave, we were also being helped.". Together, Sherri and Seth have helped thousands of bereaved families through Camp Koby and Yosef, retreats for bereaved mothers, fathers, couples, and widows. They employ many methods, including hiking therapy and psychodrama programs. She also wrote a book, *Blessing of a Broken Heart*,[434] to share her intimate story and help others dealing with loss and pain.

Sherri's difficult journey brought her to increased giving, spirituality, and learning, all of which provided her much healing. She is an incredible model of how to respond Jewishly.

Rabbi Chanina

In the year 135, after the failed Bar Kochba rebellion to free Israel from the oppressive Roman Empire, Emperor Hadrian outlawed the teaching of the Torah. Rabbi Chanina ben Teradion defied the Roman decree and continued teaching. When the Roman occupiers arrested him, they demanded to know why he was violating their laws. He replied, "as the Lord, my God commanded me," reflecting the divine obligation to learn and teach that is at the heart of Judaism.

The Romans wrapped Rabbi Chanina in the Torah scroll he was reading from, brought tufts of wool soaked them in water, cruelly placed them on his heart so that he would die slowly, and set him on fire.

As the flames consumed him, his students asked: "Our teacher, what do you see?" The Rabbi replied, "I see the parchment burning, but the Torah's letters are flying to the heavens."[435]

Rabbi Chanina's choice cost him his physical existence in this world but maintained the eternity of a Jewish People. His sacrifice reminds us that we are defined not by the oppression of even the mightiest empires, but rather, like the letters in the scroll, through our connection to the Torah and to our mission.

Liz

Liz is a Jewish woman born and raised by two Jewish parents in the Baptist Bible Belt of West Texas, living her life with very minimal Jewish involvement. None of her siblings, nor she, married Jewish spouses. When Liz became engaged to her husband-to-be, her Catholic mother-in-law-to-be was so horrified that her son was marrying a Jew that she paid a visit to her priest. The priest did not appreciate her attitude and told her that she should be very proud that her son was going to marry a member of the Chosen People; that was all her mother-in-law-to-be needed to hear.

Despite knowing next to nothing about her heritage, Liz always felt she was a Jew and tried her best to raise her three children so that they, too, would know that they were Jewish. Liz and her husband moved frequently during their 35 years of marriage, and were never involved in any of the Jewish communities, so the kids did not get any Jewish education, either.

Three years ago, Liz and her husband exchanged Christmas/Hanukkah DNA tests (they always had a tree and a "bush"); her husband, she told me, was a "mutt," composed of many different nationalities, but to her surprise, Liz turned out to be a "purebred," a 99.6% Ashkenazi Jew. This surprised her and got her thinking more about what it means to be Jewish.

And then came October 7th. Liz was so upset, so shocked, so disturbed at the evil, barbarity, and savagery of the massacre that she was "literally paralyzed" and could think of nothing else. Her first thoughts were: *Why? Why always the Jews and why always Israel?*

Five weeks later, she flew to Washington, DC, to attend the huge Pro-Israel rally, and that experience helped her begin to understand the strength, resilience, and pride of the Jewish People.

It was then, with the encouragement of a friend and the openness and welcoming from the local Chabad Rabbi, that Liz began what she calls, "an astonishingly exciting Jewish Learning Journey," her mission to finally understand what being Jewish really means. She began attending Shabbat services every Saturday morning, learning with a *"Partner in Torah"* on a weekly basis, attending a Basics of Judaism weekly learning session using a children's textbook, and going to every Chabad class and event possible; she even downloaded a language app to start learning Hebrew!

Liz believes that millions of people just like her were impacted by the sheer evil of October 7th, and she hopes to share her journey with others. As a former talk radio show host in New Hampshire, Liz has the confidence to tackle something new and will soon be launching a podcast. She believes the podcast will be her own little mitzvah or good deed, and she hopes to inspire others, Jewish or not, to learn more about the Jewish faith, the Jewish People, and the Jewish Nation of Israel…so stay tuned!

A very common Jewish response to October 7 was, like Liz's and Sapir's, to reconnect to Judaism.

Guy

One of the well-known stories is about the popular Israeli comedian

Guy, who announced in March 2024 that he plans on keeping Shabbat for the first time, and invited his hundreds of thousands of followers on social media to join him, saying that he wants at least 100,000 people to keep Shabbat for the first time.

"I may not be religious, but I'm a very proud Jew, and we all remember and need to remember October 7th," Guy said in a video message. "I'm not doing it for the *Geulah* (redemption) but for the *achdut* (unity) of the Jewish People, and for our heroic soldiers on the battlefront. Today, the heart of most of Am Yisrael is in the right place. Let's keep one Shabbat, end the divisive discourse, and bring the *ruach* (spirit) of a shared destiny from the battlefront to the homefront."

The depth of this spiritual response is profound, as he implored, "For one Shabbat, we'll turn off the screens, we won't let anyone divide us. They murdered us on Shabbat because we're Jews. On Shabbat, we'll get up and say that we're proud to be Jews so that all our enemies who thought that we're a divided nation will know that the eternal nation won't break so easily."[436]

A Choice in Every Generation

The story of the Jewish People—from Abraham to Guy and Sherri; from every young Israeli who defends his people in the IDF or learns Torah day and night in yeshiva; to Baruch and Sapir, and to every Jewish American college student like Max and Blake—is about choice. Jewish history shows us that our enemies can destroy countless Jewish bodies, but, just as the letters in Rabbi Chanina's burning Torah scroll flew to heaven, the Jewish People and the Jewish spirit will prevail.

The Jewish People have traveled most of their journey, and the destination is in sight. The choice is in front of each of us, Ze'ev Maghen exhorts:

> We have to make the conscious and collective decision to gird our creative loins, to recover the guts and the confidence, the romance and the idealism…If we revive the fire and the fascination, the study and the practice, the passion and the love; if we come home to our people with the world in our backpacks and combine what we've learned with all that we are; then the Jews will again shine their light…[437]

Find yourself in the Jewish Story, discover the collective power of your community, engage more deeply with your heritage, and let it be your shield against adversity, empowering you to carry forward the torch of your people with pride and purpose.

Rabbi Lord Sacks left this core teaching for his family, the Jewish People:

> This then, is our story, our gift to the next generation. I received it from my parents and they

from theirs across great expanses of space and time. There is nothing quite like it...it still challenges the moral imagination of mankind. I want to say to my children: Take it, cherish it, learn to understand and love it. Carry it, and it will carry you. And may you, in turn, pass it on to your children. For you are a member of an eternal people, a letter in their scroll. Let their eternity live on in you.[438]

As for me, I simply love being part of a tiny world-changing family; I am so fortunate that I know my life matters and I can make a difference in our people's wild adventure through history. I am also fortunate that I have been able to flip antisemitism on its head and filter out the negative noise that can easily weaken Jewish pride. What remains is the pure inspiration of being part of an incredible, warm, loving, caring, creative, and idealistic people. We are the most tenacious and resilient people who never lost hope in the optimistic plot line delivered to them 3,500 years ago. We never felt ourselves victims, and through it all, we have stayed resolute and happy, knowing that it's going to get really good, soon.

We Jews are compared to olives[430] because sometimes the best of us come out when we're being crushed. So, I want to thank our enemies for helping to keep us sharp, on our toes, and unified; for reminding us who we are when we sometimes forget; for forcing us to develop solutions to the challenges they throw at us, propelling us into a start-up nation; and for allowing us a pivotal role in cleaning up the world from evil. It is a privilege to face and fight evil because decreasing darkness increases light. Even if we would prefer to spend our energies on our more natural inclination to seek wisdom and spread love, we know this is part of our mission too.

I love being Jewish. I am grateful for my privilege and remain humbled by the responsibility.

This is your story too, *achi*.

Postscript

A Story Too Hard to Believe?

THE STORY OF the Jewish People is told in the greatest bestseller of all time, the Bible. This epic narrative has captivated the imaginations of billions of people around the world who have nothing else in common except that story.

In movie theaters, we see fantastic adventures brought to life with special effects, often the work of Jewish writers and directors or based on Jewish creators' work, like Marvel and DC comic book movies. These films frequently follow the plot pattern set by the original script of the Jewish People.[439] The Jewish story—starting with the underdog hero, the offer of a challenging mission (should he decide to accept it), moving through high stakes and challenges, experiencing a downfall and crisis when failure seems inevitable, and ending with resolution and a happy ending—has become humanity's legend. The characters may vary, but the core storyline remains the same.

Sometimes, superhero movies and shows seem too incredible to believe. But what about the Jewish origin story? Can we accept it to be true, or is it just too much to believe?

In some respects, it does not matter if this story is true. The Jewish impact and the backlash against it are historical facts. Our culture, technology, and history would be unrecognizable if Abraham and his descendants had never crossed and recrossed the desert. Whether divinely initiated or not, the Jewish story inspires wonder. But doesn't it pique our curiosity to know if it was?

Can we determine if the epic Jewish story, as understood by classical Judaism, is true?

I believe that we can.

Exploring the nature of God and the Torah are among the most important inquiries anyone could undertake. These topics matter because the outcomes, whatever they may be, fundamentally shape our worldview and profoundly impact our lives. They inform us about the meaning of life, the existence of free will, the concept of objective morality, and the very nature of what and who we are— whether we live only 80–90 years, or if we are souls that endure much longer.

The answer to this big question is beyond the scope of this book. However, I have written up some thoughts on the matter, what I believe to be a very strong case, in a pamphlet called "A Story Too Hard to Believe," available to my readers at my website, **RaphaelShore.com**. Please visit and download your free copy.

Acknowledgements

Writing this book has been a journey that would not have been possible without the support and contributions of many incredible friends and advisors.

A special thank you to Daniel Greenfield, whose brilliance and bravery as an author have been a guiding vision throughout this process. From research to writing, your assistance was instrumental from start to finish. You were my right hand, my sounding board, and my sparring partner in debates that clarified and sharpened this unique approach to viewing the history of the Jewish People. Your encouragement and challenges have been invaluable, and this book would not have seen the light of day without your contributions.

I am also indebted to a few friends who read the manuscript more than once and gave deep and meaningful feedback to keep me on track as I wallowed through murky and unfamiliar waters drafting my first book. Kendall Wigoda, Rabbi Chaim Willis, Ken Mischel, and Tiffany Gabbay, your contributions made a significant impact on the quality and depth of this work.

To the beta readers who provided invaluable feedback, your time and effort have not gone unnoticed. Thank you to Shoshana Palatnik, Judy Shore, Cathryn Sussman, Rachel Schultz, Shmuel Katz, Jessica Felber, Lisa Feldscher, Amy Holtz, Shmuel Katz, Philippe Lavi, Nathan Lyons, Silvia Joy Bader, and Rabbis Ken Spiro, Yaakov Palatnik, Aryeh Rosenzweig, Shaul Rosenblatt, and Shalom Schwartz. Your keen eyes and thoughtful comments have helped shape this book into its final form.

A heartfelt thank you to Dr. Yael Maoz of Beverly House Press, my publisher. Your unwavering belief in this project and steadfast support throughout the publishing process are truly appreciated.

Thank you also to the many team members and designers who helped make this project possible: Yariv Newman, Avigail Weiss Bornstein, Shmuel Lome, Dena Wimpfheimer, and Rachel Gold.

I would also like to express my deepest gratitude to the late Professor Robert Wistrich of blessed memory, who was the Director of the Vidal Sassoon International Center for the Study of Antisemitism at the Hebrew University of Jerusalem. His direction and encouragement were vital to my research, and his pioneering work in shedding light on Hitler's worldview gave me courage.

A special thank you to the late Sir Martin Gilbert of blessed memory, historian and official biographer of Winston Churchill, who motivated me to write; if he could do 80 books, I could write one. His widow, Lady Esther, remains a friend and supporter; thank you for your continued kindness.

To my wife, Rebecca, your unwavering support and boundless patience over the past three years have been nothing short of extraordinary. Your encouragement allowed me to dedicate myself fully to this project, and for that, I am forever grateful. I am blessed to have you by my side.

To anyone I may have unintentionally omitted, please know that I deeply appreciate your contributions and support. This book is a testament to the collective effort of many, and I am grateful for all the help and encouragement along the way. Thank you all.

Finally, and most importantly, I want to thank God. I have seen His hand guide me on my journey of study for 40 years, and it was not subtle, it was obvious. I thank God not only for my life and all of my blessings, which are endless, but for giving me clarity, strength, and the ability to communicate these important ideas.

Endnotes

Introduction

1 J-TV: Jewish Ideas. Global Relevance. (2023, December 6). Jewish Student Tells Congress about Antisemitism at NYU [Video]. YouTube. https://www.youtube.com/watch?v=tAF9Gu7gdzY

2 "The Jew in the Lotus," a 1994 book by Rodger Kamenetz, explores a historic and groundbreaking dialogue between rabbis and the Dalai Lama. This marked the first major recorded exchange between experts in Judaism and Buddhism.

3 Kamenetz, R. (1995). The Jew in the Lotus: A Poet's Rediscovery of Jewish Identity in Buddhist India, Harper Collins.

4 While the 'final solution' of genocide was only formalized in a commission to Nazi Reinhard Heydrich on July 31, 1941 and extended to the rest of Europe at the Wannsee Conference on January 20, 1942, it is a matter of historical debate as to when Hitler decided upon the 'solution' of genocide. There is evidence to suggest that until Hitler saw the unwillingness from all global countries to accept European Jewish refugees in any significant numbers, their expulsion from all of Europe might have been a sufficient solution for him. For our purposes, this question is not relevant, as we will see that Hitler's ideological goal was the same and required a Judenrein (Jew-free) Europe.

5 In Wisse's essay, The Functions of Anti-Semitism, National Affairs, Summer 2024

6 What I mean by the 'Jewish why' is, like Simon Senek defines it, understanding our purpose, our reason for being an independent people, our unique role and contribution to make in this world. TEDx Talks. (2009, September 29). Start with why -- how great leaders inspire action | Simon

Sinek | TEDxPugetSound [Video]. YouTube. https://www.youtube.com/
watch?v=u4ZoJKF_VuA

7 Ya, I skipped a couple steps - maybe we can cover that in a future book.

8 Talmud Sanhedrin 105B in the name of Rabbi Yochanan

9 Eaton, G. (2021, September 4). Rabbi Jonathan Sacks: "The hate that begins
with Jews never ends with Jews." New Statesman. https://www.newstatesman.
com/encounter/2018/08/rabbi-jonathan-sacks-hate-begins-jews-never-ends-
jews

"The hate that begins with Jews never ends with Jews. It was not Jews alone
who suffered under Hitler and Stalin, nor is it Jews alone suffering from the
ruthless pursuit of power that today masquerades as religion. Christians are
under assault in more than a hundred countries: put to flight in Syria, driven
out of Mosul, removed from Afghanistan, butchered, beheaded and terrorised
elsewhere. Hundreds of Muslims are dying daily, 90 per cent at the hands of
fellow Muslims. Bahais, Buddhists, Hindus and Sikhs have all suffered their
own tragedies. Yazidis are on the brink of the abyss. The world is awash with
hate across religious divides." https://rabbisacks.org/archive/hate-starts-jews-
never-ends-there/

Chapter 1

10 Since data collection in 1970. Center for Strategic and International
Studies, Hamas's October 7 Attack: Visualizing the Data, December 19, 2023.
https://www.csis.org/analysis/hamass-october-7-attack-visualizing-data

11 Natan Sharansky explains his definition here: 3D Test of Anti-Semitism:
demonization, double standards, delegitimization | Jerusalem Center for
Public Affairs. (2012, November 11). Jerusalem Center for Public Affairs.
https://jcpa.org/article/3d-test-of-anti-semitism-demonization-double-
standards-delegitimization/

12 Former Israeli Minster Moshe Arens once spoke to a program I was
directing , Senator Moynihan's Jerusalem Fellowships, and explained why
Americans often make the mistake of assuming that others think just like we
do. He said we need to understand that "The Middle East is not the Middle-
West." That message stuck with me.

13 I will never forget one personal experience I had with this folly. After my first film, Relentless: The Struggle for Peace in the Middle East was launched, one far-left Jewish fellow sought to convince me that the film had a factual error; he claimed that the PLO had changed their Charter and that it no longer called for the destruction of all of Israel. He could not bring proof for this, but still believed it based on 'media reports'. I showed him it was not true using facts and legal arguments; but to no avail - he simply did not want to believe it. Finally, he was able to 'win' the argument by showing me that Israel's Foreign Ministry website said that it had been changed; even though it was not! The Foreign Ministry of the State of Israel was also trying to convince us that Arafat and friends had changed their spots! But the PLO Charter was never legally changed.

14 This was the cause and the timing for when my filmmaking career began, first with a short to expose Arafat's double speak, called Another Way to Peace, and then with a feature length documentary called Relentless: The Struggle for Peace in the Middle East.

Wikipedia contributors. (2023, April 9). Relentless: The struggle for peace in the Middle East. Wikipedia. https://en.wikipedia.org/wiki/Relentless:_The_Struggle_for_Peace_in_the_Middle_East

15 Boyd, J. (2020, November 17). FBI: U.S. Jews by far most targeted group in Anti-Religious hate crimes. The Federalist. https://thefederalist.com/2020/11/17/fbi-u-s-jews-by-far-most-targeted-group-in-anti-religious-hate-crimes/

16 https://www.jta.org/2020/10/26/united-states/almost-all-american-jews-say-antisemitism-is-a-problem-according-to-a-new-poll-half-of-americans-dont-know-what-it-means (2020)

17 Jews again faced most hate crimes of any religious group in 2022, FBI reports | The Times of Israel. (2023, October 17). The Times of Israel. https://www.timesofisrael.com/jews-again-faced-most-hate-crimes-of-any-religious-group-in-2022-fbi-reports/

18 Breuer, B. E. (2024, February 20). Over 1,000 antisemitic incidents on college campuses since October 7. The Jerusalem Post | JPost.com. https://www.jpost.com/diaspora/antisemitism/article-787895

19 Adl, A. R. U. R. I. a. I. P. 7. |. (2024, January 4). ADL reports unprecedented rise in antisemitic incidents Post-Oct. 7 | ADL. ADL. https://www.adl.org/resources/press-release/adl-reports-unprecedented-rise-antisemitic-incidents-post-oct-7

20 UK Jewish group records all-time high in antisemitic incidents after October 7 | The Times of Israel. (2024, February 15). The Times of Israel. https://www.timesofisrael.com/uk-jewish-group-records-all-time-high-in-antisemitic-incidents-after-october-7/

21 "Poll: 96% of Jews in 13 EU Countries Say They Experience Antisemitism in Daily Life." The Times of Israel, https://www.timesofisrael.com/poll-96-of-jews-in-13-eu-countries-say-they-experience-antisemitism-in-daily-life/. Accessed 19 July 2024. In a survey of nearly 8,000 people who self-identified as Jews from 13 European countries, 96% of respondents say they encounter antisemitism in their daily lives. Some 37% of respondents say they were harassed and 4% say they were attacked in the previous year because they are Jewish. The survey is published today by the Fundamental Rights Agency of the European Union. Most respondents say they worry for their own (53%) and their family's (60%) safety and security. Three-quarters feel that people hold them responsible for the Israeli government's actions because they are Jewish, they say in the survey, which took place before the Hamas attacks on October but includes information on antisemitism collected from Jewish organizations in 2024. Just over half of respondents indicate they think that "criticizing Israel" is "probably antisemitic." A pattern of "always noting who is Jewish among [one's] acquaintances" is deemed as such by 64%, and not considering Jewish citizens as compatriots is indicated as "definitely antisemitic" by 91% of respondents. The countries surveyed are: Austria, Belgium, Czechia, Germany, Denmark, Spain, France, Hungary, Italy, the Netherlands, Poland, Romania and Sweden.

22 The ADL GLOBAL 100: An Index of Antisemitism. (n.d.). https://global100.adl.org/map/

23 2014 ADL survey found that 50 million people in Sub-Sahara Africa harbor anti-Jewish attitudes despite the presence of only 100,000 Jews in that area. The ADL GLOBAL 100: An Index of Antisemitism. (n.d.). https://global100.adl.org/map/subSaharan

24 Despite himself being born of two Jewish parents.

25 In Part II of Marx's "On the Jewish Question" which was his response to then-current debates over the 'Jewish question' about Jewish integration into European society and the granting to them of more legal rights.

26 Goebbels, J. (1935, September 13). Communism with the Mask Off. 1935 Congress of the Nazi Party.

27 Meixler, E. (2021, July 10). Malaysia's newly elected prime minister has a troubling history of hating Jews. Tablet Magazine. https://www.tabletmag.com/sections/news/articles/malaysias-newly-elected-prime-minister-has-a-troubling-history-of-hating-jews

28 Stuttaford, A. (2020, June 22). Corona conspiracies. National Review. https://www.nationalreview.com/2020/04/corona-conspiracies/

29 Gilder, George (2009). The Israel Test. Richard Vigilante Books. 241.

30 Of course not all critique of Israel crosses the line to antisemitism, as we will discuss and define in chapter 7.

31 Eric Hoffer's Defense of Israel - from LA Times 1968. (2011, June 21). The Jewish Chronicle. https://www.thejc.com/lets-talk/eric-hoffers-defense-of-israel-from-la-times-1968-sdwwsiw7

32 UN Human Rights Council: From its creation in June 2006 through June 2016, the UN Human Rights Council over one decade adopted 135 resolutions criticizing countries; 68 out of those 135 resolutions have been against Israel (more than 50%). UN Nations General Assembly: From 2012 through 2015, the United Nations General Assembly has adopted 97 resolutions criticizing countries; 83 out of those 97 have been against Israel (86%). Unwatch. (2024, January 2). The U.N. and Israel: Key Statistics from UN Watch. UN Watch. https://unwatch.org/un-israel-key-statistics/

The Security Council has not used the word "censure" since the Cold War era, and it has "censure[d]" an Entity only seven times in its history, yet Israel's actions have been the Subject of five of those seven resolutions. An Analysis of United Nations Security Council Resolutions: Are All Countries Treated Equally? Justin S. Gruenberg (2009) https://scholarlycommons.law.case.edu/

cgi/viewcontent.cgi?article=1268&context=jil Another word the Security
Council used for Israel far more commonly than other Entities during
the Cold War era is the word "deplore[d]." Israel was "deplore[d]" forty
times by the Security Council before 1990.265 The Entity "deplore[d]" the
second most regularly during this time period was South Africa, with eight
occurrences.266 In fact, Israel alone was "deplore[d]" more often than every
other Entity combined.

33 Simmons, D. (2009). Worlds Enough & Time: Five Tales of Speculative
Fiction. Harper Collin, pp. 131 https://investigationsandfantasies.
com/2014/08/06/the-once-and-future-jews-of-dan-simmons/

34 From Luther, Martin. "The Jews & Their Lies." (n.d.). Copyright 2024.
https://www.jewishvirtuallibrary.org/martin-luther-quot-the-jews-and-their-
lies-quot#google_vignette

35 Poll: 93% of Palestinians hold anti-Jewish beliefs | The Times of Israel.
(2014, May 14). The Times of Israel. https://www.timesofisrael.com/poll-93-of-
palestinians-hold-anti-jewish-beliefs/

36 The 'pay for slay' law and land laws are explained here: JNS.org. (n.d.). Pay
for Slay Archives - JNS.org. https://www.jns.org/topic/pay-for-slay/

 And Kuperwasser, B. Y. (2024, April 17). Incentivizing Terrorism: Palestinian
Authority Allocations to Terrorists and their Families. Jerusalem Center
for Public Affairs. https://jcpa.org/paying-salaries-terrorists-contradicts-
palestinian-vows-peaceful-intentions/

 and The Associated Press. (1997, May 6). Palestinians face death for selling
land to Jews. The New York Times. https://www.nytimes.com/1997/05/06/
world/palestinians-face-death-for-selling-land-to-jews.html

37 Wikipedia contributors. (2024, July 19). Expulsions and exoduses of Jews.
Wikipedia. https://en.wikipedia.org/wiki/Expulsions_and_exoduses_of_Jews

38 Rauschning, Hermann (2006). Hitler Speaks. Kessinger Publishing. 234.

39 Over a third of people in Hungary, Poland have 'extensive' antisemitic
beliefs - poll | The Times of Israel. (2023, May 31). The Times of Israel. https://

www.timesofisrael.com/over-a-third-of-people-in-hungary-poland-have-extensive-antisemitic-beliefs-poll/

40 The 10 most anti-Semitic countries | The Times of Israel. (2014, May 13). The Times of Israel. https://www.timesofisrael.com/the-10-most-anti-semitic-countries/

41 Midrash Eicha Rabbah 3:20

42 Wistrich, Robert S. (1991). Antisemitism: The Longest Hatred. Pantheon Books. xxiii-xxiv.

43 Nirenberg, David (2014). Anti-Judaism: The Western Tradition. W. W. Norton & Company.

44 Daria Horn published an article in *The Atlantic* on February 15, 2024 entitled 'Why the most educated people in the world fall for anti-semitic lies'.. A similar idea is found in the Torah; a grammatical subtlety in the Torah's words reflects the historical pattern that Jews will be identified as the 'evil force' by the society they are in. Rabbi Naftali Zvi Yehuda Berlin explains the verse in Deuteronomy 26:6, 'The Egyptians did evil to us...' to mean, "The Egyptians made the Jews into the evil ones..." in his HaEmek Davar commentary. A similar idea is found in the Torah; a grammatical subtlety in the Torah's words reflects the historical pattern that Jews will be identified as the 'evil force' by the society they are in. Rabbi Naftali Zvi Yehuda Berlin explains the verse in Deuteronomy 26:6, 'The Egyptians did evil to us...' to mean, "The Egyptians made the Jews into the evil ones..." in his HaEmek Davar commentary. You can find a copy of Daria's article here: https://jsis.washington.edu/news/some-additional-university-of-washington-community-resources/dara-horn/

45 The battle cry of giving Palestinians land 'from the river to the sea' is a call to genocide since those geographic markers include all of Israel.

46 Maharal, Gevuras Hashem, chapter 54, explains that Jew-hate is unique amongst xenophobias, because in some cases there can be no obvious external cause; others are hated perhaps because of crime, or taking jobs, or land. He mentioned Lavan (in Genesis), Pharaoh, and Haman who all tried to do genocide even though there was no external threat. So also with Hitler. As

Lucy Dawidowicz says in her The War Against the Jews (p xxiii) 1975 Bantam Books, "The final solution transcended the bounds of modern historical experience. Never before in modern history had one people made the killing of another the fulfillment of an ideology...(and not to achieve some kind of instrumental ends)."

47 I want to note that answers 1 and 3 have something in common: they both assert that the antisemites hate the Jews for a reason that relates to who they are. The scapegoat answer does not. I will ignore the second answer for now, because intuitively it makes no sense that people are hated for so long only because they are always unluckily at the wrong place and at the wrong time. It is important to note, however, that despite this answer being intuitively absurd, it has become conventional wisdom. The scapegoat theory should, however, be only a fallback position, i.e. if we cannot develop a real reason. Perhaps if we fail in answering our question, we will have no choice but to agree that antisemitism is not hatred of the Jew but simply a general hatred of the other. But I believe there is a clear answer.

48 newformofflight. (2024, March 25). Candace Owens vs Douglas Murray [Video]. YouTube. https://www.youtube.com/watch?v=biEI2rYZEg0

49 Prager, Dennis and Telushkin, Joseph (2003). Why the Jews: The Reason for Antisemitism. Touchstone. 56-64.

50 It is sad because I wish more people did this. I think it would be helpful in striving for a better world if we understood the other better, rather than projecting our own views onto them.

51 See my films Relentless, Obsession, Crossing the Line, etc. I was early to call out the ideology and threat of radical Islam, and to warn of the encroaching antisemitism on American campuses. www.raphaelshore.com

52 Gilbert, M. (2010). The Routledge Atlas of Jewish History (8th ed.). Routledge. https://doi.org/10.4324/9780203074459

Chapter 2

53 Hitler wrote this in his first written political document, in 1919, "Anti-

semitism based on purely emotional ground will always find its ultimate expression in the form of pogroms. A rational anti-semitism, however, must lead to the systematic legal fight against and the elimination of the prerogatives of the Jew…Its ultimate goal, however, must unalterably be the elimination of the Jews altogether." Jäckel, Eberhard. Hitler's World View: A Blueprint for Power, Harvard University Press, Cambridge, 1997, 48. See also "We have no intention of becoming emotional antisemites…instead our hearts are filled with a determination to attack the evil at its roots and to eradicate it root and branch." from a 1920 speech, ibid., p. 50.

54 Jäckel, Eberhard (1997). Hitler's World View: A Blueprint for Power. Harvard University Press. 48, 50.

55 Ibid. p.50.

56 Referring to his years in Vienna from 1907 to 1913, he said, "During that time a view of the world and a *Weltanschauung* grew within me which became the granite foundation of my present actions." Ibid. p.13.

57 Wistrich, Robert (1985). Hitler's Apocalypse - Jews and the Nazi Legacy. George Wiedenfeld and Nicolson Limited. 71-2.

58 Jäckel, Eberhard (1997). Hitler's World View: A Blueprint for Power. Harvard University Press. 57.

59 As mentioned in a note earlier, it is a matter of historical debate as to when Hitler decided upon the 'solution' of genocide. There is evidence to suggest that once Hitler saw the unwillingness of global countries to accept European Jewish refugees, once he understood - in Hannah Arendt's words - that the Jews were "undeportable", then genocide became the only other solution to accomplish his goal of eliminating the Jews from Europe.

60 Some military historians argue that this was not a terrible decision.

61 Wistrich, Robert (1985). Hitler's Apocalypse - Jews and the Nazi Legacy. George Wiedenfeld and Nicolson Limited. 167

62 Bullock, Alan (1971). Hitler: A Study in Tyranny. Penguin Books. 487.

63 Deutscher, Isaac (1968). The Non-Jewish Jew and Other Essays. Oxford University Press. 163.

64 The famous British playwright George Bernard Shaw also got it wrong. He had much respect for 'Herr Hitler", calling him "a very remarkable man, a very able man", Geduld, H. M. (January 1961). "Bernard Shaw and Adolf Hitler". The Shaw Review. 4 (1): 11–20., but he assumed incorrectly that Hitler's antisemitism was 'a craze, a complex, a bee in his bonnet, a hole in his armor, a hitch in his statesmanship...that has no logical connection with ... National Socialism..." Shaw, George Bernard (1936). The Millionairess. 23-27.

65 It is natural that we find the notion of an intelligent Hitler to be unsettling. I found this observation of Hitler's teen years by a friend named August Kubizek, to be interesting: "Books, books, always books! I just can't imagine Adolf without books. He had them piled up around him at home. He always had a book with him wherever he went." According to Kubizek, Hitler was registered with three libraries in Linz, Austria after the war, and spent much of his time in Vienna in the Hapsburgs' court library. "Books were his world." Hicks, S. (2016, November 6). How Smart and Well-read was Adolf Hitler? [Good Life series]. https://www.stephenhicks.org/2016/11/06/how-smart-and-well-read-was-adolf-hitler/

66 Given the cognitive dissonance at play, I have elected in the following pages to 'over-quote' from Hitler and other Nazis. It may not be the best writing style to employ, but I feel it is necessary to overcome the latent skepticism; I need to counter the feeling that I may have selected a few rare statements and pieced together 'Hitler's worldview'. On the contrary, I have selected very few from a rich treasure of possible quotations on each subject.

67 Wistrich, Robert (1985). Hitler's Apocalypse - Jews and the Nazi Legacy. George Wiedenfeld and Nicolson. 167-8; Laqueur, Walter and Rubin, Barry, eds. (1984), The Israel Arab Reader: A Documentary History of the Middle East COnflict. Penguin Books. 82. Date: November 28, 1941.

68 There were approximately 500,000 Jews in Germany in January, 1933 out of a total German population of 67 million: Wikipedia contributors. (2024, June 21). History of the Jews in Germany. Wikipedia. https://en.wikipedia.org/wiki/History_of_the_Jews_in_Germany

69 Jäckel, Eberhard (1997). Hitler's World View: A Blueprint for Power, Harvard University Press. 54.

70 Herbert Spencer in England, who coined the term 'survival of the fittest' after reading Darwin's Origin of the Species, and biologist Ernst Haeckel in Germany were amongst the leading proponents of this idea, which Haeckel called 'advanced Darwinism' — that the same law that applies in biology for the animal kingdom also applies in society, that the strong nations or races survive by eliminating the weak.

71 Hitler, Adolf (1971). *Mein Kampf.* Houghton Mifflin. 244-245.

72 Trevor-Roper, Hugh (2000). Hitler's Table Talk 1941-1944. Enigma. 38-9

73 Hitler, Adolf (1971). *Mein Kampf.* Houghton Mifflin. 135

74 Trevor-Roper, Hugh (2000). Hitler's Table Talk 1941-1944. Enigma. 28

75 Paraphrased by Rauschning from a conversation with Hitler in 1934, in Rauschning, Herman (1940). Hitler Speaks: A Series of Political Conversations with Adolf Hitler on his Real Aims. Eyre and Spottiswoode. 149.

76 Trevor-Roper, Hugh (2000). Hitler's Table Talk 1941-1944. Enigma. 141

77 Ibid. 142

78 The operation was halted at that point as a result due to of public pressure dissent, Leni Yahil, Leni (1990). The Holocaust: The Fate of European Jewry, 1932 - 1945. Oxford University Press. 307-11.

79 Trevor-Roper, Hugh (2000). Hitler's Table Talk 1941-1944. Enigma. 141.

80 Ibid. 314.

81 Ibid. 314.

82 "Mankind has grown great in eternal struggle, and only in eternal peace does it perish." Hitler, Adolf (1971). *Mein Kampf.* Houghton Mifflin. 135.

83 Hitler, Adolf (1971). *Mein Kampf.* Houghton Mifflin. 65.

84 The ancient world knew nothing of the attitudes of modem liberal democracies where stronger and weaker nations try to live happily side by side. Conquest and empire were the name of the game, and the only people not conquered by Rome were the ones they were unable to conquer.

85 Trevor-Roper, Hugh (2000). Hitler's Table Talk 1941-1944. Enigma. 314.

86 Hitler, Adolf (1971). *Mein Kampf.* Houghton Mifflin. 136.

87 Hitler bemoaned, "it was necessary for the Jew to appear on the scene and introduce that mad conception of a life that continues into an alleged Beyond." Trevor-Roper, Hugh (2000). Hitler's Table Talk 1941-1944. Enigma. 314.

88 Ibid. 44. Hitler also said, "Where a people's fight for existence is concerned, all these ideas (of humaitarianism) are of subordinate importance...The most cruel weapons are humane if they lead to a quicker victory." Jäckel, Eberhard (1997). Hitler's World View: A Blueprint for Power. Harvard University Press. 60.

89 Hitler, Adolf (1971). *Mein Kampf.* Houghton Mifflin. 65.

90 Ibid. 65.

91 Rauschning, Herman (1940). Hitler Speaks: A Series of Political Conversations with Adolf Hitler on his Real Aims. Eyre and Spottiswoode. 246-247.

92 Hitler said, "You will see how little time we shall need in order to upset the ideas and the criteria for the whole world, simply and purely by attacking Judaism." Rauschning, Herman (1940). Hitler Speaks: A Series of Political Conversations with Adolf Hitler on his Real Aims. Eyre and Spottiswoode. 233.

93 Hitler's speech in Berlin on Dec 12, 1941. Prange, Gordon W., ed. (1944). Hitler's Words: Two Decades of National Socialism, 1923-1943. American Council on Public Affairs. 97.

94 Rosenberg, Alfred (1930). The Myth of the Twentieth Century. Friends of Europe. 7-8. He also said. In Race and Race History (pp 105) that, "today it has become clear to every upright German that with the doctrine of love…a sensitive blow had been struck against the soul of Northern Europe." Rosenberg further claimed that the idea of God was the reason that the Jews had endured for so long. The Jews, Rosenberg charged, had placed God "at the center of all things" and "this has preserved and bred his thinking, his

race and his type... up to the present day." (*The Myth of the 20th Century*, 1930, pp. 30). But he also believed that God was no more than the expression of an idea that lay in the blood of the Jews and if enough Jewish blood was spilled, then God would also die He also said. In Race and Race History (pp 105) that, "today it has become clear to every upright German that with the doctrine of love…a sensitive blow had been struck against the soul of Northern Europe." Rosenberg further claimed that the idea of God was the reason that the Jews had endured for so long. The Jews, Rosenberg charged, had placed God "at the center of all things" and "this has preserved and bred his thinking, his race and his type... up to the present day." (*The Myth of the 20th Century*, 1930, pp. 30). But he also believed that God was no more than the expression of an idea that lay in the blood of the Jews and if enough Jewish blood was spilled, then God would also die.

95 Nazi Youth Song, in Grunberger, Richard (1995). The 12-Year Reich: A Social History of Nazi Germany, 1933-1945. 442, and Mazurczak, F. (2017, July 10). Dachau Golgotha. First Things. https://www.firstthings.com/web-exclusives/2017/07/dachau-golgotha

96 Trevor-Roper, Hugh (2000). Hitler's Table Talk 1941-1944. Enigma. 513.

97 Rosenberg echoed this historical perspective on the impact of the 'human concept', which "...in the course of Western history has appeared in the several forms of humaneness that have come over us like an insidious temptation. Sometimes this has called itself democracy, sometimes social compassion, sometimes humility and love." (Race History, pp.104)

98 Trevor-Roper, Hugh (2000). Hitler's Table Talk 1941-1944. Enigma. 7. Night of 11–12 July 1941

99 Ibid. 143-44.

100 Ibid. 343. December 1941.

101 Trevor-Roper, Hugh (2000). Hitler's Table Talk 1941-1944. Enigma. 7. 11–12 July 1941

102 Ibid. 51. 10 October 10, 1941. And "...(the Jew) takes them his 'Christianity'. Something which can unhinge the Roman Empire. All men are equal! Fraternity! Pacifism! No more dignity! And the Jew triumphed."

in Wistrich, Robert (1985). Hitler's Apocalypse - Jews and the Nazi Legacy. George Wiedenfeld and Nicolson Limited. 142-3. From Eckart, Dietrich (Munich) Der Bolschevismus von Moses bis Lenin – A Dialogue between Adolf Hitler and Me. 1924. 28.

103 Shirer, William L. (1960). The Rise and Fall of the Third Reich. Secker & Warburg. 240.

104 Trevor-Roper, Hugh (2000). Hitler's Table Talk 1941-1944. Enigma. 6. Date: July 11-12, 1941.

105 Ibid. 124

106 Ibid. 69

107 Ibid. 143. Date: December 13, 1941.

108 Trevor-Roper, Hugh (2000). Hitler's Table Talk 1941-1944. Enigma. 59. Date: October 14, 1941

109 Rauschning, Herman (1940). Hitler Speaks: A Series of Political Conversations with Adolf Hitler on his Real Aims. Eyre and Spottiswoode. 57. Also in Lange, Serg and Von Schenck, Ernst (1949). Memoirs of Alfred Rosenberg. Ziff-Davis. 88-89.

110 Trevor-Roper, Hugh (2000). Hitler's Table Talk 1941-1944. Enigma. 142-143. Date: December 13, 1941.

111 Ibid. 314. Also on October 21, 1941 Hitler shared, "Of old, it was in the name of Christianity. Today, it's in the name of Bolshevism. Yesterday, the instigator was Saul; the instigator today, Mordechai. Saul was changed into St. Paul and ordechai into Karl Marx. By exterminating this pest, we shall do humanity a service of which our soldiers can have no idea." 79.

112 Hitler, Adolf (1971). Mein Kampf. Houghton Mifflin. 65.

113 Prange, Gordon W., ed. (1944). Hitler's Words: Two Decades of National Socialism, 1923-1943. American Council on Public Affairs. 78.

114 Ibid. 252 Munich. May 23, 1926. And on January 27, 1932, Hitler warned Germans not to underestimate the threat, "In Germany the situation is represented as though it were merely the question of purely

abstract problems on the part of a few evil intentioned individuals. No! A *Weltanschauung* has conquered a state, and emanating from this state it will slowly shatter the entire world and bring about its collapse. Bolshevism, if unchecked, will change the world as completely as Christianity once did." Prange, Gordon W., ed. (1944). Hitler's Words : Two Decades of National Socialism, 1923-1943. American Council on Public Affairs. 253.

115 Wistrich, Robert S. (1985). Hitler's Apocalypse - Jews and the Nazi Legacy. George Wiedenfeld and Nicolson Limited. p114 - 115.

116 Forster, Jurgen (1989). The Wehrmacht and the War of Extermination against the Soviet Union.. K.G. Saur. 20 Date: September, 1941

117 Trevor-Roper, Hugh (2000). Hitler's Table Talk 1941-1944. Enigma. 5. Date: July 5, 1941

118 Breiting, Richard (1971). Secret Conversations with Hitler. John Day Company. 85. Confidential interviews of Adolf Hitler by Richard Breiting, editor of the German newspaper, the "Leipziger Neueste Nachrichten".

119 Dawidowicz, Lucy S. (1975). The War Against the Jews 1933-1945. Bantam Books. 31. From his speech at a NSDAP mtg.

120 Prange, Gordon W., ed. (1944). Hitler's Words: Two Decades of National Socialism, 1923-1943. American Council on Public Affairs. 83.

121 Spielvogel, Jackson J. (1992) Hitler and Nazi Germany: A History. Prentice Hall. 84. GHDI - document. (n.d.). https://ghdi.ghi-dc.org/sub_document.cfm?document_id=3909

As early as 1922, Hitler declared in a private conversation with Major Joseph Hell, that "The annihilation of the Jews will be my first and foremost task." Wistrich, Robert S. (1985). Hitler's Apocalypse - Jews and the Nazi Legacy. George Wiedenfeld and Nicolson Limited. 31-32.

122 Hitler, Adolf (1945) Full Text of "Political Testament of Adolf Hitler". Full text of "Political Testament of Adolf Hitler." (n.d.). https://archive.org/stream/PoliticalTestamentOfAdolfHitler/PTAH_djvu.txt

Hitler also said in his final message to the German nation, "Above all I charge the leaders of the nation and those under them to scrupulous observance of the laws of race and to merciless opposition to the universal poisoner of all peoples, International Jewry." Wistrich, Robert (1985). Hitler's Apocalypse - Jews and the Nazi Legacy. George Wiedenfeld and Nicolson Limited. 135.

123 October 4, 1943, in Remak, Yoachim, ed. (1990). The Nazi Years: A Documentary History. Simon and Schuster, and Waveland Press. 160.

124 Dawidowicz, Lucy S. (1975). The War Against the Jews 1933-1945. Bantam Books. xxiii.

125 Raymond Aron, "Existe-t-il un mystere Nazi?", in Commentaire, (1979). 349. In Friedlander, Saul (1982). From Antisemitism to Extermination: A Historiographical Study of Nazi Policies Towards the Jews and an Essay in Interpretation. Yad Vashem. p 3.

126 Friedlander, Saul (1982). From Antisemitism to Extermination: A Historiographical Study of Nazi Policies Towards the Jews and an Essay in Interpretation. Yad Vashem. p 12.

127 Lange, Serg and Von Schenck, Ernst (1949). Memoirs of Alfred Rosenberg. Ziff-Davis. 117-118.

128 Wistrich, Robert (1985). Hitler's Apocalypse - Jews and the Nazi Legacy. George Wiedenfeld and Nicolson Limited. 122. Similarly, the Nazi leader Heydrich, one of the main architects of the genocide, sai dthat Jews being deported to the East must not be allowed to go free, because those people, "...would form the germ-cell of a new Jewish development (History teaches that)." Wistrich, 124.

129 Full text of "Political Testament of Adolf Hitler." (n.d.). https://archive. org/stream/PoliticalTestamentOfAdolfHitler/PTAH_djvu.txt The Testament of Adolf Hitler (1945). N.P.C. 53-4.

130 Hitler, Adolf (1971). *Mein Kampf.* Houghton Mifflin. 306.

131 Prange, Gordon W., ed. (1944). Hitler's Words: Two Decades of National Socialism, 1923-1943. American Council on Public Affairs. 77-78. Date: April 20, 1923

132 Jäckel, Eberhard (1997). Hitler's World View: A Blueprint for Power. Harvard University Press. 52. Date: January 3, 1923 speech at Nuremberg.

133 Wistrich, Robert (1985). Hitler's Apocalypse - Jews and the Nazi Legacy. George Wiedenfeld and Nicolson Limited. 144. Date: 1924 From Eckart, Dietrich (Munich) Der Bolschevismus von Moses bis Lenin – A Dialogue between Adolf Hitler and Me. 1924. 46.

134 Rosenberg, Alfred (1930). Mythus III, from The Myth of the Twentieth Century. 10-11. Hitler said, similarly, that the Jews were a people, irrespective of their religious beliefs, "The Jewish race is first and foremost an abstract race of the mind. It has its origins, admittedly, in the Hebrew religion...however, it is in no sense of the word a purely religious entity, for it accepts on equal terms both the most determined atheists and the most sincere, practicing believers..." Hitler, Adolf (1945) Full text of "Political Testament of Adolf Hitler." (n.d.). https://archive.org/stream/PoliticalTestamentOfAdolfHitler/PTAH_djvu.txt . 56.

135 Rosenberg, Alfred (2007). Immorality in the Talmud. Preuss. 6. Date: 1919

136 Rosenberg, Alfred (1974) Race and Race History and Other Essays. Robert Pois, ed. Harper Torchbooks. 183.

137 In 1881, Karl Eugene Duehring, wrote in The Question of the Jew is a Question of Race, "The Jewish question would still exist even if every Jew were to turn his back on his religion and join one of our major churches... It is precisely the baptized Jew who infiltrates furthermost, unhindered in all sectors of society and political life. I return, therefore, to the hypothesis that the Jews are to be defined solely on the basis of race and not on the basis of religion."

138 Trevor-Roper, Hugh (2000). Hitler's Table Talk 1941-1944. Enigma. 314.

139 Hitler, Adolf (1971). *Mein Kampf.* Houghton Mifflin. 300.

140 Ibid. 64.

Chapter 3

141 He was right about Jewish influence, but he was dead wrong about what

he did with that information. He was evil, as I am explaining throughout the book.

142 Nietzsche, Friedrich (2007). Ecce Homo, trans. Antony M. Ludovici. Ware, UK : Wordsworth. 258-259. In a similar vein, Hitler said in 1942 that, "The discovery of the Jewish virus is one of the greatest revolutions that have taken place in the world." in Trevor-Roper, Hugh (2000). Hitler's Table Talk 1941-1944. Enigma. 332.

143 Nietzsche, Friedrich (1973). Beyond Good and Evil. Penguin. , Aph. 195 and 118. Also see Nietzsche's, Friedrich (2013). On the Genealogy of Morals. First Essay

144 Nietzsche, Friedrich (2013). On the Genealogy of Morals. Trans. Michael A. Scarpitti. Penguin Group. 14. (Genealogy, sec 9)

145 Nietzsche, Friedrich (1973). Beyond Good and Evil. Penguin. 125. On the Bible's impact on Western political and democratic life, see Eric Nelsons' book, The Hebrew Republic: Jewish Sources and the Transformation of European Political Thought. Harvard University Press 2011.

Hitler likewise said at a speech on September 29, 1922 in Munich, "Democracy equals capitalism equals the Jew." Prange, Gordon W., ed. (1944). Hitler's Words: Two Decades of National Socialism, 1923-1943. American Council on Public Affairs. 76. And in a speech in 1922, "... (democracy is) fundamentally not German; it is Jewish." Wistrich, Robert (1985). Hitler's Apocalypse - Jews and the Nazi Legacy. George Wiedenfeld and Nicolson Limited. 40.

146 Wistrich, Robert S. (2010). A Lethal Obsession - Anti-Semitism from Antiquity to the Global Jihad. Random House. 108. In the introduction to Robert S. Wistrich's book Antisemitism: The Longest Hatred, he discusses why this label is problematic.

147 Mendes-Flohr, Paul and Reinharz, Jehuda (1995). The Jew in the Modern World. Oxford University Press. 331-2

148 Mendes-Flohr, Paul and Reinharz, Jehuda (1995). The Jew in the Modern World. Oxford University Press. 332

149 Hitler said the same when he referred to the The Protocols of the Elders of Zion. The Protocols was a very popular but forged book that claimed to be written by a small cabal of Jews who met in a secret room to plot world domination. Hitler said he did not really care if the book was a forgery or not, because, "It is completely indifferent from what Jewish brain these disclosures originate; the important thing is that with positively terrifying certainty they reveal the nature and activity of the Jewish people and expose their inner contexts as well as their ultimate final aims." He also asked, "A question arises. Does the Jew act consciously and by calculation, or is he driven on by his instinct? I cannot answer that question." in Trevor-Roper, Hugh (2000). Hitler's Table Talk 1941-1944. Enigma. 315.

150 Nietzsche: "It was the Jews who, rejecting the aristocratic value equation (good = noble = powerful = beautiful = happy = blessed) ventured, with awe-inspiring consistency, to bring about a reversal and held it in the teeth of the most unfathomable hatred (the hatred of the powerless), saying: 'Only those who suffer are good, only the poor, the powerless, the lowly are good; the suffering, the deprived, the sick, the ugly, are the only pious people, the only ones saved, salvation is for them alone, whereas you rich, the noble and powerful, you are eternally wicked, cruel, lustful, insatiate, godless, you will also be eternally wretched, cursed and damned!' . . . the slaves' revolt in morality begins with the Jews: a revolt which has two thousand years of history behind it and which has only been lost sight of because — it was victorious . . ."

To Nietsche, as Hitler also believed, this was a deliberate strategy of sabotage, "Nothing that has been done on earth against 'the noble', 'the mighty', 'the masters' and 'the rulers', is worth mentioning compared with what the Jews have done against them: the Jews, that priestly people, which in the last resort was able to gain satisfaction from its enemies and conquerors only through a radical revaluation of their values, that is, through an act of the most deliberate (spiritual) revenge." Nietzsche, Friedrich (2018). The Genealogy of Morals, Horace B. Samuel And John McFarland Kennedy (Translators). CreateSpace. Fraser, G. (2008, November 6). On the Genealogy of Morals part 2: The slave morality. The Guardian. https://www.theguardian.com/commentisfree/belief/2008/nov/03/nietzsche-slave-morality-religion

151 Haque, O. S., De Freitas, J., Viani, I., Niederschulte, B., & Bursztajn, H. J. (2012). Why did so many German doctors join the Nazi Party early? International Journal of Law and Psychiatry, 35(5–6), 473–479. https://doi.org/10.1016/j.ijlp.2012.09.022

152 Trachtenberg, Joshua (1943). The Devil and the Jews - The Medieval Conception of the Jew and its Relation to Modern Antisemitism. Meridian Books. 99.

153 Wikipedia contributors. (2024, July 14). March 1933 German federal election. Wikipedia. https://en.wikipedia.org/wiki/March_1933_German_federal_election

154 Gilder, George (2009). The Israel Test. Richard Vigilante Books. 37-8. Gilder was acknowledging that Prager and Telushkin have a very compelling argument in explaining the deeper source of antisemitism, but argued that they ignored this critical consideration. See Prager, Dennis and Telushkin, Joseph (2003). Why the Jews: The Reason for Antisemitism. Touchstone.

155 ArchiveAuthor. (1960, December 28). Soviet Union has 30,663 Jewish scientists, handbook on Russia shows. Jewish Telegraphic Agency. https://www.jta.org/archive/soviet-union-has-30663-jewish-scientists-handbook-on-russia-shows

 And the number of Jewish scientists continued to increase even as the Jewish population declined due to antisemitism, intermarriage, and immigration. YIVO | Population and Migration: Population since World War I. (n.d.). YIVO Encyclopedia. https://yivoencyclopedia.org/article.aspx/Population_and_Migration/Population_since_World_War_I

And Burg, S. L. (1979). Russians, natives and Jews in the Soviet scientific elite [Cadre competition in Central Asia]. Cahiers Du Monde Russe Et Soviétique, 20(1), 43–59. https://doi.org/10.3406/cmr.1979.1347

156 ArchiveAuthor. (1950, August 7). Enrollment of Jews in U.S. medical schools dropped 50 percent in last 20 years. Jewish Telegraphic Agency. https://www.jta.org/archive/enrollment-of-jews-in-u-s-medical-schools-dropped-50-percent-in-last-20-years

157 Rosen, A. (2023, June 29). Ivy League exodus. Tablet Magazine. https://www.tabletmag.com/sections/arts-letters/articles/ivy-league-exodus

158 Jews or people of Jewish descent have made up 44% of the undisputed world chess champions. Jinfo, & Jinfo. (n.d.). Jewish World Chess Champions. https://www.jinfo.org/Chess_Champions.html

159 Weekends were not known to the ancient world. Judaism introduced the idea of a day off from work each week. The Bible introduced the world to the weekend through the idea of the Sabbath. See my short video on the topic Big Jewish Ideas. (2024, June 27). Shabbat: the ancient Jewish secret to mindfulness | explained [Video]. YouTube. https://www.youtube.com/watch?v=x00gN6OXDGE

160 Veblen, Thorstein (1919). The Intellectual Pre-Eminence of Jews in Modern Europe. In the Political Science Quarterly, Vol. 34, No. 1 (Mar., 1919). Oxford University Press. 39.

161 Karpen, Elizabeth. "The Real Story Behind 'Oppenheimer'" Unpacked, July 17, 2023. https://jewishunpacked.com/the-real-story-behind-oppenheimer/.

162 The 100 Most Eminent Psychologists of the 20th Century Review of General Psychology (2002) by the Educational Publishing Foundation 2002, Vol. 6, No. 2, 139–152 http://creativity.ipras.ru/texts/top100.pdf

163 In Hollywood, Samuel Goldwyn, a former glove salesman, the Warner brothers, the sons of a shoemaker, William Fox, a former newsboy, and Louis B. Mayer, the son of a junk dealer who grew up collecting scrap metal on the street, built not only their eponymous studios, but an entire industry. See Gabler, Neil (1989). An Empire of Their own: How the Jews Invented Hollywood. Anchor Books. Jewish fashion designers like Calvin Klein, Ralph Lauren, Diane Von Furstenberg, Michael Kors, and Donna Karan turned their newly adopted pseudonyms into initials marking the clothes of the world. A trip through a modern mall takes us past equally pioneering ice cream brands Häagen-Dazs and Baskin Robbins, Starbucks cafes and Dunkin Donuts, all of whom have Jewish founders or co-founders.

Movie theaters and streaming services are filled with comic book heroes

like Superman, created by Jerry Siegel and Joe Shuster, Batman created by
Bob Kane (Kahn) and Bill (Milton) Finger, and the Fantastic Four, the Hulk,
Captain America, Ant-Man, Thor, Iron Man and Black Panther created by
Stan Lee (Stanley Lieber) and Jack Kirby (Jacob Kurtzberg). And with Steve
Ditko, Lee co-created Doctor Strange and Spiderman.

164 Jews can be prominently found at all levels of politics, running for office,
leading causes, and grappling over the future of countries. The world of
political ideas would be equally unimaginable without Karl Marx and Ayn
Rand, Ludwig von Mises and Saul Alinsky.

165 Phillip Mendes, '"We are all German Jews": Exploring the Prominence of
Jews in the New Left', Melilah 2009/3. https://www.degruyter.com/document/
doi/10.31826/mjj-2011-060104/pdf , and A brief history of Jews and the
civil rights movement of the 1960s. (2014, April 7). Religious Action Center
of Reform Judaism. https://rac.org/issues/civil-rights-voting-rights/brief-
history-jews-and-civil-rights-movement-1960s

166 In fact, a survey (that I have seen referenced but not sourced) by the
American Council of Education in 1966–7 stated that "the best single
predictor of campus (civil rights) protest was the presence of a substantial
number of students from Jewish backgrounds."

167 Actually, Jews represented half that number, but it was 1899, and much of
the world had yet to be counted.

168 Twain, Mark (1963). "Concerning the Jews". Harper's Magazine (1899) in
The Complete Essays of Mark Twain. Doubleday. 249.

169 See Nelson, Eric (2011). The Hebrew Republic: Jewish Sources and the
Transformation of European Political Thought. Harvard University Press.

170 Johnson, Paul (1987). A History of the Jews. Harper & Row. 585.

171 Cahill, Thomas (1999). The Gifts of the Jews: How a Tribe of Desert
Nomads Changed the Way Everyone Thinks and Feels. Nan A. Talese/Anchor
Books. 5.

172 See also Spiro, Ken (2002). WorldPerfect-The Jewish Impact on
Civilization. Simcha Press. And (2022, August 30). Jewish ideas that

transformed the world. Aish.com. https://aish.com/jewish-ideas-that-transformed-the-world/?src=ac-rdm

173 He did not so much discover as rediscover what had been known and almost completely forgotten - and then he successfully brought this knowledge to masses. See Klinghoffer, David (2003). The Discovery of God: Abraham and the Birth of Monotheism. Doubleday. Also see Universal Jewish History where Biberfeld explains that humanity had a clear tradition of a comprehensive heritage of beliefs, principles, and laws, but they had been forgotten for the most part. Abraham was not the founder of a new belief, but rather he revived them for mankind when the principles were in danger of being forgotten. Biberfeld, Philip (1962). Universal Jewish History. Volume II, The Patriarchal Age. Feldheim. 177-197.

174 Sacks, Rabbi Jonathan (2001). Radical Then, Radical Now: On Being Jewish. HarperCollins. 55.

175 Ihaza, J. (2023, December 26). How did Kanye get here? A short history of provocation and extreme rhetoric. Rolling Stone. https://www.rollingstone.com/music/music-news/kanye-west-antisemitism-hate-speech-controversy-1234611647/

and BBC News. (2022, November 4). Kyrie Irving suspended over anti-Semitic posts. https://www.bbc.com/news/world-us-canada-63509715

176 Zaig, B. G. (2022, October 17). Kanye says 'Jewish Zionists' control the media, Jews own the Black voice. The Jerusalem Post | JPost.com. https://www.jpost.com/diaspora/antisemitism/article-719843

177 See map of the Protocols by Martin Gilbert on page?

178 PROTOCOLS of the Learned Elders of ZION, translated from the Russian by Victor E. Marsden. The Mercian Free Press. (2014). https://ia803409.us.archive.org/6/items/books_202012/The%20Protocols%20of%20the%20Learned%20Elders%20of%20Zion%20(%20PDFDrive%20).pdf

179 See The American Axis: Henry Ford, Charles Lindbergh, and the Rise of the Third Reich (2003) by Max Wallace.

180 Sachar, Howard Morley (1993). A History of the Jews in America. Vintage. 311.

181 Wilensky, D. A. (2022, March 17). In wild overestimate, Americans think 30% of the country is Jewish. J. https://jweekly.com/2022/03/17/in-wild-overestimate-americans-think-30-of-the-country-is-jewish/

182 The ADL GLOBAL 100: An Index of Antisemitism. (n.d.). https://global100.adl.org/map/subSaharan

183 The ADL GLOBAL 100: An Index of Antisemitism. (n.d.). https://global100.adl.org/map/subSaharan

184 In September 2022, a peer-reviewed study from the Institute for the Study of Contemporary Antisemitism (ISCA) revealed that antisemitism has been on the rise, and that between 2019 and 2020, an antisemitic tweet was published every 20 seconds. Shannon, M. (2022, December 14). "Jews are News" on Twitter – why? - AIJAC. AIJAC. https://aijac.org.au/australia-israel-review/jews-are-news-on-twitter-why/

185 See Twain, M. (2021, July 10). Mark Twain's "Concerning the Jews." Tablet Magazine. https://www.tabletmag.com/sections/arts-letters/articles/concerning-the-jews

186 See Gilder's 5-minute video explanation: PragerU. (2014, June 30). Do you pass the Israel Test? | 5 minute video [Video]. YouTube. https://www.youtube.com/watch?v=yfN2IvnIA4M

187 Gilder, George (2009). The Israel Test. Richard Vigilante Books. 247.

188 Ibid. 253.

189 Ibid. 251.

190 Ibid. 246.

191 Ibid. 254.

192 Ibid. 254.

193 Adams, President John, From a Letter to Dutch jurist F.A. Van der Kemp (1808) Pennsylvania Historical Society

194 Cahill, Thomas (1999). The Gifts of the Jews: How a Tribe of Desert Nomads Changed the Way Everyone Thinks and Feels. Nan A. Talese/Anchor Books. 3.

195 Gilbert, M. (2010). The Routledge Atlas of Jewish History (8th ed.). Routledge. https://doi.org/10.4324/9780203074459

Chapter 4

196 Hitler: "One may be repelled by this law of nature which demands that all living things should mutually devour one another...That's why I have the feeling that it's useful to know the laws of nature – for that enables us to obey them. To act otherwise would be to rise in revolt against heaven. If I can accept a divine commandment, it's this one: 'Thou shalt preserve the species'". Trevor-Roper, Hugh (2000). Hitler's Table Talk 1941-1944. Enigma. 140-1.

197 He did not so much discover as rediscover what had been known and forgotten - and he taught it to masses.

198 At Mount Sinai, the Torah recounts that the Jews were given the 10 Commandments, the Written Torah and the Oral tradition (that explains the Written Torah).

199 Jacobson, Simon (2002). Toward a Meaningful Life: The Wisdom of the Rebbe Menachem Mendel Schneerson. Harper Collins. 208.

200 Dawidowicz, Lucy (1976). A Holocaust Reader. Behrman House, 1976. 32. From Hitler's Memorandum on the Four-Year Plan.

201 Rabbi Shimshon Raphael Hirsch on Chumash, Genesis, Toldot.

202 The Free City of Danzig was a city-state under the protection and oversight of the League of Nations between 1920 and 1939, consisting of the Baltic Sea port of Danzig (now Gdańsk, Poland) and nearly 200 other small localities in the surrounding areas. Wikipedia contributors. (2024, July 20). Free city of Danzig. Wikipedia. https://en.wikipedia.org/wiki/Free_City_of_Danzig

203 Rauschning, Hermann (1941). The Beast From The Abyss. William Heinemann. 64.

204 Dostoevsky, Fyodor (2024). *The Brothers Karamazov* (Bicentennial Edition). Amazon.com Services. 404.

205 Ibid. 406.

206 Ibid. 408-9.

207 Dostoevsky was prophetic when he predicted that the rebellion against Judeo-Chrisitan ethics would end in violence and war: "What [does it] matter that he (humanity) now rebels everywhere against our (Christian ethics and) power? ...They will tear down the temples and drench the earth with blood." Ibid. 409. He also predicted that this rebellion would result in a lowering of moral standards in society, "Do you know that centuries will pass, and mankind will proclaim with the mouth of its wisdom and science that there is no crime, and therefore no sin..." 403.

208 Pois, Robert A. (1986). National Socialism and the Religion of Nature. Palgrave Macmillan. 57-58

209 Dostoevsky, Fyodor (2024). *The Brothers Karamazov* (Bicentennial Edition). Amazon.com Services. 406.

210 Sartre, Jean-Paul. Anti-Semite and the Jew. 53-54. He also wrote, "We must remember that a man is not necessarily humble or even modest because he has consented to mediocrity. On the contrary, there is a passionate pride among the mediocre, and antisemitism is an attempt to give value to mediocrity as such, to create an elite of the ordinary."

211 Rauschning,Hermann (1941). The Beast From The Abyss. William Heinemann. 155-156.

212 Herberg, Will (1951). Judaism and Modern Man. Farrar, Straus and Young. 273.

213 He expands on this idea, "The deeper motives of anti-Semitism have their roots in times long past; they come from the unconscious...One might say they are all 'badly christened'; under the thin veneer of Christianity, they have remained what their ancestors were, barbarically polytheistic. They have not yet overcome their grudge against the new religion which was forced upon them, and they have projected it on to the source from

which Christianity came to them…" Freud, Sigmund (1967). *Moses and Monotheism*. Vintage Books. 116-7. In a similar vein, the writer Maurice Samuel said that "They (the Christians antisemites) must spit on the Jews as 'the Christ-killers' because they long to spit on the Jews as 'the Christ-givers." Samuel, Maurice (1940). The Great Hatred. Alfred A. Knopf. 128.

214 For a full analysis of the profound Jew-hatred that is embedded in radical Islam, and its roots in and relationship with Nazism, see Kuntzel, Matthias (2007). Jihad and Jew-Hatred: Islamism, Nazism and the Roots of 9/11. Telos Press. German political scientist and historian Kuntzel argues that during and after World War II, the center for global antisemitism shifted from Nazi Germany to the Arab world.

215 Psalm 2, v 1-3

216 Talmud Shabbat 89A

217 Rauschning, Herman (1940). Hitler Speaks: A Series of Political Conversations with Adolf Hitler on his Real Aims. Eyre and Spottiswoode. 220.

218 Hitler said, "By exterminating the pest, we shall do humanity a service of which our soldiers can have no idea." Trevor-Roper, Hugh (2000). Hitler's Table Talk 1941-1944. Enigma. 79. Date: October 21, 1941. And Julius Streicher said after the enactment of the radical racist Nuremberg Laws in 1935, when many Germans thought the Jewish problem would then be solved, "Those who were, and perhaps still are, of that opinion are only soldiers who followed their leaders without knowing the ultimate goals of a wide ranging plan of war." Bytwerk, Randall L (1983). Julius Streicher. 156.

219 Song in the SS Document, "The Historical Development of the Essence of the German Reich", in Pois, Robert A. (1986). National Socialism and the Religion of Nature. Palgrave Macmillan. 46.

220 Dostoevsky, Fyodor (2024). *The Brothers Karamazov* (Bicentennial Edition). Amazon.com Services. 410.

221 The French philosopher and Christian thinker Jacques Maritain said in 1939, "Like an alien body, like an activating ferment injected into the mass, it (the Jewish People) gives the world no peace, it bars slumber, it teaches the

world to be discontented and restless as long as the world has not God, it stimulates the movement of history." And he concluded, "It is the vocation of Israel that the world execrates." Maritain, Jacques (1939). A Christian Looks at the Jewish Question. Longmans, Green and Company. 29, 30. Also see this review of his book in the journal The Catholic Worker, November 1939, https://catholicworker.org/349-html/

222 Leviticus 25:10

223 Isaiah 2:4. It is worth noting that the UN often does not live up to their ideals, as is observed in the fierce anti-Israel bias at the UN. We can say that in the UN itself we can see the challenge of Sinai and the struggle of man to live up to its higher values.

224 We hold these truths to be self-evident, that all men are created equal, that they are endowed by their Creator with certain unalienable Rights, that among these are Life, Liberty and the pursuit of Happiness. Preamble to the Declaration of Independence.

225 Steiner, George (1981). The Portage to San Cristobal of A.H. Simon and Schuster. 165. The narrative of Hitler's personal defense is fascinating: "There had to be a solution, a final solution...Was there ever a crueler invention, a contrivance more calculated to harrow human existence, than that of an omnipotent, all-seeing, yet invisible, impalpable, inconceivable God? Gentleman, I pray you, consider the case, consider it closely...

But because we are His creature, we must be better than ourselves, love our neighbor...give of what we have to the beggar...We must bottle up our rages and desires, chastise the flesh and walk bent in the rain. You call me a tyrant, an enslaver. What tyranny, what enslavement has been more oppressive, has branded the skin and soul of man more deeply than the sick fantasies of the Jew? You are not God-killers, but God-makers. And that is infinitely worse. The Jew invented conscience and left man a guilty serf...

What can be crueler than the Jew's addiction to the ideal? ...the unattainable but all-demanding God of Sinai...

It was only a small step, gentlemen, a small, inevitable step, from Sinai to Nazareth, from Nazareth to the covenant of Marxism...Three times the

Jew has pressed on us the blackmail of transcendence. Three times he has infected our blood and brains with the bacillus of perfection. Go to your rest and the voice of the Jew cries out in the night: 'Wake Up!' God's eye is upon you.

(But) Men had grown sick of it, sick to death. When I turned on the Jew, no one came to his rescue. No one. France, England, Russia, even Jew-ridden America did nothing. They were glad that the exterminator had come. Oh they did not say so openly. I allow you that. But secretly they rejoiced." 164-7.

226 Numbers 31:3, Rashi

227 Genesis 12:3

228 Gilder, George (2009). The Israel Test. Richard Vigilante Books. 3.

229 Genesis Rabbah 38:11 and Midrash Book of Straightness, Genesis, Noah

230 Palestinians: Yes to Jews, no to settlers in our state | The Times of Israel. (2014, January 27). The Times of Israel. https://www.timesofisrael.com/palestinians-yes-to-jews-no-to-settlers-in-our-state/

231 Rauschning, Herman (2003). The Voice of Destruction. Pelican. 80.

232 Erikson, Erik (1950). Childhood and Society. W.W. Norton and Company Inc. 299.

233 Genesis Rabbah 42:8

234 See Bilaam's blessing in Numbers 23:9, "The nation shall dwell alone and not be considered amongst the nations."

235 Sacks, Rabbi Jonathan. (Covenant and Conversation, 5782 on Genesis and Breishis on 'The Art of Listening'. Sacks, R. L. J. (2023, September 6). The Art of Listening | Bereishit | Covenant & Conversation | The Rabbi Sacks Legacy. The Rabbi Sacks Legacy. https://rabbisacks.org/covenant-conversation/bereishit/the-art-of-listening/

236 Montreal Jewish Forums - December 15th, 1963 - leonardcohenforum.com. (2017, July 17). https://www.leonardcohenforum.com/viewtopic.php?t=37527

237 Chief Nazi ideologist Alfred Rosenberg said, "The so-called 'Old Testament' must once and for all be abolished as a book of religious instruction." Rosenberg, Alfred (1930). The Myth of the Twentieth Century. Friends of Europe. 17.

238 Rosenstock-Huessy, E. ed. (1971). Judaism Despite Christianity - The 'Letters on Christianity and Judaism' between Eugene Rosenstock-Huessy and Franz Rosenzweig. 57, 112. He added, "For you (Jew-hater) may curse, you may swear, you may scratch yourself as much as you like, you won't get rid of us…We are the internal foe…we and you are within the same frontier, in the same kingdom." 130.

239 Talmud Avodah Zarah 2b

240 Midrash Sifri, Deuteronomy 343.

241 Dostoevsky, Fyodor (2024). *The Brothers Karamazov* (Bicentennial Edition). Amazon.com Services. 409

242 As historian David Patterson says in his analysis of the origins of Jew-hatred, "What does Stokey Carmichael have in common with Democritus? Or Henry Ford with Karl Marx? Or Immanuel Kant with John Chrysostom? Do they all need the Jews in order to have a scapegoat for society's misfortunes?" Patterson, David (2015). Anti-Semitism and Its Metaphysical Origins. Cambridge University Press. 4.

243 If it was, why did hate increase in Germany and France when we became assimilated, more 'like' Germans and French?

244 As the novelist Howard Jacobson has his character Emmy say to the 'ashamed Jew' Libor, "Can no wickedness now be done to any Jew living anywhere that doesn't have Gaza as its reasoning? That isn't tracing an effect back to its cause, Libor, that is applauding the effect." Jacobson, Howard (2010). The Finkler Question. Bloomsbury. 155.

And see chapter 7 for a full explanation of how much of the world's reaction after the October 7, 2023 massacre explains this.

245 Rauschning said, "Everything connected with anti-Semitism is paradoxical. This is so because it is not merely a phenomena of political

and social life of a particular historical situation, but it has its root in the transcendental. The very stamps on the Jews' passes in Germany are an expression of the metaphysical situation of the persecution of Israel as God's chosen people." Rauschning, Hermann (1941). The Beast From The Abyss. William Heinemann. 158.

246 The Jews become the worst violators of each day's highest mores, be they race, religion, or, today, human rights - see Rabbi Sacks in chapter 9.

247 Isaiah 43:10 "You are My witnesses…" David Patterson says, "Anti-Semitism has metaphysical origins that transcend its ontological manifestations. Because it arises from the depths…of the human soul." Patterson, David (2015). Anti-Semitism and Its Metaphysical Origins. Cambridge University Press. 5.

248   Maharal, Tiferes Yisrael ch 47, p 145.

249 Gilbert, M. (2010). The Routledge Atlas of Jewish History (8th ed.). Routledge. https://doi.org/10.4324/9780203074459

Chapter 5

250 Streicher, Nuremberg proceedings, Nuremberg Trial Proceedings Vol. 5, Thirty First Day, Thursday, 10 January 1946, Morning Session

251 Nazi Conspiracy and Aggression, Supplement B, Office of United States Chief of Counsel for Prosecution of Axis Criminality, United States Government Printing Office, Washington, 1948, pp. 1434. In 1928, Hitler's antisemitic mentor Dietrich Eckart wrote, "...the Jews have survived the greatest and most glorious nations, and will continue to survive until the end of all time, until the hour of salvation strikes for all making. The Jewish nation will not perish before this hour strikes." Eckart, Dietrich (1928) in Mosse, Mazi Culture. 75.

252 Griffin, A. (2017, February 1). Hitler accuses Roosevelt, Jews in speech at Berlin Conference. World War 2.0. https://blogs.shu.edu/ww2-0/1942/01/31/hitler-accuses-roosevelt-jews-in-speech-at-berlin-conference/

253 Linder. (n.d.). The trials of the Nuremberg Trials. http://law2.umkc.edu/
faculty/projects/ftrials/nuremberg/NurembergNews10_16_46.html
and Newsweek magazine, October 28, 1946., p 45.

254 Book of Esther, 9:14

255 KIDDUSH HASHEM Jewish Religious and Cultural Life in Poland
During the Holocaust. By Shimon Huberband. Translated by David E.
Fishman. Edited by Jeffrey S. Gurock and Robert S. Hirt. KTAV Publishing
House/ Yeshiva University Press. Cited in: Wiesel, Elie. "Praising His Name
in the Fire." New York Times, January 17, 1988, sec. 7.

256 There is an amazing Torah connection between the hanging of 10
Nazis at Nuremberg and the 10 sons of Haman. See Purimfest 1946: The
Nuremberg Trials and the Ten Sons of Haman - TheTorah.com. (n.d.).
https://www.thetorah.com/article/purimfest-1946-the-nuremberg-trials-
and-the-ten-sons-of-haman and Rosenberg, R. B. (2015, March 4). Did
Purim heroine Esther prophesy about the Nazis? Courier News. https://
www.mycentraljersey.com/story/life/faith/2015/03/04/purim-heroine-esther-
prophesy-nazis/24273719/

257 Book of Esther, 3:8

258 Book of Esther 5:13

259 Malbim on Genesis 15.5, Midrash, Rashi

260 Tablet Magazine, February 20, 2015 Geselowitz, G. (2021, July 10).
Alexander Hamilton's Jewish connection. Tablet Magazine. https://www.
tabletmag.com/sections/news/articles/alexander-hamiltons-jewish-
connection

261 Hitler, Adolf (1971). *Mein Kampf.* Houghton Mifflin. 64.

262 Hitler said: "What are the aims of the Jews? They aim to expand their
invisible state as a supreme tyranny over the world...Economically he
dominates the peoples, politically and morally he subjugates them. Politically
he accomplishes his aims through the propagation of the principals of
democracy and the doctrine of Marxism....From the ethical point of view the
Jew destroys the peoples in respect to religious and moral considerations.

Anyone who is willing to see that, can see it; and no one can help the person who refuses to see it. The Jew, voluntarily or involuntarily, consciously or unconsciously, undermines the foundation..." Prange, Gordon W., ed. (1944). Hitler's Words: Two Decades of National Socialism, 1923-1943. American Council on Public Affairs. 78.

263 Twain, Mark (1963). "Concerning the Jews". Harper's Magazine in The Complete Essays of Mark Twain. Doubleday. p 249.

264 Dawidowicz, Lucy S. (1975). The War Against the Jews 1933-1945. Bantam Books. 31.

265 Granted, many of the allied nations were not fighting just about ideology - they were trying to survive - nevertheless, they all held core values that opposed the Nazi worldview. Sadly, there are many today, from far right neo-Nazis to far left antifa radicals who still adhere to these values, but overall, it was a victory of good over evil on the long journey of progress.

266 Tolstoy, Leo Nikolayevich (1908) in "Jewish World" periodical.

267 Even Nietzsche, who hated Jewish morality, declared, "The Jews, however, are beyond any doubt the strongest, toughest, and purest race now living in Europe; they know how to prevail even under the worst conditions (in fact better than under favorable ones), by means of virtues of some sort, which one would like nowadays to label as vices – owing above all to a resolute faith which does not need to be ashamed before "modern ideas"" Nietzsche, Friedrich (2017). Beyond Good and Evil. Amazon Classics, Kindle. 169-70.

268 Psalm 20:8

269 Zecharia 4:6

270 See Horn, Dara (2021). People Love Dead Jews: Reports from a Haunted Present. W.W. Norton.

Chapter 6

271 Rabbi Samson Raphael Hirsch says: "For whilst 'theology' contains the thoughts of man on God and things Divine, the Torah contains the thoughts

of God on man and things human." Hirsch, Rabbi Samson Raphael (1984). The Collected Writings of Rabbi Samson Raphael Hirsch. Feldheim. Volume 1, p 189.

272 If you are curious about whether these ideas are God-given, see this book's postscript.

273 Maimonides, Mishneh Torah, Avoda Zara, 1.3

274 A large city in what would be today's Iraq.

275 Genesis Rabbah chapter 38

276 Yoma 28B based on Genesis 26:5

277 See Rabbi Abraham Grodzinski, Toras Abraham, p 9, 73

278 Genesis 12:1

279 Rashi on Genesis 12:1

280 Genesis 12:2-3

281 As souls, man has the potential to go beyond the solar system: Psalm 8: "When I behold Your heavens, the work of Your fingers, the moon and stars that You set in place, What is man that You have been mindful of him, mortal man that You have taken note of him? And yet You have made him little less than divine (angels) and adorned him with glory and majesty."

282 The Psalm 50 says: "I will take no bullock out of your house, nor he-goats out of your folds…I know all the fowls of the mountains; and the wild beasts of the field are Mine. If I were hungry, I would not tell you; for the world is Mine, and the fulness thereof." That Jews offered sacrifices in the Temple was because it was for them, i.e. their growth and development, not because God needed gifts or prostrations. This idea would need further explanation, but it is not for here.

283 Psalm 8:4-6

284 This is the same internal struggle that results in some becoming anti-semites and some to be philosemites.

285 Ramban on Deuteronomy 5.23: man can be nourished as animal, by

physical, or, if connected to God, nourished wholly by spiritual - unique amongst all creations. In Genesis, God creates all of the animals and their 'life' with an additional word that connects with the physical world - e.g. water or land, because they die once disconnected from their life course, just as an electrical appliance stops working once unplugged. Not so man, whose life force can alternatively be plugged into God and spirituality. Man can therefore live eternally when plugged into the Eternal Source. (I heard this idea from Rabbi Aaron Lopiansky)

286 Jacobson, Simon (2002). Toward a Meaningful Life: The Wisdom of the Rebbe Menachem Mendel Schneerson. Harper Collins. 4-5.

287 Luzzatto, Rabbi Moshe Chaim (1980). The Path of the Just - Mesilat Yesharim. Feldheim. Chapter 1.

288 Luzzatto, Rabbi Moshe Chaim. The Way of God, Derech Hashem. Feldheim. Part 1, Chapter 3.

289 Jacobson, Simon (2002). Toward a Meaningful Life: The Wisdom of the Rebbe Menachem Mendel Schneerson. Harper Collins. 129.

290 Jacobson, Simon (2002). Toward a Meaningful Life: The Wisdom of the Rebbe Menachem Mendel Schneerson. Harper Collins. 5.

291 Jacobson, Simon (2002). Toward a Meaningful Life: The Wisdom of the Rebbe Menachem Mendel Schneerson. Harper Collins. 94.

292 Genesis 9:6

293 Volozhin, Rabbi Chaim, trans Avinoam Fraenkel (2015). Nefesh HaTzimtzum - translation and commentary of Nefesh HaChaim. Urim. Volume 1, 116.

294 This idea has an interesting parallel with psychologist Abraham Maslow's not so well-known 6th level of human actualization, which he called 'transcendence'. Maslow's Hierarchy of Needs – the sixth level. (2024, January 22). BPS. https://www.bps.org.uk/psychologist/maslows-hierarchy-needs-sixth-level

295 The final goal for both Jews and non-Jews is to attain this sublime level of living.

296 Deuteronomy 30:14

297 Maharal, Gvuros Hashem. Chapter 9.

298 A mitzvah is likened to a candle, a physical vessel to contain Divine light. Mitzvot are physical acts of the soul. (Maharal in chapter 14, Tiferes Yisrael). There are 613 "Mitzvot", translated loosely as commandments, encoded in the Torah. Although they are commands, things that we should or shouldn't do, this only begins to uncover the layers of depth contained in each 'mitzvah'. Just as the Torah contains many levels beyond the literal, the same is true of the second vital tool in God's toolbox.

299 The Land of Israel is the ideal place to perform the commandments, and therefore is an inherent part of the Divine covenant with Abraham: "To your offspring I assign this land…" (Genesis 15:13). The Land of Israel is so vital to the Jewish mission that it was included in each of the first three prophecies that Abraham received from G-d.

Israel has its beautiful vistas, but what makes it special and necessary for the Jewish mission is its holiness. The connection between the Holy Land and the Holy People is more than nostalgia, nationalism or the vicissitudes of nomadic migration: it is a deep inner spiritual bond. See Kook, Rabbi Abraham Isaac, (2022). Orot. Maggid Books. p 115 - 129.

300 God revealed this to Abraham when He appointed him to the covenant, including a glimpse into the Jewish future, and some of it was not going to be fun. But as mentioned, negative prophecies do not necessarily have to be fulfilled (positive ones do). In other words, man could have used his free will to attain such purity, but God's covenantal promise seems to indicate it was an unlikely scenario.

301 Other essential Jewish tenets of faith are that God exists and is involved with everything (providence), nothing exists without Him (controls nature), and He speaks to humans. Maharal, Gevuras Hashem, chapter 47. See Weinberg, Rabbi Yaakov (1991). Fundamentals and Faith: Insights into the Rambam's 13 Principles. Targum Press.

302 In the first years of the 210, Jews were 'strangers', i.e. a second class

minority group. Slavery begins after the death of all of the brothers (tribes), and the harshest level, oppression, lasted for the last 86 years.

303 Literally the '10 Utterances'.

304 It also informed, in great detail, how history will play out. See Spiro, K. (2015, January 11). The Seven Wonders of Jewish History - Ken Spiro. Ken Spiro. https://kenspiro.com/audio-classes/the-seven-wonders-of-jewish-history/

305 Wein, R. B. (2008, June 24). Man-Made Faith • Torah.org. Torah.org. https://torah.org/torah-portion/rabbiwein-5768-korach/

306 Said in a 1974 lecture. Yosef Dov Soloveitchik. Experiencing Mesorah in the classroom. Yeshivat Har Etzion. https://www.etzion.org.il/en/philosophy/issues-jewish-thought/issues-education/experiencing-mesorah-classroom. Accessed February 2020.

307 Luzzato, Rabbi Moshe Chaim (1983). Derech Hashem - The Way Of God. Feldheim. Part 4, Chapter 2.

308 Rabbi Shimshon Raphael Hirsch attempts to summarize what cannot be categorized: "And if the Torah has eluded every comparison and every definition, so the expressions which (the people of) Israel has invented to describe the effects of the Torah on his life know no bounds. The Torah is to Israel the priceless pearl, the matchless wealth, the inexhaustible treasure, the endless field, the gold to be won from the deepest mine. The Torah is the source of knowledge and understanding, the fountain of life and peace, the well of salvation and strength, the absolute good and the tree of life which - if planted and tended with proper care - is able to bring paradise back to the world."
Hirsch, Rabbi Samson Raphael (1984). The Collected Writings of Rabbi Samson Raphael Hirsch. Feldheim. Volume 1, 195. Psalm 19: "The Torah of God is perfect, restoring the soul, the testimony of God is faithful, granting wisdom to the simple, more desirable than gold, than much fine gold; sweeter than honey, than drippings of the honeycomb."

309 Maimonides lists it as the 11th commandment. See Rothstein, G. (2022, November 21). The Mitzvah of Talmud Torah, Torah Study. Torah Musings.

https://www.torahmusings.com/2022/11/the-mitzvah-of-talmud-torah-torah-study/

310 Talmud Shabbat 88B from Song of Songs 5:6

311 Exodus 20:15

312 "It is not with you alone that I make this covenant and this oath; it is with who stands here with us today before the Lord our God, and also with who is not here with us today." Deuteronomy 29:13–14. Talmud Shabbat 146A. To be clear, this does not mean that other people cannot become very spiritual; on the contrary, everybody can.

313 Ben Yehoyada on Talmud Shabbat 146A

314 This was Abraham's original name, and it was changed by God after this prophecy took place.

315 Genesis 15:13

316 See Midrash Rabba Lech Lecha chapter 44, and Maharal, Gvuros Hashem, chapter 8, on 'The Four Exiles".

317 Deuteronomy 4:20

318 Berzovsky, Rabbi Shalom Noah. Nesivos Shalom on the Torah, Exodus. Yeshivat Beit Avraham Slonim. 8.

319 Genesis 27:40, and Rashi's commentary

320 See Maimonides, Mishneh Torah, Hilchot Teshuva, chapter 5 on the mystery and paradox of free will and God's knowledge.

321 Hess, Moses (1958). Rome and Jerusalem: A Study in Jewish Nationalism. 25.

322 Rabbi Meir Simcha HaKohen, 'Meshech Chochmah', Leviticus chapter 26

323 Talmud Sotah 9B, on midah kneged mida, the idea of 'measure for measure', regarding Shimshon - his failure started in Gaza and so his downfall was in Gaza.

324 Ezekial 20:33

325 Talmud Megillah 14A

326 "And it shall come to pass on that day, that a great shofar shall be blown, and they shall come who were lost in the land of Ashur, and the outcasts in the land of Egypt, and they shall worship the Lord on the Holy Mountain in Jerusalem." Isaiah, 27:13.

327 Described and recorded in the book Em Ubanim Smeicha, from the lecture in the Churva synagogue, Old City, Jerusalem, 1933, and also here https://mizrachi.org/hamizrachi/the-three-shofarot-of-rosh-hashanah/ where Rabbi Steven Miodownik explains Rabbi Kook's thoughts. The ideal shofar is the ram's horn that we blow on Rosh Hashana. The second shofar is the one that comes from the horn of any kosher animal; it is 'good enough', and corresponds to being 'good enough' in our behavior and spiritual growth. "The (third and) least desirable shofar comes from the horn of a non-kosher animal. This shofar corresponds to the wake-up call that comes from persecution by other nations, when we are driven to action by the piercing siren of fear. This is the shofar of affliction. This is the shofar that unites the Jewish people because of antisemitic threats. This shofar produces results, but only because it drives us to "flee from" danger instead of "running towards" redemption. There is no blessing made on such a shofar, for "we do not make a blessing on the cup of persecution." Talmud, Berachot 51A

328 Diary entry of April 11, 1944, in Frank, Anne, 1929-1945 author. The Diary of a Young Girl : the Definitive Edition. New York :Doubleday, 1995.

329 For brevity and the sake of focus, we are not delving into this deep and fascinating subject. You can learn more here: https://aish.com/why_are_ there_commandments and https://www.chabad.org/library/article_cdo/ aid/756399/jewish/The-613-Commandments-Mitzvot.htm

330 Here also, for brevity and the sake of focus, we are not delving into this deep and fascinating subject. Perhaps we will explore these in a future book. In the meantime, you can see Kook, HaRav Tzvi Yehuda HaCohen (1991). Torat Eretz Yisrael: The Teachings of HaRav Tzvi Yehuda HaCohen Kook. Torat Eretz Yisrael Publications.

331 Like the grapes of France and the wheat of Ukraine, each plant grows best in the soil and the climate that is right for it. The Jews in Israel are like

a tree planted in the perfect soil of a land whose crop is holiness. Rav Kook writes, "Israel's vital role comes to life when the nation of Israel returns to its Land…Only then can it perform its intended task of raising mankind to the knowledge and service of Hashem, the true goal and purpose of all of creation.' Kook, HaRav Tzvi Yehuda HaCohen (1991). Torat Eretz Yisrael: The Teachings of HaRav Tzvi Yehuda HaCohen Kook. Torat Eretz Yisrael Publications. 90.

332 Amos 3:2 "You alone have I singled out from all the families of the earth. That is why I will call you to account for all your iniquities." And Isaiah 43:10 "You are My witnesses, declares God…" My testifiers "eide" (i.e. witnesses).

333 Hitler said, quoted by Rauschning, "Has it not struck you how the Jew is the exact opposite of the German in every single respect, and yet is as closely akin to him as his blood brother." Rauschning, Herman (1940). Hitler Speaks: A Series of Political Conversations with Adolf Hitler on his Real Aims. Eyre and Spottiswoode. 235.

334 Wikipedia contributor Shemtov613. "Siyum HaShas," August 4, 2024. https://en.wikipedia.org/wiki/Siyum_HaShas#/media/File:13th_Siyum_HaShas_2019.jpg.

Chapter 7

335 Martin Niemöller: "First they came for the Socialists. . ." (n.d.). https://encyclopedia.ushmm.org/content/en/article/martin-niemoeller-first-they-came-for-the-socialists and Rosenwald, M. S. (2021, October 28). 'Then they came for me': A Hitler supporter's haunting warning has a complicated history. Washington Post. https://www.washingtonpost.com/news/retropolis/wp/2017/08/19/then-they-came-for-me-a-hitler-supporters-haunting-warning-has-a-complicated-history/

336 Sachs, N. (2019, January 24). Iran's revolution, 40 years on: Israel's reverse periphery doctrine. Brookings. https://www.brookings.edu/articles/irans-revolution-40-years-on-israels-reverse-periphery-doctrine/

337 Morphet, J., Oliveira, A., Fenton, R., & Griffin, A. (2024, May 7). Anti-Israel protesters vandalize WWI memorial, burn American flag after

cops block group from reaching star-studded Met Gala in NYC. New York Post. https://nypost.com/2024/05/06/us-news/over-1000-pro-palestinian-protesters-march-toward-met-gala/

338 Bernard Lewis once explained to me during filming of my film, Iranium, that in Shiite Iranian theological thinking, a global nuclear apocalypse is not a deterrent, as it was for Western countries (known as MAD - mutually assured destruction) but rather is an incentive, as it will hasten the coming of the Mahdi.

339 Egypt when the Muslim Brotherhood was elected in 2012, Gaza-Hamas 2005, Afghanistan-Taliban 1996, Iran- Islamic Republic 1979, the ISIS State 2004, to name a few.

340 After Oct. 7, UK journalist Hadley Freeman believes "the progressive left hates Jews" | The Times of Israel. (2024, June 4). The Times of Israel. https://www.timesofisrael.com/after-oct-7-uk-journalist-hadley-freeman-believes-the-progressive-left-hates-jews/ and her analysis of the left's hate of Jews: The Jewish Quarterly. (n.d.). Jewish Quarterly. https://jewishquarterly.com/essay/2024/05/blindness

341 Rust, M., Frosch, D., Bauerlein, V., Umlauf, T., & Images, A. K. (2024, April 24). The growing Pro-Palestinian protest movement, visualized. WSJ. https://www.wsj.com/politics/college-campus-pro-palestinian-protests-64115768

342 It is hard to get reliable statistics: Hamas's numbers are unreliable because they are liars and terrorists, they don't distinguish civilians from terrorists, and they show no data. Their numbers have been challenged by the UN Office for the Coordination of Humanitarian Affairs (OCHA) who halved the numbers in a study on May 11, 2024.
Abrams, E. (2024, May 12). UN halves its estimate of women and children killed in Gaza. Council on Foreign Relations. https://www.cfr.org/blog/un-halves-its-estimate-women-and-children-killed-gaza
Also see the intriguing statistical analysis by Professor Abraham Wyner in Tablet magazine Wyner, A. (2024, March 15). How the Gaza Ministry of Health Fakes Casualty Numbers. Tablet Magazine. https://www.tabletmag.com/sections/news/articles/how-gaza-health-ministry-fakes-casualty-

numbers, and Baker, G., & Sultan/Shutterstock, A. (2024, March 11). What's behind the propaganda war against Israel. WSJ. https://www.wsj.com/articles/whats-behind-the-propaganda-war-against-israel-why-biden-pushes-to-end-fighting-24694f11

343 These are the proportional numbers since Israel is a small country Eze Vidra. (2024, April 26). NYU Professor Scott Galloway on the on the double standard applied to Israel [Video]. YouTube. https://www.youtube.com/watch?v=kRWCy03dmjs

344 Maybe it was a terrible ratio of combatants to civilian deaths that so inflamed the progressive activists, a ratio perhaps unheard of in the annals of modern warfare? No. The US followed the death of 2,200 at Pearl Harbor with 3.5 million Japanese dead, and 3,000 killed on 9.11 was followed by 400,000 deaths in Afghanistan and Iraq. In the 2016-2017 Battle of Mosul, the biggest urban battles since WWII, the U.S. led Iraqi Security Force killed 10,000 civilians to destroy 4,000 ISIS in the city. That is a 1 to 2.5 combatant to civilian death ratio. https://x.com/SpencerGuard/status/1786612914117349769 These low numbers point to Israel's careful tactics, and that is why John Spencer, the chair of urban warfare studies at the Modern War Institute (MWI) at West Point said Israel's standards are the highest ever by a modern army, despite what the media hype suggests Spencer, J. (2024, March 26). Israel has created a new standard for urban warfare. Why will no one admit it? | Opinion. Newsweek. https://www.newsweek.com/israel-has-created-new-standard-urban-warfare-why-will-no-one-admit-it-opinion-1883286.
The ratio of civilian to combatant deaths in the war against Hamas is better than any US war, about 1:1, despite the fact that Hamas spent 15 years building their strategy of using the entire population as human shields by establishing their entire military infrastructure under civilian neighborhoods, schools, mosques and hospitals. (Avi Mayer אבי מאיר on X: "The average civilian casualty ratio in modern warfare is around 9:1 - that is, nine civilians killed for every combatant. In the current war, it is about 1.7:1. That's remarkable." / X. (2001, February 12). X (Formerly Twitter). https://x.com/AviMayer/status/1757065611471913161?lang=en
According to UN figures, 90% of wartime casualties in 2021 were civilians – in other words, the civilian casualty ratio was 9:1. That figure has been

roughly constant for about 40 years, though it has fluctuated from one war zone to the next. According to official Israeli estimates, more than 10,000 Hamas combatants alone (i.e., not including combatants affiliated with Islamic Jihad or other terrorist groups) have been killed since October 7. If we factor those 10,000 combatants into the overall Hamas-circulated casualty figure of 27,7000, we are left with a civilian casualty ratio of around 1.7:1 – a striking achievement that will no doubt be studied by other Western militaries for years to come. That ratio is particularly notable given the complex and dense urban combat environment in Gaza and Hamas's longstanding and well-documented practice of embedding its military infrastructure in civilian areas, operating from within population concentrations, and using civilians as human shields, all of which are intended to maximize the number of civilian casualties. (It is also important to note that the civilian casualties include those killed by misfired Palestinian rockets.))

Maybe the global community is truly sympathetic to the murder and rape of innocent Israelis, as they claim, but simply cannot abide her "disproportionate response"? When Hamas murders 1,200 Jews and hides behind its own civilians, what are the progressive pundits and leaders proposing as a solution for Israel to deal with the problem? Should Israelis stop fighting and let Hamas live to kill another day? How is Israel meant to protect its cities from the next October 7, and from Hamas's tens of thousands of missiles that have been fired at civilian populations indiscriminately in the past 15 years? When Israel acts to eliminate Hamas and some civilians are tragically killed, as they are in every war, why does the idea of "proportionate response" suddenly become a supreme moral principle that the media and pundits all cite to "prove" Israeli immorality? People did not rally in righteous indignation against Allied war crimes because more Nazis were killed than their own.

345 On the privileged Palestinian refugee status: Karsh, E. (2018, June 1). "The privileged Palestinian 'Refugees'." Middle East Forum. https://www.meforum.org/7241/the-privileged-palestinian-refugees

346 UNHCR - The UN Refugee Agency. (n.d.). Global Trends | UNHCR. UNHCR. https://www.unhcr.org/global-trends

347 Howard/Reuters, N. (2024, May 5). Biden's worst mistake of the Gaza War. WSJ. https://www.wsj.com/articles/bidens-worst-mistake-of-the-gaza-war-901efb25?mod=hp_opin_pos_2#cxrecs_s

348 Apparently, the cost to become a refugee was £250,000, as was shown in the case of the payments made (bribe?) made by the former Scottish Minister to the United Nations relief agency to get his family out.
Turner, C. (2024, July 16). Former Scottish first minister Humza Yousaf faces review over £250k Gaza funding. The Telegraph. https://www.telegraph.co.uk/politics/2024/07/13/humza-yousaf-scotland-first-minister-snp-250k-gaza-unrwa/

349 The Palestinians living there were expelled because their leadership had supported Saddam's invasion of Kuwait.

Rosen, S. J. (2012, September 1). Kuwait expels thousands of Palestinians. Middle East Forum. https://www.meforum.org/3391/kuwait-expels-palestinians

350 Wikipedia contributors. (2024, July 10). Palestinians in Syria. Wikipedia. https://en.wikipedia.org/wiki/Palestinians_in_Syria and
Wikipedia contributors. (2024, June 27). Casualties of the Syrian civil war. Wikipedia. https://en.wikipedia.org/wiki/Casualties_of_the_Syrian_civil_war

351 West Bank and Gaza - United States Department of State. (2023, December 7). United States Department of State. https://www.state.gov/reports/2019-report-on-international-religious-freedom/israel-west-bank-and-gaza/west-bank-and-gaza/

352 In Article 28 of the Hamas Charter, it declares that, "Israel, Judaism and Jews challenge Islam and the Moslem people." And Article 13: "There is no solution for the Palestinian question except through Jihad."

Iran's Supreme Leader Ayatollah Ali Khamenei regularly calls Israel a cancerous tumor: "The Zionist regime is a deadly, cancerous growth and a detriment to this region...It will undoubtedly be uprooted and destroyed." Iran leader says Israel a "cancerous tumor" to be destroyed | AP

News. (2020, May 22). AP News. https://apnews.com/article/
a033042303545d9ef783a95222d51b83

353 See https://www.jns.org/there-are-no-civilians-in-gaza/ for an interesting
angle on the matter.
Greenfield, D. (2024, June 13). There are no civilians in Gaza. JNS.org. https://
www.jns.org/there-are-no-civilians-in-gaza/

354 They are protesting genocide but supporting Hamas whose policy of
genocide is explicit. They think they are standing for peace and love, but
objectively, they are aiding and abetting Hamas who stand for hate, terrorism,
racism, mass murder and religious supremacism.

355 Preston Stewart on X: "Iran released a video directed at US university
students titled 'You are standing on the right side of history' https://t.co/
djbCtpgBXZ" / X. (n.d.). X (Formerly Twitter). https://x.com/prestonstew_/
status/1797596522177327220

356 Kukreti, S. (2024, May 30). Iran's Khamenei pens open letter to anti-
Israel US campus protesters, urges them 'to become familiar with Quran.'
Hindustan Times. https://www.hindustantimes.com/world-news/us-news/
irans-khamenei-pens-open-letter-to-anti-israel-us-campus-protesters-urges-
them-to-become-familiar-with-quran-101717059892586.html

357 Howard/Reuters, N. (2024, May 5). Biden's worst mistake of the Gaza
War. WSJ. https://www.wsj.com/articles/bidens-worst-mistake-of-the-gaza-
war-901efb25?mod=hp_opin_pos_2#cxrecs_s

358 It is a matter of serious debate as to who is to be considered innocent in a
society that elected a genocidal terror organization to power democratically,
that is the most antisemitic population in the world, and that approve of and
cheered on the October 7 massacre on a general scale. A Palestinian poll in
June 2024 shows more than 2/3 support of the October 7 massacre. Perhaps
the innocents can be defined as the very young not-yet-indoctrinated-to-hate
children and those in the minority who did not vote Hamas into power in
their one and only free, democratic election in 2005.
Bermudez, K. (2024, June 14). Most Palestinians support October 7
attack, dissatisfied with Abbas and Fatah. FDD. https://www.fdd.org/

analysis/2024/06/14/most-palestinians-support-october-7-attack-dissatisfied-with-abbas-and-fatah/

359 Some of the war crimes: Indiscriminate rocket fire - International law is clear that belligerents who fail to distinguish between combatants and civilians are guilty of war crimes. Cold blooded executions of civilian prisoners, beheadings, using human shields, shooting missiles at civilians, rape and sexual violence, hostage taking, using medical facilities for war like ambulances, hospitals, use of children to carry explosives, etc…the list goes on.

360 These low numbers point to Israel's careful tactics, and that is why John Spencer, the chair of urban warfare studies at the Modern War Institute (MWI) at West Point said Israel's standards are the highest ever by a modern army, despite what the media hype suggests.
Spencer, J. (2024, March 26). Israel has created a new standard for urban warfare. Why will no one admit it? | Opinion. Newsweek. https://www.newsweek.com/israel-has-created-new-standard-urban-warfare-why-will-no-one-admit-it-opinion-1883286
Fox, A. (2024, May 23). Israel is succeeding in Gaza. Tablet Magazine. https://www.tabletmag.com/sections/israel-middle-east/articles/israel-succeeding-gaza

John Spencer on X: "In the 2016-2017 Battle of Mosul, the biggest urban battles since WWII, the U.S. led Iraqi Security Force killed 10,000 civilians to destroy 4,000 ISIS in the city. That is a 1 to 2.5 combatant to civilian death ratio. In the 1945 Battle of Manila (which did have some variables" / X. (n.d.). X (Formerly Twitter). https://x.com/SpencerGuard/status/1786612914117349769
On the topic civilian casualties there is much to reveal. On May 11, the UN cut the number of civilian deaths by half of what Hamas had been reporting without evidence.
Abrams, E. (2024, May 12). UN halves its estimate of women and children killed in Gaza. Council on Foreign Relations. https://www.cfr.org/blog/un-halves-its-estimate-women-and-children-killed-gaza

https://twitter.com/AviMayer/status/1757065611471913161

361 Here is a thoughtful consideration of the complex issues at play in judging Israel's behavior by the late Charles Krauthammer: Judging Israel - Eassy by Charles Krauthammer. (n.d.). https://jr.co.il/articles/judging-israel. htm

362 Put starkly, the global community mobilizes - the media, the street, colleges, governments, NGOs, international institutions - to press the Jews to stop fighting. No, they are saying, the Jews must not be allowed to win a war, even against an inhuman, radical Islamist, Iran-supported, genocidal enemy who committed almost every possible war crime imaginable, are still holding over 100 men, women and children hostage, and are unrepentantly dedicated to Israel's destruction. The Jews are schooled and implored by 'moral crusaders' around the world to do the 'moral thing' and cease fire (and allow Hamas to kill and rape them some more in the near future). The inherent antisemitism was expressed well by novelist Jacobson's wanna-be Jewish character Treslove, who concludes, "The Jew would not be allowed to prosper except as they had always prospered, at the margins…Anything else would not be tolerated. A brave rearguard action in the face of insurmountable odds was one thing. Anything resembling victory and peace was another. It could not be borne, whether by Muslims for whom Jews were a sort of erroneous and lily-livered brother, always to be kept in their place, or by Christians to whom they were anathema, or by themselves to whom they were an embarrassment." (The Finkler Question, 267).

363 'Kill hostages' poster at NY parade
Fitz-Gibbon, J. (2024, June 2). Masked protester taunts NYC Israel Day Parade with vile "Kill Hostages Now" sign as families of Oct. 7th captives march. New York Post. https://nypost.com/2024/06/02/us-news/anti-israel-protester-taunts-nyc-parade-marchers-with-vile-kill-hostages-now-sign/
Anti-Israel protesters desecrate a memorial to Hamas's victims and attack the homes of Jewish museum donors.
The Editorial Board & Carlos Chiossone/Zuma Press. (2024, June 14). Celebrating the nova massacre in New York City. WSJ. https://www.wsj.com/articles/nova-massacre-remembrance-new-york-city-protesters-hamas-antisemitism-0d7f4eb0?mod=hp_opin_pos_1

Young Jewish kids don't feel safe in public schools

National Post. (2024, June 13). Nationalpost. https://nationalpost.com/
opinion/emma-teitel-jewish-kids-are-being-scapegoated-in-canada-and-
nobody-cares

364 Perhaps the most eloquent summary of the moral absurdity we are
witnessing was penned by the Russian Israeli author Dina Rubina. On May
25, in response to the Pushkin House's request for her to clarify he reposition
on the war before allowing her to speak at the University of London, Rubina
wrote this:

This is what I want to say to all those who expect from me a quick and
obsequious report on my position regarding my beloved country, which
currently lives (and always has) surrounded by ferocious enemies who seek
to destroy it . My country which is waging a just war today against a rabid,
ruthless, deceptive and cunning enemy. The last time I apologized was in
elementary school, in the principal's office, I was 9 years old. Since then, I
have been doing what I think is right, listening only to my conscience and
expressing exclusively my understanding of the world order and human laws
of justice.

On October 7, Saturday, the Jewish holiday of Simchat Torah, the ruthless,
well-trained, well-prepared and well-equipped Hamas terrorist regime
of Iran, Hamas, which rules in the Gaza enclave (which Israel left around
twenty years ago), attacked dozens of peaceful kibbutzim and bombarded
my country with tens of thousands of rockets. Hamas has committed
atrocities that even the Bible cannot describe, atrocities that rival the crimes
of Sodom and Gomorrah. Atrocities filmed by the way, by GoPro cameras,
the murderers having taken the horror to the point of sending the images
to their families or on social networks in real time. For hours, thousands
of happy, blood-drunk beasts raped women, children and men, shooting
their victims in the crotch and heads, cutting off the women's breasts and
playing football with them, cutting off the babies from the wombs of pregnant
women and immediately decapitating them, tying up and burning the small
children. There were so many charred bodies that, for many weeks, forensic
pathologists could not cope with the enormous workload of identifying
individuals.

A friend of mine, who worked in the emergency room of a New York hospital for 20 years, then in Israel for 15 years, was one of the first to arrive in the kibbutzim, as part of a team of rescuers and of doctors. She still hasn't been able to sleep since.

While she is an emergency specialist, accustomed to dissected bodies and corpses, she fainted when she saw the macabre sight and vomited all the way back in the car. Among the Hamas militants, Palestinian civilians rushed in, participating in pogroms of unprecedented scale, pillaging, killing, dragging everything they could get their hands on. Among these "Palestinian civilians" were 450 members of this highly regarded organization UNRWA (United Nations Relief Agency for Palestine Refugees in the Near East).

Judging by the utter joy of the population (also captured by thousands of mobile cameras), Hamas is supported by almost the entire population of Gaza. But the essential is there for us: More than two hundred Israelis, including women, children, the elderly and foreign workers, were dragged into the beast's den. A hundred of them are still rotting and dying in Hamas dungeons.

It goes without saying that these victims, who continue to be mocked, are of little concern to the "academic community". But that's not what I'm talking about right now. I am not writing this so that anyone will sympathize with the tragedy of my people.

During all these years, while the international community has literally poured hundreds of millions of dollars into this piece of land (the Gaza Strip) — UNRWA's annual budget alone is equivalent to a billion dollars! — During all these years, Hamas used this money to build an empire with a complex system of underground tunnels, stockpile weapons, teach schoolchildren from primary school to disassemble and assemble Kalashnikov assault rifles, print textbooks in which hatred of Israel is indescribable, in which even math problems look like this calling for the murder of Jews with every word: There were ten Jews, the shahid killed four, how many are left?

And now, when finally shocked by the monstrous crime of these bastards, Israel is waging a war of annihilation against the Hamas terrorists who so carefully prepared this war, who placed thousands of shells in all the hospitals, the schools, kindergartens…

The academic community, which was not concerned about the massacres in Syria, nor the massacre in Somalia, nor the mistreatment inflicted on the Uighurs, nor the millions of Kurds persecuted by the Turkish regime for decades, this very worried community, which wears "arafatkas" [keffiyehs], the trademark of murderers, around their necks at rallies under the slogan "Liberate Palestine from the river to the sea", which means the total destruction of Israel (and Israelis). "Academics", as polls show, have no idea where this river is, what it is called, where certain borders are located. And it is this same public which asks me "to express a position clear on the issue". Are you really serious!

As you know, I have been a professional writer for over 50 years. My novels have been translated into 40 languages, including Albanian, Turkish, Chinese, Esperanto, and many more.

Now, with great pleasure, without choosing my expressions too much, I sincerely and with all the strength of my soul send to all the brainless "intellectuals" who are interested in my position to go fuck themselves. https://quadrant.org.au/opinion/israel/2024/05/rude-and-crude-but-definitely-justified/

365 The Nobel Peace Prize 1986. (n.d.). [Video]. NobelPrize.org. https://www.nobelprize.org/prizes/peace/1986/wiesel/acceptance-speech/

366 This refers to the original Jewish idea of Tikkun, 'fixing' which refers to seeing a world filled with peace, love and awareness of God. It should not be confused with the modern usage of the term to refer to progressive social values.

367 Grossman, Vasilii (1946). "Treblinskii ad" The Hell of Treblinka in The Years of War (1941-1945), Foreign Languages Publishing House. 389-90.

Chapter 8

368 Sacks, Rabbi Jonathan (2001). Radical Then, Radical Now: On Being Jewish. HarperCollins. p 225

369 Herzl: An annotated study of "A Solution to the Jewish Question" (1896) | Sefaria. (n.d.). https://www.sefaria.org/sheets/367720.50?lang=he&with=all&lang2=he

370 David Ben Gurion, Israel's first Prime Minister, famously said, "We will know we have become a normal country when Jewish thieves and Jewish prostitutes conduct their business in Hebrew."

371 Sacks, R. L. J. (2023, February 20). What is Antisemitism? | The Rabbi Sacks Legacy. The Rabbi Sacks Legacy. https://rabbisacks.org/archive/what-is-anti-semitism-moment-magazine/

372 In fact, these people are a small, marginalized minority but they sadly represent an astonishingly high percentage of (non-Orthodox) rabbis, professors and community leaders - and they attract much media attention beyond their numbers.

373 Howard Jacobson paints an ironic picture of this type of Jew in his poignant novel, The Finkler Question, where a group is formed called the 'ASHamed Jews' who meet regularly to show that 'as Jews' they have a unique ability and even responsibility to be ashamed of their people. (The Finkler Question, p 137) They called themselves 'ashamed Jews' and not 'ashamed Zionists' because even though 'it was the Z word of which they were ashamed', because "The logic that made it impossible for those who had never been Zionists to call themselves ASHamed Zionists did not extend to Jews who had never been Jews. To be an ASHamed did not require that you had been knowingly Jewish all your life."
Jacobson, H. (2010). The Finkler question. 1st U.S. ed. New York, Bloomsbury USA. p.138.

374 For a full critique and deconstruction of the mistaken modern conception of Tikkun Olam, see Jonathan Neumann's, To Heal the World?: How the Jewish Left Corrupts Judaism and Endangers Israel. All Points Books. 2018.

375 See Chabon, M. (2023, August 2). Those people: Michael Chabon's commencement address at Hebrew Union College, Los Angeles. Tablet Magazine. https://www.tabletmag.com/sections/arts-letters/articles/michael-chabon-commencement
Rudee, E. (2018, June 6). The Chabon speech: Students and rabbis note the disconnect from graduation … and Judaism. JNS.org. https://www.jns.org/the-chabon-speech-students-and-rabbis-note-the-disconnect-from-graduation-and-judaism/

Strauchler, C. (2020, May 1). Saving Judaism from Michael Chabon. Commentary Magazine. https://www.commentary.org/articles/chaim-strauchler/saving-judaism-michael-chabon/

376 Lewis, Bernard (1999). Semites and Anti-Semites. W. W. Norton & Company. 255-256.

377 Greenfield, D. (2015, August 17). The Ghetto Jew and Israel. Israel National News. https://www.israelnationalnews.com/news/345993

378 They certainty ignored the obvious problem that the PLO (Palestine Liberation Organization) was established with the express purpose of destroying all of Israel in 1964, even before one settlement had been built (because Israel had not gained possession of the West bank and Gaza). The 'settlements' the PLO alluded to in their Charter could only mean Tel Aviv, Jaffa and Haifa; but this inconvenient fact did not disrupt their narrative.

379 One reason that many Israelis from these border villages that were so decimated on October 7 changed their political views was because they felt betrayed. Most of these kibbutzim had been the vanguard of the Israeli left's 'peace movement' and had been activists to help regular Gazans have a better life. They discovered that many of the 'innocent' Gazans that they had been helping and employing had been supplying Hamas with their community details so they could kill them, and that many of them had gleefully participated in the day's atrocities.

i24NEWS. (2024, January 19). "They killed my friends and all my beliefs" after Oct. 7, peace activists face change of heart. i24NEWS. https://www.i24news.tv/en/news/israel-at-war/survivor-testimonies/1705690765-feature

380 This confusion can also be seen subtly but powerfully in the 'Bring Them Home' slogan of the Israeli 'free-the-hostage movement'. As Steve Rosenberg points out in a JNS.org article on July 22, 2024, "Bring them home" implies that the primary responsibility for the safe return of the hostages lies with the IDF and the Israeli government. It suggests a proactive action on the part of these entities to physically bring the hostages back...this phrasing overlooks the root cause of the situation: the terrorist actions of Hamas. By focusing on "bringing" the hostages home, the narrative subtly shifts the burden of resolution onto the victims' side, rather than squarely on the perpetrators.

This can create a misleading perception that the resolution of the issue is primarily a matter of Israeli capability and willingness, rather than an act of justice and humanity that should be demanded from Hamas.

The correct focus (should be): 'Let them go'."
Rosenberg, S. (2024, July 21). 'Let them go,' not 'bring them home' JNS.org. https://www.jns.org/let-them-go-not-bring-them-home/

381 Mendes-Flohr, Paul and Reinharz, Jehuda (2010). Jew in the Modern World. p 354

382 Chappelle, Dave, host. *Saturday Night Live*. Season 48, episode 6. Aired 2022, November 12, 2022, in broadcase syndication. SNL Studios.

383 Author, N., & Author, N. (2024, April 14). A portrait of Jewish Americans. Pew Research Center. https://www.pewresearch.org/religion/2013/10/01/jewish-american-beliefs-attitudes-culture-survey/

384 Commentary, Jewish Genius, April 2007, which summarizes the research from his book, The Bell Curve. Murray and Richard Herrnstein argue that what matters most in outstanding accomplishment is genius, and that, "The key indicator for predicting exceptional accomplishment (like winning a Nobel Prize) is the incidence of exceptional intelligence…(and) the proportion of Jews with IQs of 140 or higher is somewhere around six times the proportion of everyone else"
Murray, C. (2015, November 16). Jewish genius. Commentary Magazine. https://www.commentary.org/articles/charles-murray/jewish-genius/

385 Fackenheim, Emil L. (1978). The Jewish Return to History - Reflections in the Age of Auschwitz and a New Jerusalem. Schocken. 22-24.

386 W., B., & B., D. (2019). Alcoholics anonymous: the big book : the original 1939 edition. Mineola, New York, Ixia Press, an imprint of Dover Publications, Inc.

387 Montreal Jewish Forums - December 15th, 1963 - leonardcohenforum. com. (2017, July 17). https://www.leonardcohenforum.com/viewtopic. php?t=37527

388 Cohen was probably referring to the verse in Isaiah, 43.10, where God says to the Jewish People, "You are My witnesses, declares God…"

389 Robert Weltsch, "Tragt ihn mit Stolz, den gelben Fleck," in Jüdische Rundschau, April 1933, translation from Dawidowicz, Holocaust Reader, 147–50 https://www.yadvashem.org/odot_pdf/Microsoft%20Word%20-%20 3830.pdf

390 This idea was also expressed by the Lubavitch Rebbe, Rabbi Schneerson, in an informal discussion he had with the Young Leadership Cabinet of the U.J.A. (United Jewish Appeal) on March 4, 1962: "…every one of us has an obligation to fight Hitler, [which] can be done by letting that which Hitler had in mind to annihilate, not only continue, but grow bigger and on a deeper scale. Hitler was not interested so much in annihilating the body of Jewishness as he was interested in annihilating the spirit. [He decreed that the spiritual and moral ideas which the Jewish people embodied7] must not infect the German people, the Russian people, or the Polish people—and because of that, he had all the Polish, Russian, and German people on his side. They regarded the Jews as a foreign body, and a body that does not belong must be eliminated. If you influence a Jew not to become assimilated but to profess his Jewishness, his pride and inspiration and joy, this is defeating Hitlerism. If someone does his best in his personal life to be Jewish [so that] everyone sees that in the street he is a Jew, that his home is a Jewish home, that he is proud, and that it is not a burden, but his pride, his life defeats the idea of Hitlerism." Chapter 18: The Jewish Answer to Evil. (n.d.). https://www.chabad.org/ therebbe/article_cdo/aid/3144797/jewish/Chapter-18-The-Jewish-Answer-to-Evil.htm

391 I refer to Israeli military service to defend the Jewish People, or standing up physically against Jew-hating bullies.

392 Such doubts were more typical of diaspora Jews, for example in Steven Spielberg's film, Munich, where he projected his own confusion onto the Israeli heroes who were tracking down Palestinian terrorists.

393 Gefen, Rabbi Yohonasan. (2021, December 19). All Jews are bound up with each other. Aish.com. https://aish.com/275049371/

394 These unpublished notes are preserved in the public library at Neuchatel.

Cited in Leon Poliakov, The History of Anti-Semitism (Routledge and Kegan Paul, 1975), vol. 3:104–5

395 Kook, HaRav Tzvi Yehuda HaCohen (1991). Torat Eretz Yisrael: The Teachings of HaRav Tzvi Yehuda HaCohen Kook. Torat Eretz Yisrael Publications. 90.

396 The Jews have a unique universal -particular mission, what [Rabbi Kook] calls "the perfect synthesis of the nationalist-particularist phenomena and the religious-universalist conception." Orot. 119. And, "Authentic universalism is expressed through the medium of Israel's nationhood Orot. Note 21 on p 458.

397 Maghen, Ze'ev (2014). John Lennon and the Jews: A Philosophical Rampage. Toby. 265-6.

398 Jäckel, Eberhard (1997). Hitler's World View: A Blueprint for Power, Harvard University Press. 52 Date: January 13, 1923 Speech at Nuremberg.

399 Trevor-Roper, Hugh (2000). Hitler's Table Talk 1941-1944. Enigma. 140

400 Kook, HaRav Tzvi Yehuda HaCohen (1991). Torat Eretz Yisrael: The Teachings of HaRav Tzvi Yehuda HaCohen Kook. Torat Eretz Yisrael Publications. 89. Full quote: "This spirit of idealism, to bring goodness and perfection to the world by uplifting mankind to the recognition and service of Hashem, is embodied in the inner soul of Israel."

401   Maghen, Ze'ev (2014). John Lennon and the Jews: A Philosophical Rampage. Toby. 16.

402 Maharal, Ohr Chodosh 221.

403 Maharal, Tiferes Yisrael chapter 47, 145.

404 As Rabbi Lord Sacks says, " To be a Jew is to be loved by God; it is not to be hated by Gentiles." Covenant And Conversation. Parshat Balak. https://mailchi.mp/rabbisacks/balak-246424?e=87ccc3ea4c

405 As Rabbi Lord Sacks says, "Indeed, it is only by being what we uniquely are that we contribute to humankind what we alone can give. Singular,

distinctive, countercultural – yes: these are part of the Jewish condition."
Covenant And Conversation. Parshat Balak.
https://mailchi.mp/rabbisacks/balak-246424?e=87ccc3ea4c

Chapter 9

406 Sacks, Rabbi Jonathan (2000). A Letter in the Scroll: Understanding our Jewish Identity and Exploring the Legacy of the World's Oldest Religion. Free Press.

407 Sacks, Rabbi Jonathan (2000). A Letter in the Scroll: Understanding our Jewish Identity and Exploring the Legacy of the World's Oldest Religion. Free Press. 226.

408 The Torah idea is that each person's soul is brought into the world to fulfill a special purpose. That is his/her yiud.

409 Midrash Rabbah Vayikra 32:5 and Pesikta Zuta 6:6

410 Isaiah 42:6

411 Recommended books: A History of the Jews, Paul Johnson; Crash Course in Jewish History, Ken Spiro.

412 Recommended books: Israel: A Concise History of a Nation Reborn, Daniel Gordis; The Prime Ministers: An Intimate Narrative of Israeli Leadership, Yehuda Avner; The Zionist Ideas: Visions for the Jewish Homeland? Then, Now, Tomorrow, Gil Troy.

413 Get a learning partner through https://www.partnersintorah.org/, look up your local Rabbi, or check out these fine sites: opendormedia.org, aish.com, chabad.org, torah.org.

414 Rabbi Schwartz is the founder of the Aseret movement and is also the Executive Producer of my film on this book's topic, called Tragic Awakening: A new Look at the Oldest Hatred. See www.oct7film.com.

415 Their vision is: A global effort to ensure the safety of Israel, a brighter future for citizens, and an inspired tomorrow for young Jews and youth all around the world. Visit them at www.LetsDoSomething.com

416 After his friend was killed on Oct. 7, a 25-year-old raised millions for the war effort | The Times of Israel. (2024, April 20). The Times of Israel. https://www.timesofisrael.com/after-his-friend-was-killed-on-oct-7-a-25-year-old-raised-millions-for-the-war-effort/

417 From The Inside Out w/ Rivkah & Eda. (2024, March 18). Hamas Hostage Speaks Out: Sapir Cohen's Story at Beth Tefillah Arizona Gala, PART 1 [Video]. YouTube. https://www.youtube.com/watch?v=JgFX67HE2RM

Scarr, C., & Scarr, C. (2024, April 11). Here for a reason - Mishpacha Magazine. Mishpacha Magazine - The premier Magazine for the Jewish World. https://mishpacha.com/here-for-a-reason/

418 1936 photo, in which a man alleged to be August Landmesser is conspicuously not giving the Nazi salute. https://en.wikipedia.org/wiki/August_Landmesser#/media/File:August-Landmesser-Almanya-1936.jpg Accessed July 2024.

419 Excerpt from Moral Ambition, by Rutger Bregman, which will be published in April 2025.

420 Lebor, M. (2024, April 8). ESRAMagazine. ESRAmagazine. https://magazine.esra.org.il/esramagazine/look-into-it/latest-esramagazine/entry/an-evening-with-douglas-murray.html

421 Sela Meir - Shibulat Library. (2024, June 5). "Europe owes the Jews. And if she wants to survive she should also learn from them": watch Douglas Murray's speech in Paris [Video]. YouTube. https://www.youtube.com/watch?v=b4N7JRKUE8w

422 You can check out the film at my website www.raphaelshore.com

423 Unsafe Spaces, Unpacked. (2023, February 1). Are college protests antisemitic? | Unpacked [Video]. YouTube. https://www.youtube.com/watch?v=1fZiQB2sVgg

424 Maruf, R. (2023, October 25). UPenn donors were furious about the Palestine Writes Literature Festival. What about it made them pull their funds? CNN. https://edition.cnn.com/2023/10/25/business/palestine-writes-literature-festival-what-happened/index.html

425 Ensign, R. L., & Journal, H. B. F. W. S. (2023, November 3). The billionaire donor taking on his alma mater over antisemitism. WSJ. https://www.wsj.com/us-news/education/the-billionaire-donor-taking-on-his-alma-mater-over-antisemitism-2d1637cd

426 Kirsch, N. (2024, March 11). Billionaire Marc Rowan's war with the University of Pennsylvania keeps getting hotter. The Daily Beast. https://www.thedailybeast.com/billionaire-marc-rowans-war-with-the-university-of-pennsylvania-keeps-getting-hotter

427 At one point, U.S. Rep. Elise Stefanik (R-NY), asked Magill if "specifically calling for the genocide of Jews, does that constitute bullying or harassment?" Magill initially replied "If it is directed and severe, pervasive, it is harassment."

Stefanik said, "So the answer is yes."

Magill replied "It is a context-dependent decision, Congresswoman." Lyons, K. (2023, December 8). Penn president under pressure to resign following testimony before Congress about antisemitism. Pennsylvania Capital-Star. Pennsylvania Capital-Star. https://penncapital-star.com/briefs/penn-president-under-pressure-to-resign-following-testimony-before-congress-about-antisemitism/

428 Staff, B. J. P. (2024, June 24). Marc Rowan: Campus antisemitism is bleeding into anti-Americanism. The Jerusalem Post | JPost.com. https://www.jpost.com/diaspora/antisemitism/article-805107

429 See Sacks, Rabbi Jonathan (2000). A Letter in the Scroll: Understanding our Jewish Identity and Exploring the Legacy of the World's Oldest Religion. Free Press.

430 https://en.globes.co.il/en/article-sharansky-in-prison-i-was-freer-than-my-interrogators-1001480613, https://tikvahfund.org/tikvah-online/freedom-vs-tyranny-natan-sharanskys-speech-to-the-soviet-union/
Freedom vs. Tyranny: Sharansky's "Speech to the Soviet Union" - The Tikvah Fund. (2021, July 27). The Tikvah Fund. https://tikvahfund.org/tikvah-online/freedom-vs-tyranny-natan-sharanskys-speech-to-the-soviet-union/
Whitman, A. (2024, January 7). Sharansky: In prison I was freer than my

interrogators. Globes. https://en.globes.co.il/en/article-sharansky-in-prison-i-was-freer-than-my-interrogators-1001480613

431 424,000 Jews were deported to Auschwitz in just 8 weeks - in total, 565,000 Hungariona Jews were murdered. https://www.yadvashem.org/holocaust/about/fate-of-jews/hungary.html#narrative_info
Murder of Hungarian Jewry. (n.d.). https://www.yadvashem.org/holocaust/about/fate-of-jews/hungary.html#narrative_info

432 See https://www.ladderofjacob.com/post/ki-teitzei-the-bird-s-nest and https://mosaicmagazine.com/observation/religion-holidays/2018/08/the-kabbalah-of-birds-nests/
Burton, B. (2024, July 15). Ki Teitzei: The Bird's Nest. Ladder of Jacob. https://www.ladderofjacob.com/post/ki-teitzei-the-bird-s-nest
Mosaic Magazine. (n.d.). The Kabbalah of Birds' Nests. https://mosaicmagazine.com/observation/religion-holidays/2018/08/the-kabbalah-of-birds-nests/

433 ABOUT | KobyMandellFndn. (n.d.). KobyMandellFndn. https://www.kobymandell.org/about

434 Mandel, Sherri (2009). The Blessing of a Broken Heart. Toby Press.

435 Talmud Avodah Zarah 17b, Deuteronomy 4:5

436 Israeli comedian urges 100,000 Israelis to keep Shabbos parshas Zachor. (2024, March 18). https://www.theyeshivaworld.com/news/israel-news/2269962/israeli-comedian-urges-100000-israelis-to-keep-shabbos-parshas-zachor.html

437 Maghen, Ze'ev (2014). John Lennon and the Jews: A Philosophical Rampage. Toby. 313.

438 Sacks, Rabbi Jonathan (2000). A Letter in the Scroll: Understanding our Jewish Identity and Exploring the Legacy of the World's Oldest Religion. Free Press. 229.

Postscript

439 This is a quotation from the book flap of Ken Spiro's book, Destiny: Why a Tiny Nation Plays a Huge Role in History. (2018). Gefen Books.

References

"3D Test of Anti-Semitism: demonization, double standards, delegitimization". November 11, 2024. Jerusalem Center for Public Affairs. https://jcpa.org/article/3d-test-of-anti-semitism-demonization-double-standards-delegitimization/

Abrams, Elliott. "UN Halves Its Estimate of Women and Children Killed in Gaza." Council on Foreign Relations, May 12, 2024. https://www.cfr.org/blog/un-halves-its-estimate-women-and-children-killed-gaza.

Adams, President John. "Founders Online: From John Adams to François Adriaan Van Der Kemp, 16 February 1809," University of Virginia Press, 1809. https://founders.archives.gov/documents/Adams/99-02-02-5302.

"ADL reports unprecedented rise in antisemitic incidents Post-Oct. 7". January 4, 2024. ADL. https://www.adl.org/resources/press-release/adl-reports-unprecedented-rise-antisemitic-incidents-post-oct-7

ArchiveAuthor. "Enrollment of Jews in U.S. medical schools dropped 50 percent in last 20 years." Jewish Telegraphic Agency, August 7, 1950. https://www.jta.org/archive/enrollment-of-jews-in-u-s-medical-schools-dropped-50-percent-in-last-20-years

ArchiveAuthor. "Soviet Union Has 30,663 Jewish Scientists, Handbook on Russia Shows." Jewish Telegraphic Agency, December 28, 1960. https://www.jta.org/archive/soviet-union-has-30663-jewish-scientists-handbook-on-russia-shows.

Aron, Raymond. "Existe-t-il un mystere Nazi?" Commentaire, 1979.

Baker, G., and A. Sultan. "What's behind the propaganda war against Israel." WSJ, March 11, 2024.

BBC News. "Kyrie Irving Suspended Over anti-Semitic Posts,"

November 4, 2022. https://www.bbc.com/news/world-us-canada-63509715.

Bermudez, Krystal. "Most Palestinians Support October 7 Attack, Dissatisfied With Abbas and Fatah." FDD, June 14, 2024. https://www.fdd.org/analysis/2024/06/14/most-palestinians-support-october-7-attack-dissatisfied-with-abbas-and-fatah/.

Berzovsky, Rabbi Shalom Noah. *Nesivos Shalom on the Torah, Exodus.* Yeshivat Beit Avraham Slonim.

Biberfeld, Philip. *Universal Jewish History.* Volume II, The Patriarchal Age. Feldheim, 1962. p177-197.

Big Jewish Ideas. "Shabbat: The Ancient Jewish Secret to Mindfulness | Explained." YouTube, June 27, 2024. https://www.youtube.com/watch?v=x00gN6OXDGE

Bloch, Dr. Emmanuel. and Ron, Dr. Rabbi Zvi. "Purimfest 1946: The Nuremberg Trials and the Ten Sons of Haman - TheTorah.com," n.d. https://www.thetorah.com/article/purimfest-1946-the-nuremberg-trials-and-the-ten-sons-of-haman.

Boyd, J. "FBI: U.S. Jews by far most targeted group in Anti-Religious hate crimes". November 17, 2020. The Federalist. https://thefederalist.com/2020/11/17/fbi-u-s-jews-by-far-most-targeted-group-in-anti-religious-hate-crimes/

Breiting, Richard. *Secret Conversations with Hitler.* John Day Company. 1971.

Breuer, B. E. "Over 1,000 antisemitic incidents on college campuses since October 7." The Jerusalem Post, February 20, 2024.

Bullock, Alan. *Hitler: A Study in Tyranny.* Penguin Books, 1971.

Burg, S. L. "Russians, Natives, and Jews in the Soviet Scientific Elite." Cahiers Du Monde Russe Et Soviétique 20, no. 1 (1979): 43–59. https://doi.org/10.3406/cmr.1979.1347

Burton, Ben. "Ki Teitzei: The Bird's Nest." Ladder of Jacob (blog),

August 9, 2024. https://www.ladderofjacob.com/post/ki-teitzei-the-bird-s-nest.

Cahill, Thomas. *The Gifts of the Jews: How a Tribe of Desert Nomads Changed the Way Everyone Thinks and Feels*. Nan A. Talese/Anchor Books, 1999.

Chabon, Michael. "Those People: Michael Chabon's Commencement Address at Hebrew Union College, Los Angeles." Tablet Magazine, August 2, 2023. https://www.tabletmag.com/sections/arts-letters/articles/michael-chabon-commencement.

"Chapter 18: The Jewish Answer to Evil," n.d., https://www.chabad.org/therebbe/article_cdo/aid/3144797/jewish/Chapter-18-The-Jewish-Answer-to-Evil.htm.

Dawidowicz, Lucy S. *The War Against the Jews 1933-1945*. Bantam Books, 1975.

Deutscher, Isaac. *The Non-Jewish Jew and Other Essays*. Oxford University Press, 1968.

Dostoevsky, Fyodor. *The Brothers Karamazov* (Bicentennial Edition). United Kingdom: Picador, 2021.

Dühring, Eugen. *Die Judenfrage als Racen-, Sitten- und Culturfrage: Mit einer weltgeschichtlichen Antwort* (The Jewish Question as a Question of Race, Customs and Culture: With an Answer Relating to World History). 1881.

Eaton, George. "Rabbi Jonathan Sacks: 'The hate that begins with Jews never ends with Jews.'" New Statesman, September 4, 2021. https://www.newstatesman.com/encounter/2018/08/rabbi-jonathan-sacks-hate-begins-jews-never-ends-jews

Eckart, Dietrich. *Der Bolschevismus von Moses bis Lenin – A Dialogue between Adolf Hitler and Me*. White Power Publications, 1966. https://archive.org/details/national-socialist-world-fall-1966-eckart-dietrich-bolshevism-from-moses-to-leni

Eckart, Dietrich. "Nazi Culture." As cited in Mosse, Nazi Culture, 1928. 75.

Ensign, Rachel Louise, and Hannah Beier for Wall Street Journal. "The

Billionaire Donor Taking on His Alma Mater Over Antisemitism." WSJ, November 3, 2023. https://www.wsj.com/us-news/education/the-billionaire-donor-taking-on-his-alma-mater-over-antisemitism-2d1637cd.

"Eric Hoffer's Defense of Israel - LA Times 1968". June 21, 2011. The Jewish Chronicle. https://www.thejc.com/lets-talk/eric-hoffers-defense-of-israel-from-la-times-1968-sdwwsiw7

Erikson, Erik. *Childhood and Society*. W.W. Norton and Company Inc, 1950.

Eze Vidra. "NYU Professor Scott Galloway on the double standard applied to Israel." YouTube, April 26, 2024. https://www.youtube.com/watch?v=kRWCy03dmjs

Fackenheim, Emil L. *The Jewish Return to History - Reflections in the Age of Auschwitz and a New Jerusalem*. Schocken. 1978.

Fitz-Gibbon, Jorge. "Masked Protester Taunts NYC Israel Day Parade With Vile 'Kill Hostages Now' Sign as Families of Oct. 7th Captives March." New York Post, June 2, 2024. https://nypost.com/2024/06/02/us-news/anti-israel-protester-taunts-nyc-parade-marchers-with-vile-kill-hostages-now-sign/.

Förster, Jürgen. *The Wehrmacht and the War of Extermination against the Soviet Union*. K. G. Saur, 1989.

Fox, Andrew. "Israel Is Succeeding in Gaza." Tablet Magazine, May 23, 2024. https://www.tabletmag.com/sections/israel-middle-east/articles/israel-succeeding-gaza.

Frank, Anne. *The Diary of a Young Girl*: The Definitive Edition. Doubleday, 1995. Diary entry of April 11, 1944.

Fraser, Giles. "On the Genealogy of Morals part 2: The Slave Morality." The Guardian, November 6, 2008.

"Freedom vs. Tyranny: Sharansky's "Speech to the Soviet Union."" The Tikvah Fund, July 27, 2021. https://tikvahfund.org/tikvah-online/freedom-vs-tyranny-natan-sharanskys-speech-to-the-soviet-union/

Friedlander, Saul. *From Antisemitism to Extermination: A Historiographical*

Study of Nazi Policies Towards the Jews and an Essay in Interpretation. Yad Vashem. 1982.

Freud, Sigmund. *Moses and Monotheism.* Vintage Books, 1967. p116-7.

From The Inside Out w/ Rivkah & Eda. "Hamas Hostage Speaks Out: Sapir Cohen's Story at Beth Tefillah Arizona Gala, PART 1," March 18, 2024. https://www.youtube.com/watch?v=JgFX67HE2RM.

Gabler, Neil. *An Empire of Their Own: How the Jews Invented Hollywood.* Anchor Books, 1989.

Geduld, H. M. "Bernard Shaw and Adolf Hitler." The Shaw Review 4, no. 1 (January 1961): 11–20.

Gefen, Rabbi Yehonasan. "All Jews Are Bound up With Each Other." Aish.com, December 19, 2021. https://aish.com/275049371.

Geselowitz, Gabriela. "Alexander Hamilton's Jewish Connection." Tablet Magazine, July 10, 2021. https://www.tabletmag.com/sections/news/articles/alexander-hamiltons-jewish-connection.

Gilbert, M. (2010). The Routledge Atlas of Jewish History (8th ed.). Routledge. https://doi.org/10.4324/9780203074459

Gilder, George. *The Israel Test.* Richard Vigilante Books, 2009.

Goebbels, Joseph. Communism with the Mask off. *Speech Delivered in Nurenberg on September 13th, 1935 at the Seventh National Socialist Party Congress.* M. Müller. 1935.

Greenfield, Daniel. "The Ghetto Jew and Israel." *Israel National News,* August 17, 2015. https://www.israelnationalnews.com/news/345993.

Greenfield, Daniel. "There Are No Civilians in Gaza." JNS.org, June 13, 2024. https://www.jns.org/there-are-no-civilians-in-gaza/.

Griffin, Anna. "Hitler Accuses Roosevelt, Jews in Speech at Berlin Conference." World War 2.0, February 1, 2017. https://blogs.shu.edu/ww2-0/1942/01/31/hitler-accuses-roosevelt-jews-in-speech-at-berlin-conference/.

Grodzinski, Rabbi Abraham. *Toras Abraham*. 1962. https://tablet.otzar.org/#/b/103789/p/1/t/1670122892800/fs/0/start/0/end/0/c

Grossman, Vasilii. *"Treblinskii ad" The Hell of Treblinka in The Years of War (1941-1945)*. Foreign Languages Publishing House, 1946.

Gruenberg, Justin S. (2009) "An Analysis of United Nations Security Council Resolutions: Are All Countries Treated Equally?" Case Western Reserve Journal of International Law, Vol. 41, Issue 2, Article 12. https://scholarlycommons.law.case.edu/cgi/viewcontent.cgi?article=1268&context=jil

Grunberger, Richard. *The 12-Year Reich: A Social History of Nazi Germany, 1933-1945*. Holt, Rinehart and Winston, 1979.

Guest, Hazel Skelsey. "Maslow's Hierarchy of Needs – the Sixth Level," BPS. January 22, 2024. https://www.bps.org.uk/psychologist/maslows-hierarchy-needs-sixth-level.

"Hamas's October 7 Attack: Visualizing the Data", December 19, 2023. Center for Strategic and International Studies. https://www.csis.org/analysis/hamass-october-7-attack-visualizing-data

Hadley Freeman. "The progressive left hates Jews." The Times of Israel, June 4, 2024.

Haggbloom, Steven J., Renee Warnick, Jason E. Warnick, Vinessa K. Jones, Gary L. Yarbrough, Tenea M. Russell, Chris M. Borecky, et al. "The 100 Most Eminent Psychologists of the 20th Century." *Review of General Psychology* 6, no. 2 (June 1, 2002): 139–52. https://doi.org/10.1037/1089-2680.6.2.139.

Haque, O. S., J. De Freitas, I. Viani, B. Niederschulte, and H. J. Bursztajn. "Why did so many German doctors join the Nazi Party early?" International Journal of Law and Psychiatry 35, no. 5–6 (2012): 473–479. https://doi.org/10.1016/j.ijlp.2012.09.022

Herberg, Will. *Judaism and Modern Man*. Farrar, Straus and Young, 1951. p273.

"Herzl: An Annotated Study of 'a Solution to the Jewish Question' (1896) " n.d. https://www.sefaria.org.il/sheets/367720.50.

Hess, Moses. *Rome and Jerusalem: A Study in Jewish Nationalism*. 1958.

Hicks, Stephen. "How Smart and Well-read was Adolf Hitler?" Good Life series, November 6, 2016. https://www.stephenhicks.org/2016/11/06/how-smart-and-well-read-was-adolf-hitler/

Hirsch, Rabbi Samson Raphael. *The Collected Writings of Rabbi Samson Raphael Hirsch*. Volume 1. Feldheim, 1984.

Hitler, Adolf. *Mein Kampf*. Houghton Mifflin. 1971.

Hitler, Adolf. "Political Testament of Adolf Hitler". Full text of "Political Testament of Adolf Hitler." (n.d.). 1945. https://archive.org/stream/PoliticalTestamentOfAdolfHitler/PTAH_djvu.txt

Hoffer, Eric. "Israel's Peculiar Position." *Los Angeles Times*, May 26, 1968.

Horn, Dara. *People Love Dead Jews: Reports from a Haunted Present*. W.W. Norton. 2021.

Huberband, Shimon. *Jewish Religious and Cultural Life in Poland During the Holocaust*. Translated by David E. Fishman. Edited by Jeffrey S. Gurock and Robert S. Hirt. KTAV Publishing House/ Yeshiva University Press. 1987.

i24NEWS. "'They Killed My Friends and All My Beliefs' After Oct. 7, Peace Activists Face Change of Heart." *i24NEWS*, January 19, 2024. https://www.i24news.tv/en/news/israel-at-war/survivor-testimonies/1705690765-feature.

Ihaza, J. "How did Kanye get here? A short history of provocation and extreme rhetoric." Rolling Stone, December 26, 2023. https://www.rollingstone.com/music/music-news/kanye-west-antisemitism-hate-speech-controversy-1234611647/

"Israeli Comedian Urges 100,000 Israelis to Keep Shabbos Parshas Zachor," March 18, 2024. https://www.theyeshivaworld.com/news/israel-news/2269962/israeli-comedian-urges-100000-israelis-to-keep-shabbos-parshas-zachor.html.

J-TV: Jewish Ideas. Global Relevance. "Jewish Student Tells Congress About Antisemitism at NYU," December 6, 2023. https://www.youtube.com/watch?v=tAF9Gu7gdzY.

Jäckel, Eberhard. *Hitler's World View: A Blueprint for Power.* Harvard University Press, 1997.

Jacobson, H. *The Finkler Question.* Bloomsbury, 2010.

Jacobson, Simon. *Toward a Meaningful Life: The Wisdom of the Rebbe Menachem Mendel Schneerson.* Harper Collins, 2002.

"Jews again faced most hate crimes of any religious group in 2022, FBI reports." The Times of Israel. October 17, 2023. https://www.timesofisrael.com/jews-again-faced-most-hate-crimes-of-any-religious-group-in-2022-fbi-reports/

Jinfo, and Jinfo. "Jewish World Chess Champions," n.d. https://www.jinfo.org/Chess_Champions.html.

JNS.org. (n.d.). "Pay for Slay Archives" JNS.org. https://www.jns.org/topic/pay-for-slay/

Johnson, Paul. *A History of the Jews.* Harper & Row, 1987.

Kamenetz, Rodger. *The Jew in the Lotus: A Poet's Rediscovery of Jewish Identity in Buddhist India.* Harper Collins, 1995.

Karsh, Efraim. "The privileged Palestinian 'Refugees.'" Middle East Forum, June 1, 2018. https://www.meforum.org/7241/the-privileged-palestinian-refugees

Kaufman, Elliot. "Biden's Worst Mistake of the Gaza War." *WSJ*, May 5, 2024. https://www.wsj.com/articles/bidens-worst-mistake-of-the-gaza-war-901efb25?mod=hp_opin_pos_2#cxrecs_s.

Kirsch, Noah. "Billionaire Marc Rowan's War With the University of Pennsylvania Keeps Getting Hotter." *The Daily Beast*, March 11, 2024. https://www.thedailybeast.com/billionaire-marc-rowans-war-with-the-university-of-pennsylvania-keeps-getting-hotter.

Klinghoffer, David. *The Discovery of God: Abraham and the Birth of Monotheism.* Doubleday, 2003.

Kook, HaRav Tzvi Yehuda HaCohen. *Torat Eretz Yisrael: The Teachings of HaRav Tzvi Yehuda HaCohen Kook.* Torat Eretz Yisrael Publications, 1991.

Kook, Rabbi Abraham Isaac. *Orot*. Maggid Books, 2022.

Kukreti, Shweta. "Iran's Khamenei Pens Open Letter to anti-Israel US Campus Protesters, Urges Them 'To Become Familiar With Quran.'" *Hindustan Times*, May 30, 2024. https://www.hindustantimes.com/world-news/us-news/irans-khamenei-pens-open-letter-to-anti-israel-us-campus-protesters-urges-them-to-become-familiar-with-quran-101717059892586.html.

Kuntzel, Matthias. *Jihad and Jew-Hatred: Islamism, Nazism and the Roots of 9/11*. Telos Press, 2007.

Kuperwasser, B. Y. Incentivizing Terrorism: Palestinian Authority Allocations to Terrorists and their Families. Jerusalem Center for Public Affairs, April 17, 2024. https://jcpa.org/paying-salaries-terrorists-contradicts-palestinian-vows-peaceful-intentions/

Lange, Serg and Von Schenck, Ernst. *Memoirs of Alfred Rosenberg*. Ziff-Davis. 1949.

Laqueur, Walter, and Barry Rubin, eds. *The Israel Arab Reader: A Documentary History of the Middle East Conflict*. Penguin Books, 1984.

Lebor, Marian. "ESRAmagazine." *ESRAmagazine* (blog), April 8, 2024. https://magazine.esra.org.il/esramagazine/look-into-it/latest-esramagazine/entry/an-evening-with-douglas-murray.html.

Lewis, Bernard. *Semites and Anti-Semites*. W. W. Norton & Company, 1999.

Linder. "The Trials of the Nuremberg Trials," n.d. http://law2.umkc.edu/faculty/projects/ftrials/nuremberg/NurembergNews10_16_46.html.

Luther, Martin. "*The Jews & Their Lies*." (n.d.). 2024. https://www.jewishvirtuallibrary.org/martin-luther-quot-the-jews-and-their-lies-quot#google_vignette

Luzzatto, Rabbi Moshe Chaim. *Derech Hashem - The Way Of God*. Feldheim, 1983.

Luzzatto, Rabbi Moshe Chaim. *Mesilat Yesharim - The Path of the Just*. Feldheim, 1980.

Lyons, Kim. "Penn President Under Pressure to Resign Following Testimony Before Congress About Antisemitism • Pennsylvania Capital-Star." Pennsylvania Capital-Star, December 8, 2023. https://penncapital-star.com/briefs/penn-president-under-pressure-to-resign-following-testimony-before-congress-about-antisemitism/.

Maghen, Ze'ev. *John Lennon and the Jews: A Philosophical Rampage*. Toby Press, 2014.

Maimonides. Mishneh Torah, *Avoda Zara*.

Maharal. *Gvuros Hashem*.

Maharal. *Tiferes Yisrael*.

Mandel, Sherri. *The Blessing of a Broken Heart*. Toby Press, 2009.

Maritain, Jacques. *A Christian Looks at the Jewish Question*. Longmans, Green and Company, 1939.

Marsden, Victor E. *PROTOCOLS of the Learned Elders of ZION*, trans. by Victor E. Marsden. The Mercian Free Press, 2014. https://ia803409.us.archive.org/6/items/books_202012/The%20Protocols%20of%20the%20Learned%20Elders%20of%20Zion%20%28%20PDFDrive%20%29.pdf

"Martin Niemöller: 'First they came for the Socialists...'" United States Holocaust Memorial Museum. https://encyclopedia.ushmm.org/content/en/article/martin-niemoeller-first-they-came-for-the-socialists

Maruf, Ramishah. "UPenn Donors Were Furious About the Palestine Writes Literature Festival. What About It Made Them Pull Their Funds?" CNN, October 25, 2023. https://edition.cnn.com/2023/10/25/business/palestine-writes-literature-festival-what-happened/index.html.

Mayer, Avi. "The average civilian casualty ratio in modern warfare is around 9:1 - that is, nine civilians killed for every combatant. In the current war, it is about 1.7:1. That's remarkable." X (Formerly Twitter), February 12, 2024. https://x.com/AviMayer/status/1757065611471913161

Mazurczak, F. "Dachau Golgotha." First Things. July 10, 2017. https://www.firstthings.com/web-exclusives/2017/07/dachau-golgotha

Mendes, Phillip. "'WE ARE ALL GERMAN JEWS': EXPLORING THE PROMINENCE OF JEWS IN THE NEW LEFT." *Melilah Manchester Journal of Jewish Studies (1759-1953)* 6, no. 1 (January 1, 2011): 22–38. https://doi. org/10.31826/mjj-2011-060104.

Mendes-Flohr, Paul, and Jehuda Reinharz, eds. *The Jew in the Modern World*. Oxford University Press, 1995.

Meixler, E. (2021, July 10). "Malaysia's newly elected prime minister has a troubling history of hating Jews." Tablet Magazine. https://www.tabletmag. com/sections/news/articles/malaysias-newly-elected-prime-minister-has-a-troubling-history-of-hating-jews

Miller, Elhanan. "Palestinians: Yes to Jews, No to Settlers in Our State." Times of Israel, January 27, 2014. https://www.timesofisrael.com/palestinians-yes-to-jews-no-to-settlers-in-our-state/.

Miodownik, Rabbi Steven. "The Three Shofarot of Rosh Hashanah &Ndash; World Mizrachi." World Mizrachi, September 18, 2022. https://mizrachi.org/hamizrachi/the-three-shofarot-of-rosh-hashanah/.

Montreal Jewish Forums - December 15th, 1963 - leonardcohenforum.com. (2017, July 17). https://www.leonardcohenforum.com/viewtopic.php?t=37527

Morphet, Jack, Alex Oliveira, Reuven Fenton, and Allie Griffin. "Anti-Israel Protesters Vandalize WWI Memorial, Burn American Flag After Cops Block Group From Reaching Star-studded Met Gala in NYC." *New York Post*, May 7, 2024. https://nypost.com/2024/05/06/us-news/over-1000-pro-palestinian-protesters-march-toward-met-gala/.

Mosaic Magazine. "The Kabbalah of Birds' Nests," n.d. https://mosaicmagazine.com/observation/religion-holidays/2018/08/the-kabbalah-of-birds-nests/.

"Murder of Hungarian Jewry," n.d. https://www.yadvashem.org/holocaust/about/fate-of-jews/hungary.html#narrative_info.

Murray, C. "Jewish genius. Commentary Magazine". November 16, 2015. https://www.commentary.org/articles/charles-murray/jewish-genius/

Nelson, Eric. *The Hebrew Republic: Jewish Sources and the Transformation of European Political Thought*. Harvard University Press, 2010.

newformofflight. "Candace Owens vs Douglas Murray." YouTube, March 25, 2024.

Newsweek Magazine. "Newsweek (US Edition) 1946-10-28: Vol 28 Iss 18 : Free Download, Borrow, and Streaming : Internet Archive," October 28, 1946. p 45. https://archive.org/details/sim_newsweek-us_1946-10-28_28_18/page/44/mode/2up.

New York Time (Associated Press). "Palestinians Face Death for Selling Land to Jews." *The New York Times*, May 6, 1997. https://www.nytimes.com/1997/05/06/world/palestinians-face-death-for-selling-land-to-jews.html.

Nietzsche, Friedrich. *Beyond Good and Evil*. Penguin Books, 1973.

Nietzsche, Friedrich. *Ecce Homo*. Trans. by Antony M. Ludovici. Wordsworth, 2007.

Nietzsche, Friedrich. *On the Genealogy of Morals*. Trans. by Michael A. Scarpitti. Penguin Group, 2013.

Nirenberg, David. *Anti-Judaism: The Western Tradition*. W. W. Norton & Company, 2014.

Office of United States Chief of Counsel for Prosecution of Axis Criminality. *Nazi Conspiracy and Aggression, Supplement B*. United States Government Printing Office, Washington. 1948. p 1434.

"Over a third of people in Hungary, Poland have 'extensive' antisemitic beliefs – poll". May 31, 2023. The Times of Israel. https://www.timesofisrael.com/over-a-third-of-people-in-hungary-poland-have-extensive-antisemitic-beliefs-poll/

Patterson, David. *Anti-Semitism and Its Metaphysical Origins*. Cambridge University Press, 2015.

Pearlman, Jonathan. "Blindness: October 7 and the Left." The Jewish Quarterly, May 2024. https://jewishquarterly.com/essay/2024/05/blindness.

Philpot, Robert. "After Oct. 7, UK Journalist Hadley Freeman Believes 'the

Progressive Left Hates Jews." Times of Israel, June 4, 2024. https://www.timesofisrael.com/after-oct-7-uk-journalist-hadley-freeman-believes-the-progressive-left-hates-jews/.

Pois, Robert A. *National Socialism and the Religion of Nature.* Palgrave Macmillan, 1986. p46,57-58.

"Political Testament of Adolf Hitler." (n.d.). 1945. https://archive.org/stream/PoliticalTestamentOfAdolfHitler/PTAH_djvu.txt

"Poll: 93% of Palestinians hold anti-Jewish beliefs." The Times of Israel. May 14, 2014. The Times of Israel. https://www.timesofisrael.com/poll-93-of-palestinians-hold-anti-jewish-beliefs/

"Poll: 96% of Jews in 13 EU Countries Say They Experience Antisemitism in Daily Life." The Times of Israel. July 19, 2024. https://www.timesofisrael.com/poll-96-of-jews-in-13-eu-countries-say-they-experience-antisemitism-in-daily-life/.

Prager, Dennis and Telushkin, Joseph (2003). *Why the Jews: The Reason for Antisemitism.* Touchstone. 56-64.

Prange, Gordon W., ed. *Hitler's Words: Two Decades of National Socialism, 1923-1943.* Washington, D.C.: American Council on Public Affairs, 1944.

Preston Stewart on X: "Iran released a video directed at US university students titled 'You are standing on the right side of history' https://t.co/djbCtpgBXZ." X (Formerly Twitter).

Rauschning, Herman. *Hitler Speaks: A Series of Political Conversations with Adolf Hitler on his Real Aims.* Eyre and Spottiswoode, 1940.

Rauschning, Herman. *The Beast From The Abyss.* William Heinemann, 1941.

Rauschning, Herman. *The Voice of Destruction.* Pelican, 2003.

Religious Action Center of Reform Judaism. "A Brief History of Jews and the Civil Rights Movement of the 1960s," April 7, 2014. https://rac.org/issues/civil-rights-voting-rights/brief-history-jews-and-civil-rights-movement-1960s.

Remak, Yoachim. *The Nazi Years: A Documentary History.* Simon and Schuster, and Waveland Press. 1990.

Rosen, Armin. "Ivy League Exodus." Tablet Magazine, June 29, 2023. https://www.tabletmag.com/sections/arts-letters/articles/ivy-league-exodus.

Rosen, Steven J. "Kuwait expels thousands of Palestinians." Middle East Forum, September 1, 2012. https://www.meforum.org/3391/kuwait-expels-palestinians

Rosenberg, Alfred. *Immorality in the Talmud.* Preuss. 6. Franz Eher Verlag, 1943.

Rosenberg, Alfred. *Race and Race History and Other Essays.* Robert Pois, ed. Harper Torchbooks. 1974. p183.

Rosenberg, Alfred. *The Myth of the Twentieth Century.* Friends of Europe, 1930. p 10-11.

Rosenberg, Rabbi Bernhard. "Did Purim Heroine Esther Prophesy About the Nazis?" *Courier News*, March 4, 2015. https://www.mycentraljersey.com/story/life/faith/2015/03/04/purim-heroine-esther-prophesy-nazis/24273719/.

Rosenberg, Steve. "'Let Them Go,' Not 'Bring Them Home'," JNS.org, July 21, 2024, https://www.jns.org/let-them-go-not-bring-them-home/.

Rosenstock-Huessy, E. ed. *Judaism Despite Christianity - The 'Letters on Christianity and Judaism' between Eugene Rosenstock-Huessy and Franz Rosenzweig,* 1971.

Rosenwald, Michael S. "'Then They Came for Me': A Hitler Supporter's Haunting Warning Has a Complicated History." *Washington Post*, October 28, 2021. https://www.washingtonpost.com/news/retropolis/wp/2017/08/19/then-they-came-for-me-a-hitler-supporters-haunting-warning-has-a-complicated-history/.

Rothstein, R. Gidon. "The Mitzvah of Talmud Torah, Torah Study." Torah Musings, November 21, 2022. https://www.torahmusings.com/2022/11/the-mitzvah-of-talmud-torah-torah-study/

Rubina, Dina. "Rude and Crude but Definitely Justified - Quadrant

Online." Quadrant Online, May 28, 2024. https://quadrant.org.au/opinion/israel/2024/05/rude-and-crude-but-definitely-justified/.

Rudee, Eliana. "The Chabon Speech: Students and Rabbis Note the Disconnect From Graduation ... and Judaism." JNS.org, June 6, 2018. https://www.jns.org/the-chabon-speech-students-and-rabbis-note-the-disconnect-from-graduation-and-judaism/.

Rust, M., D. Frosch, V. Bauerlein, T. Umlauf, and A. K. Images. "The growing Pro-Palestinian protest movement, visualized." WSJ, April 24, 2024.

Sachar, Howard Morley. *A History of the Jews in America*. Vintage. 1993. p311.

Sachs, N. "Iran's revolution, 40 years on: Israel's reverse periphery doctrine." Brookings, January 24, 2019. https://www.brookings.edu/articles/irans-revolution-40-years-on-israels-reverse-periphery-doctrine/

Sacks, Rabbi Jonathan. *A Letter in the Scroll: Understanding our Jewish Identity and Exploring the Legacy of the World's Oldest Religion*. Free Press, 2000.

Sacks, Rabbi Lord Jonathan. *Radical Then, Radical Now: On Being Jewish*. HarperCollins, 2001.

Sacks, Rabbi Lord Jonathan. "The Art of Listening | Bereishit | Covenant &Amp; Conversation | the Rabbi Sacks Legacy." The Rabbi Sacks Legacy, September 6, 2023. https://rabbisacks.org/covenant-conversation/bereishit/the-art-of-listening/.

Sacks, Rabbi Lord Jonathan. "What is Antisemitism?" The Rabbi Sacks Legacy, February 20, 2023. https://rabbisacks.org/archive/what-is-anti-semitism-moment-magazine/

Sales, B. "Almost all American Jews say anti-Semitism is a problem, according to a new poll. Half of Americans don't know what it means." Jewish Telegraphic Agency, October 27, 2020. https://www.jta.org/2020/10/26/united-states/almost-all-american-jews-say-anti-semitism-is-a-problem-according-to-a-new-poll-half-of-americans-dont-know-what-it-means

Samuel, Maurice. *The Great Hatred*. Alfred A. Knopf, 1940. p128.

Sela Meir - Shibulat Library. "Europe owes the Jews. And if she wants to survive she should also learn from them": watch Douglas Murray's speech in Paris [Video]. YouTube, June 5, 2024. https://www.youtube.com/watch?v=b4N7JRKUE8w

Shannon, Michael. "'Jews Are News' on Twitter – Why? - AIJAC." AIJAC, December 14, 2022. https://aijac.org.au/australia-israel-review/jews-are-news-on-twitter-why/.

Sharansky, Natan. "Freedom vs. Tyranny: Sharansky's "Speech to the Soviet Union" Tikvah Fund, July 27, 2021. https://tikvahfund.org/tikvah-online/freedom-vs-tyranny-natan-sharanskys-speech-to-the-soviet-union/

Shaw, George Bernard. *The Millionairess*. 1936.

Shirer, William L. *The Rise and Fall of the Third Reich*. Secker & Warburg, 1960.

Simmons, D. Worlds Enough & Time: Five Tales of Speculative Fiction. Harper Collin, 2009. https://investigationsandfantasies.com/2014/08/06/the-once-and-future-jews-of-dan-simmons/

Sinek, Simon. "Start with Why - How Great Leaders Inspire Action. TEDxPugetSound." YouTube, September 29, 2009. https://www.youtube.com/watch?v=u4ZoJKF_VuA

Soloveitchik, Yosef Dov. "Experiencing Mesorah in the Classroom." Yeshivat Har Etzion, 1974. https://www.etzion.org.il/en/philosophy/issues-jewish-thought/issues-education/experiencing-mesorah-classroom

Spencer, John. 'in the 2016-2017 Battle of Mosul, the Biggest Urban Battles Since WWII, the U.S. Led Iraqi Security Force Killed 10,000 Civilians to Destroy 4,000 ISIS in the City. That Is a 1 to 2.5 Combatant to Civilian Death Ratio. In the 1945 Battle of Manila (Which Did Have Some Variables.' X (formerly Twitter), n.d. https://x.com/SpencerGuard/status/1786612914117349769.

Spencer, John. "Israel Has Created a New Standard for Urban Warfare. Why Will No One Admit It? | Opinion." *Newsweek*, March 26, 2024. https://www.

newsweek.com/israel-has-created-new-standard-urban-warfare-why-will-no-one-admit-it-opinion-1883286.

Spiro, Ken. *Destiny: Why a Tiny Nation Plays a Huge Role in History.* Gefen Books, 2018.

Spiro, Ken. "Jewish Ideas That Transformed the World." Aish.com, August 30, 2022. https://aish.com/jewish-ideas-that-transformed-the-world/?src=ac-rdm.

Spiro, Ken. "The Seven Wonders of Jewish History." Ken Spiro, January 11, 2015. https://kenspiro.com/audio-classes/the-seven-wonders-of-jewish-history/

Spiro, Ken. *WorldPerfect-The Jewish Impact on Civilization.* Simcha Press, 2002.

Staff, By Jerusalem Post. "Marc Rowan: Campus Antisemitism Is Bleeding Into anti-Americanism." *The Jerusalem Post | JPost.Com*, June 24, 2024. https://www.jpost.com/diaspora/antisemitism/article-805107.

Steiner, George. *The Portage to San Cristobal of A.H.* Simon and Schuster, 1981.

Stewart, Preston. "Iran released a video directed at US university students titled 'You are standing on the right side of history' https://t.co/djbCtpgBXZ" . X (Formerly Twitter). https://x.com/prestonstew_/status/1797596522177327220

Strauchler, Chaim. "Saving Judaism From Michael Chabon." Commentary Magazine, May 1, 2020. https://www.commentary.org/articles/chaim-strauchler/saving-judaism-michael-chabon/.

Streicher, Julius. "Nuremberg Trial Proceedings" Vol. 5, Thirty-First Day, Thursday, Morning Session. *Nuremberg Proceedings.* January 10, 1946.

Stuttaford, A. "Corona conspiracies." National Review. June 22, 2020. https://www.nationalreview.com/2020/04/corona-conspiracies/

Teitel, Emma. "Emma Teitel: Jewish Kids Are Being Victimized in Canada and Nobody Cares," National Post. June 13, 2024. https://nationalpost.com/

opinion/emma-teitel-jewish-kids-are-being-scapegoated-in-canada-and-nobody-cares.

"The 10 most anti-Semitic countries." The Times of Israel, May 13, 2014. https://www.timesofisrael.com/the-10-most-anti-semitic-countries/

The ADL GLOBAL 100: An Index of Antisemitism. (n.d.). https://global100.adl.org/map/subSaharan

The Annotated U.S. Constitution and Declaration of Independence. United Kingdom: Harvard University Press, 2009.

The Associated Press. (1997, May 6). Palestinians face death for selling land to Jews. The New York Times. https://www.nytimes.com/1997/05/06/world/palestinians-face-death-for-selling-land-to-jews.html

The Editorial Board and Carlos Chiossone/Zuma Press. "Celebrating the Nova Massacre in New York City." *WSJ*, June 14, 2024. https://www.wsj.com/articles/nova-massacre-remembrance-new-york-city-protesters-hamas-antisemitism-0d7f4eb0?mod=hp_opin_pos_1.

The Jewish Chronicle. "Eric Hoffer's Defense of Israel - From LA Times 1968," June 21, 2011. https://www.thejc.com/lets-talk/eric-hoffers-defense-of-israel-from-la-times-1968-sdwwsiw7.

The Tikvah Fund. "Freedom Vs. Tyranny: Sharansky's 'Speech to the Soviet Union' - the Tikvah Fund," July 27, 2021. https://tikvahfund.org/tikvah-online/freedom-vs-tyranny-natan-sharanskys-speech-to-the-soviet-union/.

Tolstoy, Leo Nikolayevich. In *Jewish World* periodical. 1908.

Trachtenberg, Joshua. *The Devil and the Jews - The Medieval Conception of the Jew and its Relation to Modern Antisemitism.* Meridian Books, 1943. p99.

Trevor-Roper, Hugh. *Hitler's Table Talk 1941-1944.* Enigma, 2000.

Turner, Camilla. "Former Scottish First Minister Humza Yousaf Faces Review Over £250k Gaza Funding," *The Telegraph*, July 16, 2024, https://www.telegraph.co.uk/politics/2024/07/13/humza-yousaf-scotland-first-minister-snp-250k-gaza-unrwa/.

Twain, Mark. (1963). "Concerning the Jews". In *Harper's Magazine* in *The Complete Essays of Mark Twain*. Doubleday. 1963. p 249.

Twain, Mark. *The Complete Essays of Mark Twain*. Doubleday, 1963.

"UK Jewish group records all-time high in antisemitic incidents after October 7." The Times of Israel, February 15, 2024. https://www.timesofisrael.com/uk-jewish-group-records-all-time-high-in-antisemitic-incidents-after-october-7/

UNHCR - The UN Refugee Agency. "Global Trends | UNHCR." UNHCR, n.d. https://www.unhcr.org/global-trends.

United States Department of State. "West Bank and Gaza - United States Department of State," December 7, 2023. https://www.state.gov/reports/2019-report-on-international-religious-freedom/israel-west-bank-and-gaza/west-bank-and-gaza/.

Unpacked. "Are College Protests Antisemitic?" Unpacked, February 1, 2023. https://www.youtube.com/watch?v=1fZiQB2sVgg.

Unwatch. "The U.N. and Israel: Key Statistics from UN Watch." UN Watch, January 2, 2024. https://unwatch.org/un-israel-key-statistics/

Vahdat, Amir and Gambrell, Jon. "Iran Leader Says Israel a 'cancerous Tumor' to Be Destroyed." AP News, May 22, 2020. https://apnews.com/article/a033042303545d9ef783a95222d51b83.

Veblen, Thorstein."Political Science Quarterly: March 1919: The Intellectual Pre-Eminence of Jews in Modern Europe," Oxford University Press, 1919. https://www.psqonline.org/article.cfm?IDArticle=2999.

Volozhin, Rabbi Chaim, trans Avinoam Fraenkel. *Nefesh HaTzimtzum - translation and commentary of Nefesh HaChaim*. Urim. Volume 1, 116. 2015.

W., B., & B., D. *Alcoholics Anonymous: The Big Book* : The Original 1939 Edition. Ixia Press, 2019.

Wallace, Max. *The American Axis: Henry Ford, Charles Lindbergh, and the Rise of the Third Reich*. St. Martin's Publishing Group, 2004.

Wein, Rabbi Berel. "Man-Made Faith." Torah.org, June 24, 2008. https://torah.org/torah-portion/rabbiwein-5768-korach/

Weinberg, Rabbi Yaakov. *Fundamentals and Faith: Insights into the Rambam's 13 Principles.* Targum Press, 1991.

Wiesel, Elie. "The Nobel Peace Prize 1986," n.d. https://www.nobelprize.org/prizes/peace/1986/wiesel/acceptance-speech/.

Wilensky, David A.M. "In Wild Overestimate, Americans Think 30% of the Country Is Jewish." *J.*, March 17, 2022. https://jweekly.com/2022/03/17/in-wild-overestimate-americans-think-30-of-the-country-is-jewish/.

"West Bank and Gaza - United States Department of State." United States Department of State, December 7, 2023. https://www.state.gov/reports/2019-report-on-international-religious-freedom/israel-west-bank-and-gaza/west-bank-and-gaza/

Whitman, Ariel. "Sharansky: In Prison I Was Freer Than My Interrogators." *Globes*, January 7, 2024. https://en.globes.co.il/en/article-sharansky-in-prison-i-was-freer-than-my-interrogators-1001480613.

Wikipedia contributors. "August Landmesser," August 20, 2024. https://en.wikipedia.org/wiki/August_Landmesser#/media/File:August-Landmesser-Almanya-1936.jpg.

Wikipedia contributors. "Casualties of the Syrian Civil War." Wikipedia, June 27, 2024. https://en.wikipedia.org/wiki/Casualties_of_the_Syrian_civil_war.

Wikipedia contributors. "Palestinians in Syria." Wikipedia, July 10, 2024. https://en.wikipedia.org/wiki/Palestinians_in_Syria.

Wikipedia contributors. "Relentless: The struggle for peace in the Middle East." Wikipedia, April 9, 2023. https://en.wikipedia.org/wiki/Relentless:_The_Struggle_for_Peace_in_the_Middle_East

Wikipedia contributors. "History of the Jews in Germany." Wikipedia, June 21, 2024. https://en.wikipedia.org/wiki/History_of_the_Jews_in_Germany

Wikipedia contributors. "Expulsions and exoduses of Jews." Wikipedia, July 19, 2024. https://en.wikipedia.org/wiki/Expulsions_and_exoduses_of_Jews

Wilensky, David A.M. "In Wild Overestimate, Americans Think 30% of the

Country Is Jewish." *J.*, March 17, 2022. https://jweekly.com/2022/03/17/in-wild-overestimate-americans-think-30-of-the-country-is-jewish/.

Wisse, R. R. (n.d.). *The functions of Anti-Semitism*. National Affairs. https://www.nationalaffairs.com/publications/detail/the-functions-of-anti-semitism

Wistrich, Robert S. *Antisemitism: The Longest Hatred*. Pantheon Books, 1991.

Wistrich, Robert S. *Hitler's Apocalypse - Jews and the Nazi Legacy.* George Wiedenfeld and Nicolson Limited, 1985.

Wistrich, Robert S. *A Lethal Obsession - Anti-Semitism from Antiquity to the Global Jihad*. Random House, 2010.

Wyner, A. "How the Gaza Ministry of Health Fakes Casualty Numbers." Tablet Magazine, March 15, 2024.

Yahil, Leni. *The Holocaust: The Fate of European Jewry, 1932 - 1945*. Oxford University Press. 1990.

YIVO Encyclopedia. "YIVO | Population and Migration: Population Since World War I," n.d. https://yivoencyclopedia.org/article.aspx/Population_and_Migration/Population_since_World_War_I.

Zaig, Gadi. "Kanye Says 'Jewish Zionists' Control the Media, Jews Own the Black Voice." *The Jerusalem Post | JPost.Com*, October 17, 2022. https://www.jpost.com/diaspora/antisemitism/article-719843.

About the Author

Raphael Shore is an acclaimed filmmaker, educator, human rights activist, and educational entrepreneur dedicated to empowering the Jewish community and all people of goodwill with actionable solutions to combating hatred and delivering a universal message of hope and tolerance.

As founder of OpenDor Media and the Clarion Project, Shore has established himself as a voice of truth and reason in a crowded and often hostile media landscape. His 18 documentaries and feature films (*Obsession; Beneath the Helmet; Crossing the Line*) have amassed over 150 million views to date and won multiple awards, reflecting Shore's unique ability to connect with and deliver a message that resonates with people of all walks.

His first book, *Who's Afraid of the Big Bad Jew? Learning to Love the Lessons of Jew-Hatred* unravels the warped origins of antisemitism to unexpectedly reveal a message of hope and beauty rooted in the very essence of Judaism itself. Complementing this seminal work is his feature film **Tragic Awakening: A New Look at the Oldest Hatred**, in which Shore explores, along with Arab Zionist Rawan Osman, the genesis of Jew-hatred and how it can be harnessed into a force for good.

Shore's works have catalyzed profound change, earning hundreds of media placements and Capitol Hill screenings. In addition, the NYPD has even included Shore's documentaries in its training materials. In the wake of the October 7 pogrom in Israel – the single worst attack on Jews since Kristallnacht – Shore's works and thought-provoking questions bear all the more significance and a place in our collective discourse.

Find out more at RaphaelShore.com.